Object-Oriented Systems Development: a gentle introduction

Carol Britton
University of Hertfordshire

and

Jill Doake
Anglia Polytechnic University

THE McGRAW-HILL COMPANIES

London · Burr Ridge IL · New York · St Louis · San Francisco · Auckland
Bogotá · Caracas · Lisbon · Madrid · Mexico · Milan
Montreal · New Delhi · Panama · Paris · San Juan · São Paulo
Singapore · Sydney · Tokyo · Toronto

Published by
McGraw-Hill Publishing Company
SHOPPENHANGERS ROAD, MAIDENHEAD, BERKSHIRE, SL6 2QL, ENGLAND
Telephone +44 (0) 1628 502500
Fax: +44 (0) 1628 770224 Web site: http://www.mcgraw-hill.co.uk

British Library Cataloguing in Publication Data

A catalogue record for this book is available from the British Library

ISBN 0 07709544 8

Library of Congress Cataloguing-in-Publication Data

The LOC data for this book has been applied for and may be obtained from the Library of Congress, Washington, D.C.

Further information on this and other McGraw-Hill titles is to be found at http://www.mcgraw-hill.co.uk
Authors' Website address: http://www.mcgraw-hill.co.uk/textbooks/britton

Every effort has been made to ensure the accuracy of material in this book. The authors and publisher cannot accept any responsibility for errors or omissions or the consequences thereof.

Publisher: David Hatter
Produced by: Steven Gardiner Ltd
Cover by: Hybert Design
Printed at the University Press, Cambridge

Trademarks

Macintosh is a trademark of Apple Computer Inc.
Access and Windows are trademarks of Microsoft Corporation

For
Lisa, Tom, James, Matthew, Beccy and Ed

Contents

ACKNOWLEDGEMENTS

PREFACE

1   INTRODUCTION   **1**
    1.1   Background to the case study: the *Just a Line* security problem   1
    1.2   How we use the case study in this book   1
    1.3   What is a system?   2
    1.4   Developing systems   3
    1.5   Why object-orientation?   4
    1.6   What you will find in this book   4
    1.7   The structure of the book and the web site   6
    Exercises   6
    References and further reading   7

2   BACKGROUND AND BASICS   **8**
    2.1   Why an object-oriented approach is needed   8
        2.1.1   Maintaining software   8
        2.1.2   Testing software   11
        2.1.3   Reusing software   11
        2.1.4   Large and complex systems   12
    2.2   Background to object-orientation   13
    2.3   Object-oriented concepts   13
    Exercises   25
    References and further reading   26

3   DEVELOPMENT APPROACHES   **27**
    3.1   The system life cycle   27
        3.1.1   The traditional system life cycle   27
        3.1.2   The life cycle using prototyping   28
        3.1.3   The object-oriented system life cycle   29
        3.1.4   Features of the object-oriented system life cycle 35
    3.2   Methodologies   36
        3.2.1   Why do we need a methodology?   36
        3.2.2   Early methodologies   37
        3.2.3   Object-oriented methodologies   38
        3.2.4   Choosing a methodology   39
    Exercises   42
    References and further reading   42

4   ENGINEERING THE SYSTEM REQUIREMENTS   **43**
    4.1   The role of the requirements engineer   43
    4.2   The requirements engineering process   46
    4.3   Requirements elicitation   48
        4.3.1   Requirements elicitation methods   48
    4.4   Requirements specification   56

	4.5	Requirements validation	58
		4.5.1 Requirements validation methods	59
	4.6	The difficulties of requirements engineering	61
	Exercises		63
	References and further reading		64

5   **OBJECT MODELLING**   **66**

	5.1	Modelling	66
		5.1.1 What is a model?	66
		5.1.2 Using models for communication	68
		5.1.3 Using models to tackle complexity	68
		5.1.4 Different stages of development	69
	5.2	The class diagram	69
		5.2.1 Stages in building a class diagram	70
	5.3	Data dictionary	82
		5.3.1 Value of a data dictionary	84
		5.3.2 Data dictionary notation	84
	Exercises		90
	References and further reading		96

6   **MODELLING THE BEHAVIOUR OF THE SYSTEM**   **97**

	6.1	Use cases and scenarios	97
		6.1.1 Working with use cases and scenarios	99
		6.1.2 The advantages of use cases and scenarios	100
		6.1.3 Use cases and scenarios in the *Just a Line* car park case study	101
	6.2	Interaction diagrams	103
		6.2.1 Sequence diagrams	103
		6.2.2 Collaboration diagrams	106
	6.3	State diagrams	107
	6.4	Good practice in modelling	110
	Exercises		114
	References and further reading		118

7   **MOVING TOWARDS IMPLEMENTATION**   **119**

	7.1	The design view	119
		7.1.1 Notation for the design model	120
		7.1.2 Detail in the design model	120
	7.2	The class diagram at the design stage	120
		7.2.1 The Barrier class	121
		7.2.2 The Simulator class	124
		7.2.3 The CarParkSystem class	127
	7.3	Relationships at the design stage	127
		7.3.1 The analysis model relationships	128
		7.3.2 The design model relationships	128
	7.4	Sequence diagrams at the design stage	135
	Exercises		142
	References and further reading		142

8   **IMPLEMENTATION**   **143**

	8.1	Implementing the class diagram	143

		8.1.1	The Card class	145
		8.1.2	The StaffCard class	146
		8.1.3	The VisitorCard class	147
	8.2	Implementing the dynamic model		148
		8.2.1	Creation of the objects	148
		8.2.2	Following the sequence of messages	149
	8.3	Code fragments		151
	Exercises			159
	References and further reading			166

9   DEALING WITH PERSISTENT DATA   **167**

	9.1	The problem of persistent data	167
	9.2	Different types of database	168
	9.3	Microsoft Access: a typical relational database	168
	9.4	Implementing object-oriented models in a relational database, such as Microsoft Access	170
		9.4.1 Converting a class diagram into tables	170
	9.5	Linking Java code to a relational database	177
	Exercises		178
	References and further reading		180

10   TESTING   **181**

	10.1	Stages of testing	181
		10.1.1 Pre-implementation testing	181
		10.1.2 Post-implementation or code testing	182
	10.2	Special requirements for testing O-O software	187
		10.2.1 Class/object testing	187
		10.2.2 Object integration testing	191
		10.2.3 Coverage criteria	192
	Exercises		192
	References and further reading		194

APPENDIX A   Background material for the case study   **195**

APPENDIX B   Models for the car park system   **204**

APPENDIX C   Java code for the *Just a Line* car park simulation   **213**

APPENDIX D   Summary of UML notation   **223**

APPENDIX E   Java code for the family hierarchy example   **229**

ANSWERS TO SELECTED EXERCISES   **232**

BIBLIOGRAPHY   **262**

GLOSSARY   **265**

INDEX   **271**

Acknowledgements

There are several people whom we would like to thank for their help and support. First of all, we are both extremely grateful to David "Sherlock" Howe for putting the whole book under a magnifying glass and uncovering a multitude of errors and inconsistencies; any that still remain are entirely our own fault. We would also like to thank our publisher, David Hatter, for his support, patience and good humour, particularly when it looked as if the book was going to be fifty pages short. At Anglia Polytechnic University Alan Curtis wrote the Java program and was an unfailing source of help and support, Sarah Ratcliffe wrote the code to link Java to Microsoft Access, Ishbel Duncan gave us valuable advice on testing and Ian Oxford provided technical first-aid when we really made a mess of things. At the University of Hertfordshire Mick Wood and Wilf Nicholls were a source of useful ideas and where to find information on the web, and Jonathan Wilson provided technical help with diagrams and Chapter 8.

On a personal level, we would like to thank Jill's parents, Ian and Vicki Paterson, for their very generous hospitality, Sue Long for advice on Chapter 5, and Beccy Doake for sorting out the diagrams in Chapter 2 when we were both completely defeated by them. Finally, again, a very big thank you is due to our husbands for putting up so cheerfully with yet another book (not to mention doing all the cooking).

Preface

There are so many books on all aspects of object-oriented development that it is difficult, if not impossible, for someone who is new to the subject to know where to start. You may have picked up this book because you liked the cover, or because it was nearest on the shelf, but how will you know if it's actually worth your while reading it? We can't answer that here, but we can try to give you some idea of the type of person that we had in mind when we wrote the book.

Object-orientation is not an easy subject; it is essential to have a good grasp of the key concepts before moving on to more complex topics. This book is for people who want to achieve exactly that: a sound understanding of the basic ideas that underpin the development of object-oriented systems. Many books on the subject provide a comprehensive and detailed account of all features of object-orientation, or an academic discussion of advanced issues, but this can be overwhelming for beginners. If you simply want a gentle introduction to object-oriented systems development, then we hope that you will find this book useful.

Our principal aim, throughout the book, is to make the material accessible to beginners and to non-computer specialists. We hope that it will be helpful as a course text for two main groups: those studying object-oriented development at first-year degree level, and students of related subjects, such as business, management and accountancy. The book is also designed for introductory reading on conversion MSc courses in Computer Science. Finally, we have tried to present the material in such a way that the book can be read by anyone who is considering installing or upgrading a software system and wants to understand the process of object-oriented development. Increasing numbers of people today come into contact with computer systems and need to know something about how these systems are developed. We hope that this book is simple enough to give these readers a clear introduction to the subject, and interesting enough to persuade them to follow up the suggestions for further reading.

The book follows the development of a small system from the initial awareness of the problem through to the completed software product. It is designed to be worked through from start to finish but, for those people who are interested in particular topics, it can be used as a reference manual since each chapter can be read in isolation. In the latter case, it is also advisable to look briefly at the introductory material on the *Just a Line* car park case study in Chapters 1, 4 and 5, or the material in Appendix A.

Carol Britton and Jill Doake
Cambridge, March 2000

1

Introduction

1.1 Background to the case study: the *Just a Line* security problem

Just a Line is a company that designs and sells greeting cards for all occasions. The company was founded in the early 1990's by Harry and Sue Preston to sell their own card designs by mail order, but has grown so rapidly that *Just a Line* products have now taken over a large share of the market, both at home and abroad. Much of this success is due to Harry's flair for innovative ideas and understanding of the market; his edible cards and non-crease wrapping paper have been especially popular, while the 'Juvenile Jokes' and 'Tasteless Titters' card ranges are regular best sellers. Sue, meanwhile, has been in charge of managing the company, making sure that profits are healthy, staff happy and that everything runs smoothly.

On the whole, things are going well and recently *Just a Line* has moved into large new premises on the edge of town. Sue's only problem at present concerns security at the new company site. A few months ago *Just a Line*'s new line of 'touchy-feely' card sculptures was scooped by *Global Greetings,* a rival company. Harry is devastated that his ideas have been stolen, and is convinced that there must have been a leak from someone inside *Just a Line*. He wants to tighten security, so that management can see which employees are in the *Just a Line* building at any time and casual visitors are discouraged from wandering around the site.

Sue is sympathetic to Harry's point of view and agrees that stricter security is needed, but she is worried that new security measures may be unpopular with the staff, many of whom have been with them since the early days of *Just a Line.* She decides to talk to D&B Systems, the company who developed the original computer system for *Just a Line*, to discuss the situation and see what solutions might be available. During the past few years, D&B have expanded from business application software, such as the system they developed for *Just a Line,* into computer security products and integrated systems providing computerized control of buildings and site access.

Extracts from an interview of Sue and Harry carried out by Mark Barnes of D&B Systems can be found in Chapter 4.

1.2 How we use the case study in this book

The main purpose of this book is to explain the object-oriented development process in such a way that newcomers to the subject can understand it. The *Just a Line* case study is used throughout to show how a small, but complete, system would be developed from the initial requirements through to the working code.

Even at an introductory level, there are some hard steps in the process, which it would be unrealistic to gloss over. In particular, what most students find very difficult is the uncomfortable shift from viewing the system as a set of real-world objects, behaving in a recognizable way, to seeing it as a set of software objects, behaving as they must to achieve the overall system functionality.

One of the main claims of an object-oriented approach to developing systems is a seamless transition from real-world to software objects; and it is the case that we find many of the same objects in the final code as in the original problem domain. However, the behaviour of the objects in the code is in many ways different from the behaviour of their real-world counterparts.

Once we have identified the objects, we then have to sort out what functionality the system must support. The nature of object-orientation means that this functionality can only be achieved by being divided up amongst objects. What dictates this division is no longer rooted in the real-world, but depends on what will produce software that is robust, reliable, maintainable and reusable.

You will therefore find some unexpected behaviour in the car park case study, such as an entrance barrier object telling a car park object to decrement its space count, and a car park object asking a card reader object if a card is valid.

Before we embark on developing the case study, we discuss in general terms what we mean by a system, and what distinguishes the object-oriented approach.

1.3 What is a system?

'System' is a word that is used all the time in a wide range of subject areas; biological systems, weather systems, political systems and computer systems are just a few examples. Yet most people, although they use the word freely and with confidence, would find it difficult to define exactly what they mean by a system. We are not going to embark on a discussion of system theory here, but it is useful at this stage to give some idea of what we mean when we use the term 'system'. In this book, we define a system as an interrelated set of objects or elements that are viewed as a whole and designed to achieve a purpose.

We must add to this definition that a system has a boundary. The system in question lies inside the boundary; outside the boundary is the environment with which the system interacts. The environment is defined as being the surrounding conditions, outside the boundary, which affect the system and are affected by it, but not controlled by it. For example, we might define weather conditions as being part of the environment of a central heating system. Sometimes the boundary of a system is clear and obvious. If we view a person as a system, the boundary is clear, since normally one person is clearly separate from another and from the environment; similarly with a car. In computer systems, however, it is usually hard to define the boundary; it is dictated by which elements we think of as being within the system, and which as being part of the environment. The normal rule is that inside the boundary are things that the system is designed to control; outside the boundary are things that the system is not designed to control. The boundary may be set because we cannot design-in control; in a central heating system the weather must be considered to be outside the boundary of the system since we cannot control it. The boundary may also be set because we choose not to include certain elements. This choice may be dictated by:

- Money constraints. We may find that it will cost too much to computerize more than a limited set of system functions.
- Time constraints. The more functions we computerize the longer it will take.
- Resources available. We may, for example, have to work on existing hardware or with an established database.

- Cost effectiveness. Sometimes limited benefits are gained from expensive computerization.

The boundary in software systems is often difficult to define; developers, clients and users must all have a role in deciding what is to be included in the system.

When we talk about a system we understand by this term that it is a set of interrelated objects or elements that are viewed as a whole and designed by humans beings to achieve a purpose; it has a boundary within which it lies and outside of which is the environment. In this book, when we refer to a system, we base our understanding on this description, but more specifically, we interpret the word as comprising the software, documentation, methods of operation, hardware, users and operators which make up a software system.

1.4 Developing systems

System development is a gradual progression from the client's initial vague ideas about the problem, via a series of transitional stages, to a completely formal statement, expressed in a programming language, which can be executed on a machine. A diagram of the process can be seen in Figure 1.1. At each stage of development, the problem is expressed in an appropriate modelling notation or programming language.

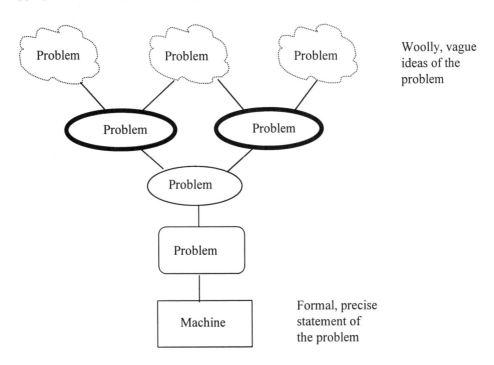

Figure 1.1 A view of the system development process

Traditionally, system developers have worked within the context of some framework or methodology, which provides an agreed structure for the development process. Normally, an organization will adopt a specific approach to developing software systems, which may be referred to as the system or project life cycle, methodology or project plan. The same framework will often be used for all projects developed within an organization and provides the basis for a standard approach to developing software.

However, it is increasingly being realized that different applications require different approaches. The approach used to develop a particular software system should be the one that is most suitable for the type of system being developed, the clients, the users, the developers and the tools and techniques they have at their disposal. System developers are becoming aware that it is impossible for one single development approach to prescribe how to tackle the great variety of problems, tasks and situations encountered. The diversity of applications undertaken means that there cannot be a universal way of developing systems.

1.5 Why object-orientation?

The aim of this book is to introduce the reader to the object-oriented way of developing systems. Although object-orientation is still seen as a relatively new approach, it has in fact been around for some time and the ideas on which it is based go back as far as the late sixties. Early interest in the object-oriented approach focused on programming language issues, but over the years this has grown to cover the whole of the system development process, from capturing initial requirements right through to the final software product. One of the most important features of object-orientation is that the whole development process is based around a single, central concept—that of the object, for example, a customer or an order. Objects in the real world become components in analysis and design models and, eventually, part of the final code. Structuring development around objects provides conceptual simplicity, promoting understanding and supporting all stages of the development process. A structure based on objects rather than function is more robust and less vulnerable to the changes that inevitably occur, since objects are less volatile than function. Object orientation is an approach that is theoretically sound and has also proved over the years to be a practical and popular way of developing software systems.

1.6 What you will find in this book

Different problems and applications require different methods of development. No single method has been proved as appropriate for all development situations and it is most unlikely that such a method does, or could, exist. Because of this, we concentrate in this book on describing the techniques that we feel are important in the development of an object-oriented system, with minimal emphasis on a prescribed method or sequence of events. Once the techniques have been understood, they can be used in different situations as the developer sees fit.

We outline a skeleton development process to indicate how analysis and design models should be developed, both in relation to each other and in relation to other software development activities such as requirements elicitation and coding. We also discuss the differing interpretation of models according to which stage in the development process they describe. The stages of development we use are analysis, design and implementation; in each of these stages there can be many iterations. The activities undertaken during the stages are not very different from those in a traditional systems life cycle; the differences lie in the type of models used and in the iterative nature of the object-oriented development process.

We discuss an analysis, a design model and an implementation model, exploring the differences between them and introducing the idea of classes. The analysis model is based on the application domain; the classes identified will be based entirely on things that are familiar to the client. The functionality specified is drawn from the user requirements (not necessitated by any requirements of implementation) and relationships between classes model real-life relationships.

In the design model we introduce further classes necessitated by the nature of the implementation, such as an interface class to cope with the human-computer interface, and classes to facilitate storage of data. At this stage the relationships change to reflect connections necessitated by implementation considerations and anticipate the way in which they will be implemented in the final code.

Throughout the book we have chosen notations and languages that are both theoretically sound and widely used in industry. The models at the analysis and design stages are in UML notation and the code is written in the Java programming language. Examples in the brief discussion about persistent data in Chapter 9 are shown in Microsoft Access.

No technical knowledge is assumed; where computer terminology is used, this is explained in the glossary at the back of the book. As this book is written for newcomers to object-oriented development, we have tried to present an overall view of the subject. Some topics are discussed at an introductory level only, with suggestions for further reading at the end of each chapter. There is also an annotated bibliography at the end of the book. Examples of code are written in Java, but it is not necessary to have any detailed knowledge of the Java programming language.

There are many different topics in object-oriented system development and no book of this size could hope to do justice to them all. We have chosen to concentrate on three main aspects:

- a general introduction to object-orientation, so that the reader will have an idea of what it is all about, where it came from and how it differs from traditional software development. You can find this in Chapters 2 and 3 and 10;
- an illustration, by means of a case study, of how initial requirements for a software system are eventually implemented in code. This is covered in Chapters 4 to 9;
- instructions on how to construct the models that are central to the object-oriented development process. You can find the models for the analysis stage in Chapters 5 and 6, and the design stage models in Chapter 7. In these chapters, particularly 5 and 6, our aim is to teach readers to use the object-oriented modelling techniques with a certain degree of confidence and competence. Learning to use a modelling technique is rather like learning to swim. You can spend hours reading all about it, even learn the instructions off by heart, but when you jump into the swimming pool, you will still sink like a stone. The only way to learn this sort of skill is to practise it. Accordingly, in Chapters 5 and 6, you will find not only explanation and examples, but also a large number of exercises. Answers to these are at the back of the book after the appendices.

1.7 The structure of the book and the web site

The book follows the development of a small software system from the initial identification of the problem through to the final software product. You will get most benefit from the book if you read it through from start to finish, but we realize that many people will not have time for that, or may already be familiar with some parts of the material. In this case, it is possible to pick out specific topics, as all the chapters are designed to be read independently. However, as the same case study is used throughout, it would be a good idea to also have a look at the background material; parts of the material appear in Chapters 1, 4 and 5, or you can find it collected together in Appendix A.

Chapter 2 of the book introduces the basic concepts of object-orientation and Chapter 3 covers the development life cycle and some of the object-oriented methods. Development of the case study starts in Chapter 4 on requirements engineering, which covers a range of techniques used in the elicitation, specification and validation of requirements. The principal object-oriented analysis techniques are introduced in Chapter 5, which describes how to construct a class diagram, and Chapter 6, which discusses how to model the behaviour of the system. The principal modelling techniques covered here are use cases, scenarios, sequence diagrams and state diagrams. Chapter 7 follows the models produced during analysis through to the design stage of development, and Chapter 8 shows how the models are finally turned into code. In Chapter 9 we briefly discuss the problem of persistent data, and look at how object-oriented code written in the Java programming language can access data that is stored in a relational database, such as Microsoft Access. Finally, Chapter 10 looks at testing in an object-oriented context.

There are five appendices. Appendix A contains all the background material for the case study, Appendix B a set of analysis and design models, and Appendix C the Java code for the final system. In Appendix D you can find a summary of the modelling notation used in the book and Appendix E contains the family hierarchy example used in Chapters 2 and 10.

All the chapters and two of the appendices include exercises, and answers to the majority of these can be found at the end of the book. There is also a full glossary of technical terms and a bibliography.

This book is supported by a web site, which can be found at http://www.mcgraw-hill.co.uk/textbooks/britton. In addition to links to a range of useful sites, the web site contains the background material and set of analysis and design models for the *Just a Line* car park case study, and Java code for the implementation of the car park system, the JDBC link to the data stored in Microsoft Access and the family hierarchy example.

Exercises

1.1   Imagine that you have been asked to develop an information system for your local area. Discuss the factors that will influence your choice of boundary for the system.

1.2   The diagram in Figure 1.1 is only one way of visualizing the system development process. Look up some of the books on this subject in your college library and compare the diagrams in them with the one given here.

References and further reading

Bennett, S., McRobb, S. and Farmer, R. *Object-Oriented Systems Analysis and Design using UML,* London: McGraw-Hill, 1999.

Britton, C. and Doake, J. *Software System Development: a gentle introduction,* 2nd edn, London: McGraw-Hill, 1996.

Carter, R., Martin, J., Mayblin, B. and Munday, M. *Systems, Management and Change—A Graphic Guide,* Paul Chapman in association with The Open University, 1988.

Kaposi, A. and Myers, M. *Systems Models and Measures,* Springer Verlag, 1994.

2

Background and Basics

2.1 Why an object-oriented approach is needed

The rapid increase in the power, speed and capacity of computers over the last four decades has encouraged software developers to tackle increasingly large and complex systems. Software developers in the late sixties made little attempt to change the way such systems were developed. As a result, software produced at this time was typically delivered years late, very over budget, did not do what it was supposed to, frequently failed and was impossible to maintain. Software systems developed over the last thirty years using structured methods (see Chapter 3) have shown significant improvements in terms of robustness, reliability and maintainability. However, as the problems tackled by software developers have become progressively larger and more complex, it has become apparent that structured methods are not a complete answer. Despite all the effort that has gone into improving the software development process, the software crisis is growing worse each year. It is still rare for a project to be delivered on time, within budget and without serious faults. What software practitioners are looking for, and what object-orientation promises, is a new approach to system development which will produce software that is more:

- maintainable
- testable
- reusable
- able to cope with large and complex systems.

In the following sections we discuss each of these features of software and then introduce the O-O concepts that aim to deliver them.

2.1.1 Maintaining software

Maintaining software starts the moment a software system is handed over to the client. The term maintenance should refer to the introduction of enhancements to delivered software, however, it is frequently used as a euphemism for finding and correcting errors that were not detected while the system was being built. Despite improved practice, maintaining software is still extremely problematic. Software projects of any size take a long time, and therefore cost a great deal to develop. If a company has invested huge amounts of money in a software application, it will expect the software to function for a significant amount of time. During its lifetime an application will be required to change in order to meet new requirements. Even with improved techniques introduced with the structured approach, studies have shown that each time a change is made, new bugs are often introduced. Three commonly identified causes of maintenance problems are:

- functional decomposition
- poor modularity
- visibility of data.

Functional decomposition

Structured methods use a procedural approach to software design, that is, the structure of the software is based on top-down functional decomposition. This means that a system is partitioned into its main areas or activities, each area corresponding to something that the system *does*—one of its major activities. Each of these areas may be viewed as a sub-system; i.e. each area is part of a bigger system and may itself be partitioned into smaller areas or activities. Data is passed freely between the sub-systems. For example, consider a typical mail order system as modelled in Figure 2.1. The mail order system is divided into three sub-systems:

- Handle customer orders
- Order stock
- Keep accounts.

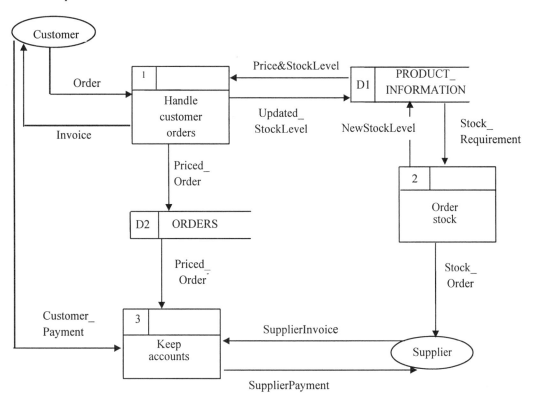

Figure 2.1 A mail order system showing functional decomposition

Figure 2.1 uses a standard data flow diagram notation to represent the activities and flow of data through the system. In the diagram each of the three sub-systems is represented by a rectangle labelled with a brief description of what the sub-system does. Data stores, which will eventually become computer files, are represented as open-ended rectangles. In the diagram there are two: D1 PRODUCT_INFORMATION and D2 ORDERS. Movement of data is represented by labelled arrows. In the diagram we see data, such as orders, customer payments and supplier invoices pass between the three sub-systems.

A program produced from a functional design echoes the design structure—the modules of the software are defined by what they do, i.e. each module executes a separate function. This structure has proved to be one of the things that makes such software hard to maintain. During the life-time of a software application the types of change most often implemented are changes to what the software must do—its functionality. If the structure of the software is based on its functionality, radical alterations to what the program does will affect its underlying structure. The essential shape of the software becomes masked and can disappear entirely. It does not take long for a program to degenerate into a fragile, incomprehensible monster that no-one dares to touch.

Poor modularity

It is unusual for programmers to maintain their own code. It is more likely that maintenance will be done by someone who has never seen the code before. Often maintenance is done by new, inexperienced programmers. The more of the code they have to read and understand the harder the task of these programmers. If modules are properly decentralized, then each module is autonomous—it is self contained and independent. If this is the case, a maintaining programmer need only read and understand the module he or she has to change, or perhaps this and one or two closely related modules. If a program module is not autonomous the programmer may find that he or she has to read and understand large sections of the rest of the program in order to understand it well enough to carry out the required update.

Poor modularity is also one of the causes of the well-recognized knock-on effect of introducing changes to working code where a change in one part of the program can have a dramatic effect on some other part that is not obviously related. The more autonomous the module, i.e. the less it depends on and communicates with other parts of the program, the less chance there is of a small change to one module causing a chain reaction throughout the program. Functional decomposition, unfortunately, does not promote properly decentralized, autonomous modules.

Another aspect of modularity is the cohesion of a module. A module is cohesive if it has a clearly defined role—a single, obvious purpose in the application. A module with a clearly defined purpose is easier for a maintaining programmer to read and understand.

Visibility of data

Another cause of the knock-on effect of introducing changes is high visibility of data: data being too visible and therefore too accessible to parts of the program that do not need to access it. Changes made to the data in one part of the program can cause mysterious errors and unpredictable behaviour in other parts. The most notorious culprit in this respect was the COMMON block of data in early FORTRAN programs. This was a block of data to which all parts of the program had unlimited access. Block structured programming languages introduced the concept of scoping which limited data visibility, however it did not entirely succeed in making data invisible to parts of the program that did not need it, and the knock-on effect of changes continued to be a problem.

The structured approach to software development was a great improvement on anything that preceded it, but it still left much to be desired, particularly in the area of software maintainability. For software to be easy to maintain, four things are required:

- Software needs to have a robust structure that is based on something less liable to change than its functionality.
- Modules need to be cohesive to be easily understood by maintaining programmers who come across them for the first time.
- Program modules need to be as independent as possible. If this can be done then the effect of any change will be confined to the module being changed. This should also have the effect of limiting the amount of code a programmer has to understand when he or she is required to maintain the program.
- Data needs to be less visible.

The object-oriented approach to software development promised to deliver all of these features.

2.1.2 Testing software

The computing world has recognized for many years that it is not feasible to completely test any but the most trivial program. Even if project managers were prepared to allocate significant time, money and trained people to the task, most software is too complicated and has too many possible paths through it for it to be possible, far less economically viable, to test it with all possible combinations of data. Instead software developers develop acceptable standards of test coverage (see Chapter 10). In the last decade there has been a lot of talk about the value of software testing, however it remains an activity which is unpopular with both project managers and programmers. The computing fraternity realizes that testing is important, but doesn't like doing it. Any approach that seems likely to reduce the testing burden will find favour with software practitioners.

Object-orientation (O-O) promised to simplify testing. Software units built using an O-O approach are self-sufficient and independent with clearly defined interfaces. This means that each unit can be carefully tested in isolation before being plugged into the system. Integration can take place gradually so that faults found can be readily traced to the offending module. Data in an O-O system is encapsulated (see Section 2.3) inside an object: it is hidden and therefore inaccessible to parts of the program that do not need to see it. Data can only be manipulated in a strictly controlled way, by using those procedures that have been defined publicly in the class interface. O-O encourages reuse of library modules. In theory this also reduces the testing burden as library modules will be already tried and tested. It was thought that the use of inheritance (see Section 2.3) would also mean less testing as the descendant unit would only need to be tested where it differed from its parent.

2.1.3 Reusing software

Ever since software has been used commercially, there has been talk of software reuse. The theory is that, since so many problems contain similar features, the obvious way to produce software efficiently is to reuse existing software solutions rather than rewrite them from scratch each time. There has always been some software reuse, notably of mathematical and numerical routines. We also reuse software whenever we purchase a package to perform special purpose jobs, e.g. spreadsheets, word-processors and databases. However, to date, the normal pattern of software development does not include a significant amount of reuse. Various problems have prevented reuse being a standard approach to software development:

- Some software construct is needed that is smaller and more flexible than the off-the-shelf package and more powerful than the mathematical routine. Purchased software is usually hard to tailor to specific requirements; mathematical routines are useful but don't do enough.
- Library modules written for reuse (whether purchased or in-house) have a tendency to be all things to all people. The module writer tries to build in all the functionality that he or she thinks a user could ever possibly need. This results in white elephants, such as a generic linked list module found in one company's software library which had 2000 functions for handling linked lists. If a module has this number of functions it becomes impossible to find the one you actually want to use. What is required is a library of fairly simple modules offering basic functionality and a mechanism for readily tailoring those modules to fit requirements precisely.
- There needs to be some way that programmers can easily access and understand library modules. There is no point in having a good library of software modules if no-one knows what is in it and it takes the programmer longer to find and understand a module than it would to write it from scratch.
- If a module is to be included in a library of reusable software, it has to have a clear and easily identifiable purpose (i.e. to be cohesive) and it needs to be self-contained—it must not rely on any part of the program for which it was originally written. Software designed using functional decomposition rarely produces modules with these qualities.
- One approach software developers can take to the building of a library of reusable modules is to look at completed software projects for modules that might prove useful in the future. Any modules identified in this way will inevitably require a certain amount of cleaning up, since they will almost certainly contain references to other parts of the program for which they were originally written. This cleaning up takes time and programmer effort; time which the company may not have and which may not have been budgeted for. The building of a software library is expensive and needs to have management commitment and resources allocated to it.
- Programmers seem to have a built-in reluctance to use other people's code. This tendency is so widespread and well-recognized that it has been dubbed the 'not invented here' syndrome. Whatever the reason, programmers seem to prefer to write their own routine rather than look for, read, understand and then use an existing module.

2.1.4 Large and complex systems

Software systems today are larger and more complex than ever before. A few years ago we were happy with simple menu-driven systems. The structured approach with functional decomposition was well suited to the design of such software. Now most software applications seem to require a graphical user interface (GUI) to be acceptable. The top-down structured design approach has proved inadequate to cope with the scale and complexity of such systems.

In the past, every time an approach to software development has proved inadequate, a new approach has been found. Machine code was fine for a simple application of a few hundred lines of code. When larger applications were required, assembly language was invented—the use of mnemonics freed the programmer's mind to some extent from detailed concentration on the structure of machine instructions. When huge commercial systems and other ambitious software projects were required, high level programming languages came into common use. Subsequently fourth generation languages (4GLs) and other programming tools were invented and used to meet the demands of the commercial programming world. Each time a new software tool is developed a step forward is taken in terms of the size and complexity of the problems that can be successfully undertaken. The mathematician Whitehead claimed that every time a successful new notation is invented, it frees the human brain from the drudgery of concentration on the technicalities of an inferior notation and allows it to tackle more difficult problems. He points out that the Romans, with their clumsy Roman numerals could not manage long division. It was not until the current Arabic numeric system came into common use that the human mind could cope with long division and any more complicated mathematical calculations.

Software developers are looking for a new approach to tackle the complexity of today's software problems. In recent years, the answer has appeared to lie in the O-O approach to developing software systems.

2.2 Background to object-orientation

Concepts from which the object-oriented approach is derived have been around since the 1960s. The programming language Simula was developed to write computer simulations of real processes. Program units in Simula were not based on functionality but on the real-world objects to be simulated in the software. Ideas generated by the Simula experiment were taken up and developed by the team that produced Smalltalk in the Xerox Palo Alto Research Center. There are now many object-oriented programming languages, including Smalltalk, C++, Java and Eiffel.

The initial interest in object-orientation focused on programming language issues. More recently, however, O-O ideas have been applied to the whole software development process—analysis, design and implementation (see Chapter 3). New modelling techniques, the equivalent of techniques that were used in structured modelling, have been developed to model the application domain in object-oriented terms (see Chapters 5 and 6).

2.3 Object-oriented concepts

Object-orientation has its own specialized vocabulary which must be mastered if the technology is to be understood. The principal terms are introduced in Table 2.1. The underlying concepts are explained below. Further explanations of terms can be found in the glossary.

Objects

The basic building block of object-oriented software is the object. Software objects are derived from and model the real-world objects in the application domain. That is, whatever

Table 2.1 Object-oriented terminology

Term	Definition
Object	Software unit packaging together data and methods to manipulate that data
Class	Template or factory for creating objects
Attribute	Data item defined as part of a class or object
Operation	Procedure or function defined as part of a class or object; using this term refers to the procedure's public interface with the rest of the software
Method	Procedure or function defined as part of a class or object; using this term refers to the procedure's implementation
Message	Request sent to an object to execute one of its methods
Encapsulation	Packaging data and operations into an object
Data hiding	Making the internal details of an object inaccessible to other objects
Inheritance	Mechanism for defining a new class in terms of an existing class
Polymorphism	The ability to hide different implementations behind a common interface

type of software system you are developing, whatever problem you are trying to solve, it will feature certain entities, objects or things. These objects or things form the subject matter of the system. A mail order system will feature objects such as customers, orders and products; a library system will feature objects such as members, books, loans and reservations; a restaurant booking system will have customers, tables, reservations and cancellations; a system to simulate traffic behaviour might have traffic lights, cars, bicycles and pedestrians. All of these objects are understandable features of their problem domain and will have a software representation in the system being written. Objects in the real-world therefore translate into objects in the software system.

Objects in an O-O system can represent physical things (such as customers, products, members, and books), conceptual things (such as orders, loans, reservations and cancellations) or organizational things (such as companies or departments). Objects can also be computer implementation features such as GUI windows, files or linked lists, but this type of object is ignored in the early stages of O-O system development.

Real-world objects will have certain properties or attributes that are of interest to the system developer: a customer in a mail order system will have a name, a telephone number, an address for invoicing purposes and possibly a separate delivery address. A product will have a product number, a description and a price. A car knows the amount of fuel it has in its tank, the speed at which it is moving, the temperature of its engine. Real-world objects also have characteristic behaviour which the system developer will wish to capture in his or her software representation of the object: a customer can change his or her address or telephone number, a product can be withdrawn or have its price changed, a car can stop, start, move forward or backwards.

Like the real-world object it models, a software object packages together data and behaviour. A software object consists of certain data items and knows how to perform certain functions. To represent the real-world car as a software object, its data (amount of fuel, speed, temperature) will be translated into variables, and its behaviour (start, stop, move etc.) into procedures. In O-O terminology these variables are known as attributes and the procedures as operations. Both attributes and operations are an integral part of the software object. Figure 2.2 shows the car as a real-world object; Figure 2.3 shows how the car would be represented as a software object in the UML (Unified Modelling Language).

Figure 2.2 A real-world car

Jemima : Car

fuel = 6.4 litres
speed = 32 mph
temperature = cool

Figure 2.3 The car represented as a software object

The first line of the object shown in Figure 2.3 specifies the object name—Jemima, the class of the object (see below), in this case Car; the other lines specify the values of its three data attributes—fuel, speed and temperature. Notice that the name of the class that the object belongs to is always underlined and preceded by a colon, e.g. :Car. The object name is often omitted (see Figure 2.6), but if mentioned, it comes before the colon. Conventionally, operations are not mentioned in a diagram of an object; these are specified in the class description (see below). It is understood that all objects of a given class know about and have access to these operations. A diagram of an object concentrates on showing what is unique to each object, such as the object name and its attribute values.

An object-oriented system is made up of such objects which collaborate to achieve the functionality required by the system. An object will be sent a request to perform its part in the functionality. In turn, it may send a request to another object to perform the next part of the functionality. The sending of such requests to achieve inter-object collaboration and communication is known as message passing.

Software objects model objects in the real world. This offers a conceptual simplicity which promotes ease of understanding. These software objects, persist through the development stages of requirements capture, analysis, design and into code. This offers a seamless development process. The objects identified in the initial stages of the development process will still be there at the implementation stage. They may have a few more features that are revealed as development progresses, and by the time we get towards implementation, objects and their classes will be specified in more technical detail, but they are still the same objects and classes. We may also find that as we approach implementation, we need to add classes that are to do with the way we plan to implement the software rather than to do with the problem domain; for example nodes in a linked list, and classes to handle the user interface. However, there will be enough objects and classes based in the problem domain, derived from real-world objects to offer a maintaining programmer considerable assistance in understanding the code and its structure.

Class

An object is defined in terms of its class. When we specify that a class will have certain attributes and certain operations, we determine that all objects of that class, i.e. all instances of that class, will have the same structure—precisely those attributes and precisely those operations. The terms object and instance (of a class) are used interchangeably. The process of creating an instance of a class is known as instantiation.

We can think of a class as being an object factory, a template for all objects of that class. Diagrammatically, classes are represented as rectangles with three sections: one for the name of the class, one for the class attributes and one for the operations. The class for the car object described above is shown in Figure 2.4. Notice that a car object (being a particular instance) has values for its attributes (e.g. 6.4 litres in Figure 2.3), but a class (being a general representation) does not.

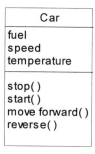

Figure 2.4 The class for the car object

If the mail order system shown in Figure 2.1 were redesigned using an O-O approach, it might have classes such as those shown in Figure 2.5.

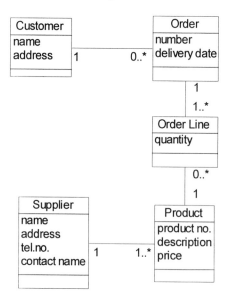

Figure 2.5 Classes in the mail order system

The lines that connect the classes are known as associations (see Chapter 5) and indicate that these classes have some sort of relationship. The numbers and asterisks (*) indicate the multiplicity of the relationship. The asterisk means an arbitrary number—zero, one or many. In Figure 2.5 the multiplicity symbols tell us that:

- a customer may have any number of orders between zero and many (number unspecified)
- an order is for only one customer
- an order may have one to many order lines
- an order line will belong specifically to one order
- an order line will refer to only one product
- product may appear on zero or many different order lines
- a product will be supplied by only one supplier
- a supplier may supply one or many products.

In traditional data modelling terms, a class is to an object what an entity is to occurrence of that entity; or in programming terms what a type, especially a user-defined type, is to a variable of that type.

Attribute

The attributes of a class are the data items that define it; for example, name and address might be two attributes of a class Customer. The attributes recorded in a class are only those that are of interest to the system under development. For example, in a mail order system we would not include attributes such as a customer's passport number or taste in beer. All the objects in a class have the same set of attributes, but the attributes have different values. This is illustrated in Figure 2.6, below, which shows three objects of a Customer class. Notice that the object names are omitted on these diagrams; they are anonymous objects of class :Customer

: Customer	: Customer	: Customer
name = Jane Lyon	name = Miles Dunn	name = Les Doolan
address = 4 High St	address = 32 Green Lane	address = 102 High St
Anytown	Anytown	Anytown

Figure 2.6 Three objects of class Customer, with specific values

Operation

The O-O equivalent of a function or procedure is an operation. The difference is that an operation is always defined as part of a class, it cannot exist separately. The operations on a class combine to form the class behaviour. The operations, attributes and associations together achieve the responsibilities of a class. A class is usually responsible for some part of the overall system functionality. In the mail order system shown in Figure 2.5 the class Customer is responsible for recording and maintaining data about the company's customers; the class Order maintains a list of outstanding orders; the class Product maintains a list of company products and the class Supplier maintains a list of suppliers.

The operations can be defined as public or private. Public operations are those which are available to be used by any other part of the program—objects of any other class in the system; these operations are said to form the class's public interface. Private operations are procedures used internally by a class to achieve its responsibilities—they are not available to other parts of the program: they do not form part of the class's public interface.

An operation is invoked when a message is sent to an object of the class containing that operation. A message is the O-O equivalent of a procedure call.

Method

Methods are closely related to operations; both terms refer to the procedures that form part of a class's structure—the procedures that a class and all objects of that class know about, and which will be executed upon receipt of an appropriate request. The term operation tends to be used in the early stages of software development and the term method as we move towards implementation. More precisely, the term operation refers to a class's public interface—public procedure names that other objects in the system know and can name when sending a request for a service. The term method is used to refer to the actual implementation of that procedure—the body of code that is executed in response to a request from other objects in the system. This has important implications for polymorphism (see below).

Message

The overall functionality, in an object-oriented system, is achieved by objects interacting with each other. They do this by sending messages to each other requesting services. A message normally takes the form of the name of the receiving object followed by the name of the operation to be executed. Let us assume that the software using our car object also has a person object, and that person is called Tom. If Tom wants the car to start he must send it a message telling it to execute its start operation (see Figure 2.7). The message will only work if it is sent to the right object and it is a message the object recognizes, i.e. it corresponds to one of the operations defined in its class.

Figure 2.7 Tom sends a start message to Jemima

The initiating object is referred to as the client or sender, the receiving object as the server or receiver. When a server object receives a message it executes the appropriate operation.

To achieve a task of any size several of the objects in a system have to co-operate with each other—this will be done by message passing between the objects involved. In a well-structured O-O system the responsibility for achieving the required system functionality is evenly distributed amongst its classes. No one class should have overall control, or do all the work (see Chapter 6). For example, to produce an invoice in the mail order system shown in Figure 2.5 will require co-operation between all of the classes shown, except Supplier.

Message passing is important because it represents two definitive aspects of the O-O approach to software design. One big difference between the procedural and the O-O approach is that, in procedural code, data is passed between functions; for example, a sine function will be sent an angle, will calculate its sine and send back the answer. In an O-O program, the sine function is an operation defined on the class Angle and therefore all objects of the Angle class will know about this operation and be able to calculate their sine on demand. Typically, in an O-O system, data is encapsulated in an object and the object itself will have operations (defined in its class) to do any processing of the data that is required. A list object will have built-in sort, insert and find operations, a stack object will have built-in push and pop operations. The Customer class in the mail order example (Figure 2.5) will have operations to find a given customer, update customer details, insert a new customer and delete a customer.

The other aspect of the O-O approach, highlighted by message passing, is the emphasis placed on building objects that are independent and self-sufficient. We want objects, once activated by a message, to take charge of executing their responsibilities. For example, in Figure 2.8 we have a mother object and a son object.

Figure 2.8 Mother tells son to pull up his socks

The mother wants her son to pull up his socks. To be truly object oriented she must tell her son to pull up his socks (message) and have trained him to know how to pull up his own socks (operation) in response to her message. What she must not do is to pull up her son's socks herself—this would be violating the principle of data encapsulation—she would be directly changing the state of her son (manipulating his data), not using the defined operation (that he pull up his socks himself).

A slightly more complicated example of message passing and devolved responsibility is shown in Figure 2.9.

Figure 2.9 Father tells mother to get his tea

Here the father tells the mother to get his tea. Getting the tea is one of the mother's responsibilities—it is an operation she knows about and can execute. As we can see from Figure 2.9, she co-operates with others in the execution of her duty: she tells the children to do certain jobs. What makes this a good O-O situation (although perhaps politically incorrect) is that responsibility is devolved. We have a group of co-operating objects sharing responsibility. As soon as she gets the message 'get my tea' the mother takes charge—she issues the orders (sends messages) to the children. If the father issued the orders directly to the children and the mother, this would mean that one person was too much in charge, had too much responsibility. In O-O terms the father would become a 'god' class (see Chapter 6).

Encapsulation and data hiding

Packaging related data and operations together is called encapsulation. The encapsulation mechanism provides three desirable software qualities:

* proper modularity
* data abstraction
* data hiding.

Modularity The encapsulation of data and operations into a single software construct—the object—provides a useful building block for software systems. This software construct provides software modules ideal for producing reusable units of code. It is larger than the mathematical functions mentioned in Section 2.1.3 and therefore can provide a more useful bundle of functionality. But it is smaller and more flexible than off-the-shelf packages such as spreadsheets and databases. The object has other qualities that should promote reuse. It models real-world objects and so is inherently easy to understand—the reader comes to the code (or design) with a ready made understanding of the software object he or she is going to examine, based on his or her understanding of how it behaves in the real world. The objects are designed to be as independent as possible, so they should not have many dependencies on other parts of the code and should be easily transformed into candidates for a software library.

Data abstraction An object's name, class and the names of its operations form its public interface. This provides the abstraction—all the object's clients need to know about is the information provided in the public interface while the internal representation of the object's data and operations is irrelevant and invisible to the client.

Data hiding The data encapsulated in an object can only be accessed by using that object's operations—operations designed to ensure that the data is handled properly. We can think of the data as being surrounded by a protective outer ring of operations (see Figure 2.10).

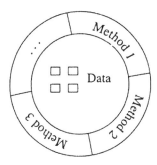

Figure 2.10 Data inside an object is surrounded by a protective ring of methods

Client modules cannot access that data directly; they can only send a message to the object requesting that it execute one of its methods. This method in turn will access the data in the proper way. Encapsulation ensures that the internal representation of the data and operations is concealed. The external interface of an object does not tell the world details of how data is stored or what algorithm is used by a method. This is what is known as data hiding.

For example, suppose we want to define a counter to keep track of the score in a game. Let us suppose that we want to define it, in accordance with the rules of the game, so that the score can be incremented by one when a goal is scored and decremented by one when a foul is made. To implement this counter in a programming language which does not support data hiding, we might declare a variable 'score' to be an integer and write procedures to do the incrementing and decrementing as specified. However, the variable 'score' will be visible—some parts of the program will know that it is implemented as an integer. There is nothing to stop these parts of the program from using normal integer arithmetic on it rather than the defined procedures. It is quite possible that 'score' might inadvertently have 5 added to it or 10 subtracted; it might even be multiplied by 100—none of which are in line with the rules of the game. The data is not protected. However, using the O-O approach, we can define an object, 'Counter' with 'score' as an attribute. In this case the representation of score is hidden, the rest of the world does not know or care whether it is implemented as an integer, a real, or a pointer to an integer. We can define two methods, increment and decrement, and implement them so that the rules of the game are adhered to (see Figure 2.11).

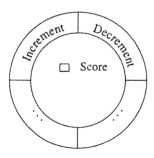

Figure 2.11 Counter implemented as an object

We can then rest assured that our 'score' attribute will only be updated by invoking these methods. Data hiding is enforced.

Data hiding has another benefit. If we want to change any of the implementation details of an object, any of its internal representation, we can do so without affecting any other part of the program—any client object. We can, for example, change the algorithm we use to perform a calculation without changing the public interface to the object. If we wanted to change the way our counter is implemented so that every goal increments the score by 2 and every foul decrements it by 1, we can implement this without any change to the interface. A goal still increments the score and a foul decrements it. The two methods are still increment and decrement, they are just implemented differently. We might also decide to change the representation of the data from an integer to a pointer to an integer. This can also be done without having any effect on the public interface.

The main advantage of data hiding is that it provides a robustness to maintenance changes made to code. It effectively limits the knock-on effect of introducing changes to working code.

Inheritance

Inheritance is a mechanism which allows new classes to be defined in terms of existing classes; a new class can be defined as a specialization of one that has already been written. The specialized class automatically includes or inherits the features (operations and attributes) of the class it is created from. O-O terminology has different ways of describing this relationship:

the	**specialized** class	inherits from the	**general** class
the	**child** class	inherits from the	**parent or ancestor** class
the	**sub**-class	inherits from the	**super**-class

The child class automatically inherits the characteristics of the parent class and can then add features to reflect its specialization, change or suppress inherited features. In a true inheritance relationship, the child class is said to have an IS-A relationship with its parent class. This means that it is of the same kind (but with some specialization) as its parent; just as a Labrador is a kind of dog, or a car is a kind of vehicle. A more detailed example can be found in the mail order system mentioned above. This system might have a class, Customer, which could usefully have two specialized versions: Local Customer and Retail Customer, as in Figure 2.12.

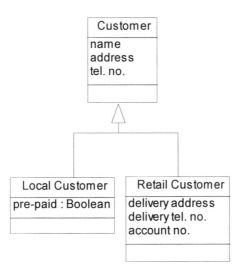

Figure 2.12 Specializations of the Customer class

A retail customer will typically be a large department store, such as Harrods. This type of customer might have an account, payable at the end of the month, and therefore will need an account number. A retail customer might have two addresses, one for billing purposes and one for delivery. These new requirements will feature in the specialized classes. A local customer must pay in advance, and have the same address for billing and delivery. Both the Local Customer class and the Retail Customer class have an IS-A relationship with the parent class Customer.

An inheritance relationship is indicated, diagrammatically, by a line between classes with a triangle pointing towards the parent class. Conventionally, inherited features are not shown in the specialized classes, but features which are introduced in the specialization, (e.g. account number and delivery address) are shown.

Polymorphism

The term polymorphism means the ability to define program entities, e.g. operations, that take more than one form. Polymorphism linked with an inheritance hierarchy allows a single message to be interpreted differently by different objects. Which method is executed will depend on which object receives the message.

We distinguish, in the section above on methods, between an operation and a method. What happens in an inheritance hierarchy is that a single operation may be implemented by more than one method. For example, in the inheritance hierarchy shown in Figure 2.13, the operation talk is first defined in the class Person. Each of the specialized classes: Baby, Toddler, Teenager, Mother, Father, Grandad, Granny, specializes this operation, so that each has a different method associated with the operation. A complete implementation of the family hierarchy can be found in Appendix E.

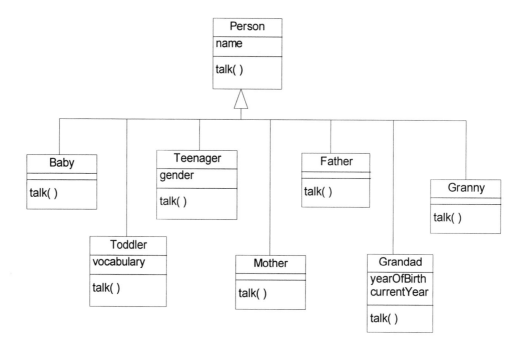

Figure 2.13 The talk operation is implemented differently in each class in the hierarchy

The message, talk, will produce a different response depending on the class of the object it is sent to. Let us assume that the method implementation is as shown in Table 2.2.

Table 2.2 Different implementations of the talk operation

Class	Method implementation
Person	I'm not saying anything
Baby	Wah, Wah
Toddler	Contents of the attribute vocabulary
Teenager	(male) Grunt, Grunt
Teenager	(female) Where is my mascara?
Mother	Have you tidied your room?
Father	I'm going to football
Grandad	I'm (currentYear minus yearOfBirth) years old
Granny	When's the boxing on?

This means that if we send an object of class Baby the message 'talk', it will respond 'Wah Wah'. If an object of class Toddler is sent the message 'talk', it will respond by outputting the entire value of the attribute 'vocabulary'. An object of class teenager will respond variously depending on the value of the attribute 'gender': if male it will respond 'Grunt, Grunt'; if female 'Where is my mascara?'. If an object of class Grandad is sent the message 'talk', it will subtract its year of birth from the current year and tell us its age.

Let us imagine that we have created objects from our class hierarchy as follows:

a Baby	named Amber	
a Toddler	named Noah	whose vocabulary is 'Mama' and 'NO'
a Teenager	named Edward	of male gender
a Teenager	named Lisa	of female gender
a Mother	named Lola	
a Father	named Matthew	
a Grandad	named David	born 1901, current year is 1999
a Granny	named Janet	

If we send all of these objects the talk message, they will respond as follows:

Amber	'Wah, Wah'
Noah	'Mama, NO'
Edward	'Grunt, Grunt'
Lisa	'Where is my mascara?'
Lola	'Have you tidied your room?'
Matthew	'I'm going to football!'
David	'I'm 98 years old'
Janet	'When's the boxing on?'

Since the original software crisis of the late sixties and early seventies, methodologies and software design and development techniques have emerged for improving the quality of delivered software. However, they have only been partially successful. Software developers continue to tackle problems of ever-increasing size and complexity. Methodologies and techniques continue to lag behind what is required to cope with today's software problems. Software is still delivered late, over-budget, is unreliable and inadequately tested.

The O-O approach promises to offer many improvements in the development process, to provide the next big step forward in terms of methodology, techniques and notations. Many of the problems identified as those causing software to be insufficiently robust and hard to maintain are specifically addressed in the O-O approach. These improvements are claimed to be across the whole software development process—requirements capture, analysis, design and code.

Exercises

2.1   Software designed used structured methods has proved to be difficult to maintain. Discuss the causes of these problems.

2.2   Briefly explain the difference between the following pairs of terms. You should
       include small examples to illustrate your answers.

a)   class / object
b)   attribute / operation
c)   association / multiplicity
d)   subclass / superclass
e)   message / method
f)   encapsulation / data hiding

2.3   In what ways does the object-oriented approach to software development hope to
       address the problems which continue to cause the software crisis

References and further reading

Bennett, S., McRobb, S. and Farmer, R. *Object-Oriented Systems Analysis and Design using UML,* London: McGraw-Hill, 1999.

Booch, G., Rumbaugh, J. and Jacobson, I. *The Unified Modeling Language User Guide,* Reading, Massachusetts: Addison-Wesley, 1999.

Fowler, M. with Scott, K. *UML Distilled: Applying the Standard Object Modeling Language,* Reading, Massachusetts: Addison-Wesley, 1997.

Rumbaugh, J., Blaha, M., Premerlani, W., Eddy, F. and Lorensen, W. *Object-Oriented Modeling and Design,* Englewood Cliffs, N.J.: Prentice-Hall, 1991.

3

Development Approaches

Traditionally, the development of a system is divided into several main stages. The progression of a system through these stages is known as the system life cycle. In this chapter we discuss the reasons for splitting up the system development in this way and how an object-oriented approach affects the nature and content of the stages.

There is no single generally accepted life cycle. Various methodologies have evolved which do precisely define the stages into which the development process should be split, and the exact sequence of tasks to be performed at each stage. A methodology gives a recipe for the development of systems. We introduce the concept of a methodology and briefly describe currently popular methodologies used in object-oriented development.

The choice of development methodology can be a major contributor to the success or failure of a system development project. We discuss briefly the factors that should be taken into account by developers when deciding the approach for particular development projects.

3.1 The system life cycle

The traditional system life cycle divided the development of a system into stages. It specified the general nature of the activities involved at each stage, the sequence in which these activities should be ordered and the output or deliverables from each stage. There were several advantages to this approach to system development. The activities involved at each stage were defined, documented and agreed. This helped when training new staff, and amongst established staff it meant that a consistent approach to system development was achieved. Communication between teams of system developers was also improved by adopting an agreed approach. For managers, the advantage was that each stage could be used as a milestone. Managers could put a date to that milestone and use it to monitor the development of the project. Having the activities involved at each stage specified beforehand brought tremendous advantages in terms of estimating the timescale for the project, costing and controlling the system development. Figure 3.1 shows an example of the stages in a typical system life cycle.

3.1.1 The traditional system life cycle

Computer science is a young discipline, which is still evolving. It has never agreed on a single right way to develop a system and, given the enormous diversity in the types of system it tackles, it probably never will. However, most system development approaches do partition the development process into a more or less agreed sequence of stages. The process begins with an initial attempt to define the problem and identify feasible solutions to it. The client's requirements are then fully analysed and recorded before decisions about design or implementation are made. In the early stages of development, system requirements are deliberately expressed in non-technical terms so that they can be understood and checked by the client. Once the requirements have been agreed, design of the system can be tackled; at this stage the developer establishes the overall structure of the system and proposes the hardware and software that will meet the client requirements. When the design is complete, the system is implemented in a programming language, tested and handed over to the client. From this point, work on the system is regarded as maintenance (correcting errors and implementing changes).

```
Problem Definition

Feasibility Study

Analysis

Design

Implementation
```

Figure 3.1 Stages in a typical system life cycle

3.1.2 The life cycle using prototyping

Designing systems, like designing anything else, involves building models. As we shall see in this book, there is a wide range of techniques for modelling both the original problem and the system that is to solve it. Some of these techniques are automated, but many are based on pencil and paper. Some paper-based techniques use diagrams, some are based on text, but all have one thing in common: a model created in one of these ways will always be just that—a model. However much care, time and effort the developer puts into it, the model will never itself become a working system.

Prototyping, on the other hand, is based on the concept of a working model. There are different ways of prototyping and different uses of prototypes, but what is common to all these is that not only the system developer but also the client and users will be able to see and experiment with part of the system on the computer from a relatively early stage in the development process.

With a disposable prototype, a model of the system (or part of it) is developed very quickly and refined in frequent discussions with the client. This type of model shows the client what the system will do, but is not backed up by detailed structured design. It is similar to a dress designer who makes up the pattern for an exclusive outfit in cheap material to see how it will look. Once the designer and client have tried out various ideas on this model, and are happy about the design of the final garment, the actual outfit is made up exactly like the model, but in fabric of a much higher quality.

Prototypes like this, in dress design or systems development, are very helpful in capturing requirements at an early stage in development, especially if the client is not sure where the problems lie. In the area of computer systems these prototypes are also an essential tool in designing and refining the user interface—what the system will look like to the people who are actually going to use it.

One of the most important things about this sort of prototype is that it is sooner or later discarded for all but documentation purposes. It is very tempting for designer and client alike to allow the model to be developed as the basis for the final system, but this is a path to disaster. The essence of prototyping like this, to capture client requirements, is speed. There is no place here for the detailed analysis and design that are essential for robust, reliable and maintainable systems. Keeping a prototype that has been built in this way, and developing it to become the final system, is as inappropriate as a dress designer selling the model made up in cheap material as an exclusive outfit. If the system developer decides to build this sort of prototype, it is also essential to decide exactly when and how it will be set aside, and then ensure that this is done when the time comes.

One widely used approach to developing systems is rapid prototyping, where the aim is to develop the model into the final system. This means that the system will be developed more quickly than by other, more traditional, methods and that the cost should be lower. It is important that extensive and detailed analysis of the problem is carried out before rapid prototyping begins, otherwise the final system will be like a house built on sand without any solid structural foundations. In this sort of approach, modern automated tools really come into their own; most developers will not attempt to develop a system using rapid prototyping without automated modelling tools and a powerful, high-level implementation language.

The typical life cycle for rapid prototyping is different from the one for full life cycle development, as can be seen from the diagram in Figure 3.2 on the following page. After the initial requirements are agreed, these are analysed and split into different areas in order to provide the basis for initial prototypes of different parts of the system; each prototype is demonstrated to the client and then refined to incorporate further requirements and modifications. The cycle of demonstration and refinement continues until both client and developer are satisfied. This process is carried out for each part of the system. The final prototypes are integrated and the complete system is then tested and eventually handed over to the client.

3.1.3 The object-oriented system life cycle

Object-oriented system development is based on the principal stages of the traditional system life cycle: analysis, design, implementation and maintenance. However, development tends to be viewed as a single, seamless process, with smoother transitions between different stages than in the traditional life cycle. Fundamental object-oriented concepts, such as objects, classes, associations and inheritance drive the development process from its very early stages and provide a single, unifying foundation for the life cycle.

The object-oriented life cycle is much less obviously linear than its predecessor; iteration of the various stages (which was seen as an add-on in the traditional life cycle) is an essential part of object-oriented development. One of the advantages of the iterative approach in object-oriented system development is that it is compatible with the use of prototypes throughout the development process. Rapid prototyping may be used to develop a small part of the system, which is then validated by users and continuously improved in an iterative and incremental development cycle.

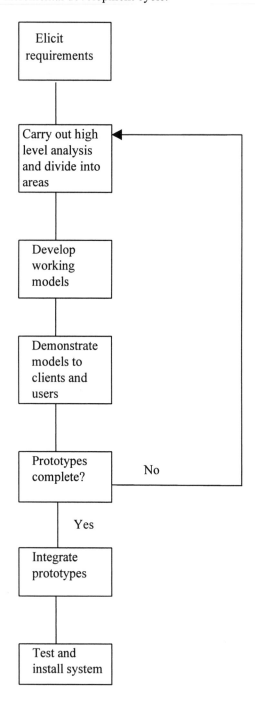

Figure 3.2 A life cycle for development using rapid prototyping

As with the traditional system life cycle, the exact content of each stage in the object-oriented cycle—the steps and activities involved—will vary from one practitioner to the next. If a standard methodology (see Section 3.2) is used, precise details are given as to what should be done and what techniques should be used. A rough guide to the nature of each stage in the object-oriented life cycle is outlined below.

Analysis

It is increasingly realised that successful system development depends on 'getting it right' in the early stages. It doesn't matter how elegant the coding, nor how friendly the interface, if the system doesn't do what is required, then it is a failure. The discipline which has grown up to address this problem is known as requirements engineering and is divided into elicitation (gathering the requirements), specification (modelling the requirements) and validation (checking that the requirements are correct). Requirements engineering is discussed in detail in Chapter 4.

The analysis stage of system development begins with a period of fact finding during which the system developer investigates the current system. The investigation is part of the process of requirements elicitation (see Chapter 4) and must be tackled methodically and thoroughly. Key members of staff must be interviewed to establish in detail how the present system works and what the problems are. In a large system it may be impossible, because of time or financial constraints, to interview everyone concerned. The system developer may be forced to concentrate on key staff and obtain any information required from other potential users by the use of carefully designed questionnaires.

Another useful source of information is the documentation of the present system. The system developer should collect and study copies of such documents as reports, invoices, order forms, information recorded in files about, for example, customers, suppliers or stock levels. In a large system there may also be documentation in the form of job descriptions, office procedures and user manuals, etc. The developer may also find it useful simply to observe the normal operation of the current system. This may reveal features not discovered by any other fact-finding technique and will help the system developer understand the staff interviewed and the documents studied.

Facts will rarely emerge in a neatly ordered fashion. It is much more usual for system developers to discover by the end of the fact-finding stage that they have a mass of detailed, unstructured and probably conflicting information. The next job is to sort out what has been discovered and document it in a way that will help organize the material. This must then be discussed with the clients to check that the system developer has correctly understood what was said in the interview, fill in any gaps and resolve any apparent conflicts.

In object-oriented development it is seen as essential to spend time getting to grips with the problem in its real-world context. Object-orientation views any system as a collection of collaborating objects, which means that identifying the 'right' objects early on is crucial to success. The aims of the analysis stage of object-oriented system development are:

- to determine the scope of the system and establish the business case for developing it, including risk assessment and criteria for success;
- to establish an agreed set of requirements (although these will inevitably change during development of the system);
- to identify a set of objects which will fulfil these requirements;

- to describe the attributes and observable behaviour of these objects;
- to identify relationships and patterns of communication between the objects;
- to chronicle events which may occur in the system and describe the way in which the objects may be affected by these events.

The objects identified in the problem domain and specified during analysis form the basis for all subsequent development of the system. Information about the objects is held in models, which are refined and extended during the later stages of development. The most important of these is the class diagram, which records class names, attributes, operations, and relationships between the objects. The class diagram is central to object-oriented system development; it is discussed in detail in Chapter 5.

The other main model that is constructed during the analysis stage of development is the dynamic model. Dynamic modelling is concerned with events that occur during the life of a system and the effects these have on the objects and their relationships. The techniques for dynamic modelling that are covered in this book are use cases, scenarios, interaction diagrams and state diagrams. These are discussed in Chapter 6.

During the analysis stage of development, both the class diagram and the dynamic models concentrate on information that is relevant to the user's view of the system. The models at this stage are implementation independent; depending on decisions yet to be taken, they may be implemented in several different ways. Experience has shown that if implementation decisions are made too soon, the design of the new system can be unnecessarily constrained by the limitations of the hardware or software selected. For example, if the developer decides at an early stage that the system will be implemented using a commercial package, this may preclude the opportunity to use a system architecture that would have been more elegant. If the developer is committed from the start to a certain type of hardware, this may mean that it is impossible to use a particular item of software that would have been ideal for the system. Sometimes there is no choice in the matter—it may be necessary to use existing client software and hardware—but if there is a free choice, decisions about implementation issues should not be made until the analysis stage has been completed.

The physical deliverable from the analysis stage of object-oriented development is a validated specification of requirements which has been agreed with the client and which contains the initial class diagram and dynamic models of the system. The specification should also include details of non-functional requirements, such as those relating to system response times, security and the user interface. A less tangible, but equally important deliverable from the analysis stage is a sound understanding in the mind of the developer of the nature of the problem and its domain, the requirements established so far, the objects that will fulfil those requirements and the ways in which the system will react to external events.

Design

Once the developers feel that they have a sound grasp of the problem to be solved, the next step is to determine how this is going to be achieved. It is probable that the client will be offered a choice of different technical solutions that will meet the requirements specified. Typical alternative solutions may be:

- A very cheap solution which does the job and no more.

- A medium price solution which does the job well and is convenient for the user; it will probably have additional features the client did not request but which the system developer knows from experience will be needed.
- A high cost solution—everything the client could ever need, but at a price.

Solutions may differ in their:

- *System boundaries*: the proposed systems might affect, though not necessarily computerize, different parts of an organization's functions.
- *Automation boundaries*: one proposed solution might leave some functions to operate manually, while another computerizes them.
- *Hardware and networking*: one solution might propose the use of a large central computer with a number of terminals and laser printers. A cheaper solution might recommend a network of personal computers (PCs) and less sophisticated printers.
- *Software*: the advantages of object-oriented system development are most fully exploited when the system is implemented in an object-oriented programming language or an object-oriented database management system. However, systems where analysis and design have been carried out on an object-oriented basis may be successfully implemented in a language such as Visual Basic or a procedurally-based programming language, such as Pascal.
- *Design strategies*: the system developer might choose to follow a full life cycle approach, or to develop the system incrementally, using a series of prototypes.
- *User interface*: the design of the user interface will be determined by the type of people using the system. Someone who is not used to computers and who uses the system only occasionally will need more help than someone who has been trained to use computers and sits at a screen all day. User interface design is a crucial part of all system development, since a system which users find unfriendly and hard to use will be rejected and must count as a failure. Prototyping, which is the most effective way to design user-friendly systems, is facilitated and encouraged by object-oriented system development. One widespread application of object-orientation is the design and implementation of graphical user interfaces (GUIs), such as Windows and the Apple Macintosh.
- *Cost and time*: all of the factors discussed above will affect the cost of the system and the time it will take to develop it.

The principal task of the design stage in object-oriented system development is to determine the architecture of the system to be built: how the system as a whole is to be organized into smaller, more manageable components or subsystems. Whereas analysis concentrates on understanding the user's view of the system, system design is driven by implementation concerns. The models that were constructed during the analysis stage are still at the centre of the development process, but during the design stage they are adapted and expanded to take account of technical considerations and constraints arising from the implementation environment. Details added to the analysis models address issues such as flow of control, data storage, concurrency and potential reuse. The aim of system design is to create a model that can be implemented and which captures all relevant features of the system, relating both to what the system is to do and how it is to do it. The output from the design stage should therefore contain all the information that the programmers need to code the system.

At the design stage, too, decisions have to be taken as to whether parts of the new system can be constructed from reusable components. One of the main claims of object-oriented development is that it encourages reuse of code and designs, and that this leads to more efficient development and more reliable systems. Two important aspects of the design stage of object-oriented development are to identify any appropriate components in a class library that may be reused in the new system (known as design with reuse) and to identify new classes that can subsequently form part of a library of classes for future use (known as design for reuse).

Implementation

During this stage the system is physically built; the program code is written and tested, and supporting documentation is produced. The output from this stage of the life cycle includes:

- Program listings, test plans and supporting documentation
- Manual of operating procedures
- Manual of clerical procedures
- User manual.

Object-oriented system development is based on a set of concepts, including classification, association and inheritance, that apply throughout the life cycle, and is built around a set of models that are started during analysis and gradually refined and extended as development progresses. This continuity means that the later stages of development are a natural consequence of earlier stages and, as such, involve less time and effort than the equivalent stages in the traditional system life cycle. This is particularly evident when the system is implemented in an object-oriented programming language, such as C++ or Java. However, even when an object-oriented programming language is not used for implementation, the emphasis placed on the analysis and design stages of the life cycle by the object-oriented approach means that less time and effort have to be spent on implementation, testing and maintenance. The potential for reuse in object-oriented development also means that, in many cases, there is less work during the later life cycle stages.

Once coding is complete and the system has been exhaustively tested, it must be installed at the clients' site on their equipment and the changeover from the old to the new system supervised. This will involve training users and ensuring that the data from the old system is successfully taken on by the new system. There is often a hand-holding period before the new system is formally handed over to the clients. Installation is sometimes regarded as a separate stage in the life cycle. After installation, the system development team will only be involved in maintaining and modifying the system.

Maintenance

The maintenance stage starts as soon as the system is formally handed over to the clients. The term 'maintenance' is often used as a euphemism for finding and correcting errors that were not detected before the system was handed over. True maintenance is modifying the system to meet evolving requirements. In either case the system developer must start again at the beginning of the cycle by ascertaining the client and user requirements.

Figure 3.3 models a simplified system life cycle as a completed circle, starting and ending with client requirements. Note also the backward-pointing arrows at each stage which indicate the iterative nature of system development. At each stage the system development team must check back to the requirements specified in the previous stage, and re-do the work if necessary.

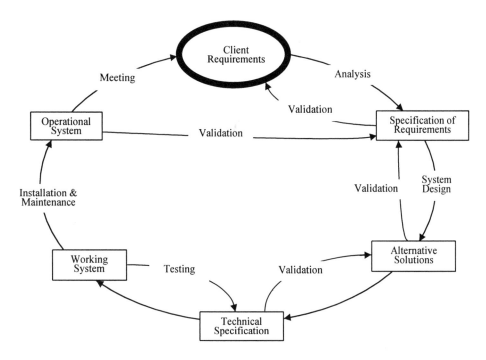

Figure 3.3 A simplified system life cycle

3.1.4 Features of the object-oriented system life cycle

Although the object-oriented life cycle is, in many ways, similar to the traditional system life cycle, there are differences that have a significant impact on the development process.

- The object-oriented approach places most emphasis on the early stages of development: understanding the problem, establishing the requirements and identifying the data objects that will satisfy these. This type of development not only means that later stages of the life cycle involve less time and effort, but also leads to more robust, adaptable and dependable systems.
- Object-orientation encourages developers to think about issues, such as maintenance, modification and possible reuse, throughout the development life cycle. Anticipating these issues at an early stage means that they are more easily and efficiently dealt with when they do occur.

- Object-orientation has a common shared terminology, covering key concepts, such as encapsulation, class and inheritance. Such terms are an important part of the object-oriented system life cycle, since they enable developers to share understanding of complex concepts and to communicate their ideas on the system more effectively.
- The aim of object-oriented development is a seamless transition from original idea to finished system; this means that the separate stages of the life cycle are much less distinct than in traditional system development.
- Object-orientation actively supports iteration throughout the development process; it is therefore equally suitable for full life cycle development as well as for incremental development, based on rapid prototyping.
- In object-oriented development the emphasis on data leads to a single, unifying concept (the object) throughout the life cycle and, ultimately, to more stable software.
- The object-oriented approach refines and extends models built in the early stages of development, rather than creating new models at each stage. This eliminates the need for shifts between different representations of the problem, ensures that important information is preserved and supports seamless system development.
- The seamless approach to development facilitates traceability: the tracking of features from initial requirements through to program code.

3.2 Methodologies

A software development methodology is usually based on a life cycle model of system development and has a number of development stages with a set of steps and rules for each stage. Whereas a life cycle coarsely partitions the development of a system into stages, a methodology takes a life cycle and further divides each of the stages into a number of steps. A methodology will prescribe in great detail what tasks are involved in each step, the nature of each task, the order in which the tasks need to be done, what documents are required as input to each stage, and what documents are produced from it. In fact, it provides a detailed plan for producing a system.

3.2.1 Why do we need a methodology?

Comparisons are often made between the stages involved in designing and building software and other artefacts such as houses or bridges. Relatively speaking, methodologies for developing software have not been around for very long. However, they embody knowledge and wisdom gained by system developers through trial and error over a number of decades. For example, it is now generally accepted that one of the first and most important tasks in system development is to find out exactly what the new system is required to do. This may involve a detailed and time-consuming study of the existing system and its immediate environment. Experience has shown that failure to do this successfully is what causes the type of error that is hardest to find and most expensive to correct. Most methodologies incorporate this experience by prescribing a set of tasks designed to ensure that requirements are successfully captured, specified and validated with the client and users of the system.

Building a system involves constructing many different models of the system (see Chapters 5, 6 and 7 on modelling). Each model is only a partial description of the system. To understand the whole system, we have to understand how the models relate to and complement each other. A methodology provides a framework, an agreed structure, in which these models can be related to each other.

A methodology provides inexperienced system developers with a recipe to follow. Some methodologies are specifically designed for this purpose. Each step along the development process is prescribed, as are the required documents for the step and the nature of the output from it. Methodologies vary in the amount of direction that they provide: some (often referred to as 'cookbook' methodologies) are highly prescriptive, with detailed instructions and descriptions of deliverables. Other methodologies advocate a 'toolbox' approach. This is similar to the case where a craftsman is asked to design and build a table; the craftsman will select certain tools for the job and will go about the task in a certain way. If asked to make a picture frame, the craftsman will select some of the same tools and some different ones. The process of constructing the frame is different in many ways from that of building the table. System development methodologies that use the toolbox approach provide the system developer with a range of techniques that are helpful for developing systems. For each new application, appropriate techniques are selected and used in an appropriate way by the system developer. What is important is that the choice of techniques should be determined by the nature of the problem, not predetermined by a methodology.

Building a system, especially a large and complex system, is a long and complicated process during which a great number of tasks have to be accomplished. Many of the tasks are interdependent; often, large teams of developers will be involved and their work will need to be co-ordinated. Using a methodology helps with the management of the whole project by breaking down the development process into small tasks, specifying the order in which they should be done and the interdependencies of the tasks. This helps with planning, scheduling and monitoring the progress of the system.

3.2.2 Early methodologies

Over the years there have been many different methodologies, each offering its own view of how to go about building a system. Different methodologies are suitable for developing different types of system. Some that have been used for developing real-time systems are Yourdon, Mascot3, JSD (Jackson System Development). Methodologies used for developing information systems include SSADM (Structured Systems Analysis and Design Method), JSD (Jackson System Development) and Information Engineering (James Martin).

Different methodologies place emphasis on different aspects of system development. Some concentrate on the flow of data through the system, modelled using data flow diagrams, others consider the structuring and interrelationships of the stored data in the system, modelled using entity relationship diagrams, to be of primary importance.

Methodologies are constantly changing to accommodate new technological advances and new ideas in system development. For example, the development of automated CASE tools, such as Rational Rose and end-user programming languages, such as Visual Basic, together with a change in client attitudes to system development, has led to radically different approaches to software development.

3.2.3 Object-oriented methodologies

There is a wide range of object-oriented methodologies, each with its own view of the development process. Some focus on design and implementation, some on analysis, some concentrate on a particular modelling technique, while others are specifically geared towards a particular implementation language. However, there is one feature that all these methodologies have in common: they organise the development of systems around objects. New methodologies are constantly being developed and old ones are continually being updated, so it is not possible to give a definitive picture of all the object-oriented methodologies that are used in industry and academia at any one time. In the section below, we briefly introduce and provide references for some of the main methodologies that have appeared in recent years.

Responsibility-Driven Design (Wirfs-Brock et al., 1990)

This methodology focuses on the early stages of system development. It claims to be suitable for any programming medium, not only object-oriented languages. Responsibility-Driven Design advocates putting a lot of effort into determining the responsibilities which different classes have towards others in the system and how the various classes collaborate with each other. The responsibilities of a class indicate its purpose, and the collaborators are the other classes needed for the class to carry out its responsibilities. Once objects and classes in the system have been established, scenarios are used to identify the responsibilities and collaborations.

Booch (1994)

Grady Booch was one of the first authors to suggest an approach to developing object-oriented systems, gearing his original methodology towards implementation in specific languages. Booch's approach is much less prescriptive than many of the other methodologies; he advocates an incremental and iterative development process, which he calls 'round-trip gestalt design'. Booch provides a rich set of notations for modelling object-oriented systems; many of his ideas have been incorporated in the Unified Modelling Language (UML).

Objectory (Jacobson et al., 1992)

The main contribution of this methodology is the use case, which specifies the functionality that the system will offer from the users' perspective. A use case specifies a set of interactions between a user and the system to achieve a particular goal. A use case, such as 'make phone call', is refined by a number of scenarios, each of which describes what happens in a specific situation. For example, scenarios for 'make phone call' could include 'dialling tone, dial number, ringing tone, connect, talk, hang up' and 'dialling tone, dial number, number unobtainable, hang up'. Use cases and scenarios are a very effective way of identifying the initial user requirements for the system; they are an important element of UML.

Object Modelling Technique (OMT) (Rumbaugh et al,. 1991)

OMT was originally developed by James Rumbaugh at General Electric as a series of steps for the production of software systems, with associated techniques and notations. OMT claims to be suitable, both for full life-cycle development, and for development using rapid prototyping. The methodology has three main stages: analysis, design and implementation, but it strongly emphasises the idea of a seamless development process. Central to this process is a model of objects in the problem domain to which design and implementation details are added during development. Rumbaugh's version of the object model has been widely used in object-oriented system development and is one of the principal components of UML.

Second generation methodologies

Some of the more recent object-oriented methodologies claim to be 'second generation', integrating and extending the best features of the early methodologies. Two examples of second generation methodologies are Fusion (Coleman et al., 1994), which is based on elements of OMT, Objectory, Booch and Responsibility-Driven Design, and Syntropy (Cook and Daniels, 1994) which incorporates elements of formal methods into the object-oriented development process.

So many new methodologies, and variants of previous ones, constantly appear on the market, that it is difficult to keep track of them all. The ones that we mention here have provided the foundations for a structured and systematic approach to object-oriented development and, in several cases, they have contributed to the Unified Modelling Language (UML).

A standardised notation: the Unified Modelling Language (UML)

One of the difficulties arising from the popularity of the object-oriented approach to developing systems is lack of standardization. Although the underlying concepts remain the same, there is a huge variation in notation and process among the object-oriented methodologies. The Unified Modelling Language aims to address this problem by combining the best elements of the main object-oriented methodologies while, at the same time, reflecting best practices in industry.

UML was started in the mid-90's by James Rumbaugh (OMT) and Grady Booch; they were later joined by Ivar Jacobson (Objectory). It is a very ambitious project and, at the time of writing, is still not complete. The UML standard notation has solid foundations, is well-documented and is already in use, but development of a standard development process has proved much more difficult. However, work continues and it is hoped that a full methodology, which will be widely supported by industry, will be available in the near future.

3.2.4 Choosing a methodology

The way in which a software system is developed has a huge influence on the final software product and can make the difference between success and failure in a development project. Developers frequently do not have the opportunity to choose which methodology they will use on a particular project; the development approach may be predetermined by such factors as company policy, resources, available support tools or preferences of the project manager. However, where the situation does allow the developer to choose the development methodology, it is important that the choice should be soundly based. The three main issues that should be considered are:

- who are the stakeholders?
- what type of system is to be developed?
- what are the principal features of the environment in which the system is to be developed?

A stakeholder, in the context of developing software systems, is anyone who either contributes to the system development or who is affected by it. This will include, among others, the developers who are working on the system, the clients who are paying for the development and who are the principal source of requirements for the system, and the users who will be operating the system on a day to day basis. For each of these groups, it is important to establish their previous experience of software system development, their understanding of and familiarity with the problem domain, and the extent of their planned involvement in the development.

As regards the type of system to be developed, questions that the developer has to determine include the extent to which it is safety-critical (where failure would cause severe hardship or even loss of life) or security-critical (where failure would cause loss of crucial information). It is also very useful to establish system priorities: for example, whether the most important aspect is the way the data is structured, the complexity of processing required, or the way that information is to be presented (such as using a multimedia interface).

The environment in which a system is developed is influenced by a wide variety of factors, including the cultural and social aspects of the developing and client organisations, the tools that are available to support development, and constraints of time or money. In making a choice of methodology the developer also has to bear in mind the nature of the existing system, whether manual or computerized, and whether the new system has to be implemented in a particular programming language or commercial package. Figure 3.4, on the following page, shows features of the *Just a Line* security problem: stakeholders, type of system and development environment, and Exercise 3.4 asks you to identify features for different types of software systems.

Once the developer has got an overall picture of the different factors that make up the development context of the particular project, this should provide a sound basis on which to make the choice of suitable methodology. Many methodologies, particularly those that have been around for some time, are appropriate for specific types of development; others are more general, but may be geared towards a particular programming language; yet others depend heavily on the involvement of clients throughout the development process. With a good knowledge both of different methodologies and of the features of the development context, the developer can select the best match to ensure a successful outcome for the project.

Stakeholders:
- Sue and Harry Preston
- *Just a Line* employees
- visitors to the *Just a Line* site
- the local council (if the car park is to be affected)
- the developers.

Type of system:
- security, but not safety-critical
- processing of data and interface both important.

Development environment:
- need to investigate thoroughly how access is controlled at present
- need to be aware that the proposed measures may be unpopular with employees
- the system should be in operation relatively soon
- money is presumably not a problem
- prototyping is a feasible approach.

Figure 3.4 Features of the *Just a Line* security problem

The system life cycle approach was developed in response to the software problems of the sixties and seventies. It partitioned the development of a system into predetermined stages, each of which had to be completed and agreed with the client before progressing to the next stage. The particular contributions this brought to improving the quality of the delivered system were in concentrating more attention on capturing client requirements, enforcing a more structured approach to system development and allowing much more effective project management. More recently, the object-oriented view of the life cycle emphasises the importance of seamless development based on fundamental object-oriented concepts.

Progressing from the coarse partitioning of the life cycle, methodologies refine each of the stages into a prescribed series of activities with precisely defined inputs and outputs. There are already a large number of methodologies based on the object-oriented approach, which has led to problems of standardisation. However, this is now being addressed by the Unified Modelling Language (UML) which aims to provide a standard notation for object-oriented system development.

Using a methodology for system development has tremendous advantages in terms of improved communication between clients, system developers and project managers. However, it is very important that the methodology chosen is appropriate for the particular development context, since the methodology used is a major factor in the success or failure of a project.

Exercises

3.1   What are the main benefits of the system life cycle?

3.2   What do you think are the advantages and disadvantages of developing a system using rapid prototyping?

3.3   In what ways does the object-oriented approach claim to improve the system development process?

3.4   Imagine that you are a member of a team developing the following systems:

- a public information system for your local area;
- a system to monitor heart patients in hospital;
- a system to handle orders from a charity's Christmas catalogue;
- a system to control traffic lights at the junction near a village school.

For each case write down as much as you can about the development environment, the type of system and the stakeholders.

References and further reading

Booch, G. *Object-oriented Analysis and Design with Applications,* 2nd edn, Redwood City, California: Benjamin/Cummings, 1994.

Coleman, D., Arnold, P., Bodoff, S., Dollin, C., Gilchrist, H., Hayes, F. and Jeremaes, P. *Object-Oriented Development: The Fusion Method,* Englewood Cliffs, N.J.: Prentice-Hall, 1994.

Cook, S. and Daniels, J. *Designing Object Systems. Object-Oriented Modelling with Syntropy,* Hemel Hempstead: Prentice-Hall, 1994.

Fowler, M. with Scott, K. *UML Distilled: Applying the Standard Object Modeling Language,* Reading, Massachusetts: Addison-Wesley, 1997.

Henderson-Sellers, B. *A Book of Object-Oriented Knowledge,* 2nd edn, Upper Saddle River, N.J.: Prentice-Hall, 1997.

Jacobson, I., Christerson, M., Jonsson, P. and Overgaard, G. *Object-Oriented Software Engineering: A Use Case Driven Approach,* Wokingham: Addison-Wesley, 1992.

Rumbaugh, J., Blaha, M., Premerlani, W., Eddy, F. and Lorensen, W. *Object-Oriented Modeling and Design*, Englewood Cliffs, N.J.: Prentice-Hall, 1991.

Sommerville, I. *Software Engineering,* 5th edn, Wokingham: Addison-Wesley, 1995.

Wirfs-Brock, R., Wilkerson, B. and Wiener, L. *Designing Object-Oriented Software,* Englewood Cliffs, N.J.: Prentice Hall, 1990.

4

Engineering the System Requirements

It is generally accepted that many systems fail because they do not satisfy the requirements of clients and users. The process of ensuring that software systems deliver what is wanted is known as requirements engineering and is divided into three stages: elicitation, specification and validation. In this chapter we describe the role of the requirements engineer and discuss each of the three stages of requirements engineering. The chapter includes examples from the requirements engineering process for the *Just a Line* security case study.

4.1 The role of the requirements engineer

Requirements engineering is one of the most important activities in the system development process. If the final system does not satisfy the clients' and users' requirements, then it is a failure. It is therefore essential that what is wanted is clearly identified, documented and agreed as early as possible and that any changes are handled in an equally rigorous way.

The role of the requirements engineer in the development of a software system is similar to that of an architect in a building project. We can get a good idea of what he or she has to do by looking at the part an architect plays in a typical building project.

Let us imagine a family with three children whose present house is a bit on the small side. The family's aim is to get more living space and there are various ways in which they might do this: move house, extend their present house, or build a new one (see Figure 4.1).

Figure 4.1 Options for solving the problem of lack of space

There are certain constraints on how the family solves the space problem; it is not feasible, for example, to reduce the number of children, and there is likely to be a limit on how much money they can afford to spend. We will assume that the family members have decided to build an extension to their house and have called in an architect for preliminary discussions. In establishing the precise requirements for the proposed extension, the architect has several distinct tasks to carry out. First, he or she will have to identify the users of the extension; in this case these will obviously be the parents (who are paying for the work to be done) and the children. However, on talking to the family, the architect discovers several more potential users (see Figure 4.2). It turns out that one of the reasons for the extension is that an elderly grandmother is going to come and live with the family; she will also be a user of the extension. There is also a large and very energetic dog whose needs must be taken into account.

Figure 4.2 The users of the new extension

On top of all these direct users of the extension, there are other people who are not direct users, but who will nonetheless have the right to comment on aspects of its design; these are the neighbours and the local council.

It is important, in the early stages of the project, for the architect to become familiar with the environment in which the extension is going to be situated; this includes the layout of the existing house, its position, the size and shape of the garden and its immediate neighbourhood. This is shown is Figure 4.3, below.

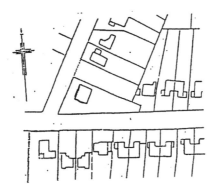

Figure 4.3 Plan of the neighbourhood, showing the position of the house

Once the clients and users have been established and the architect has a clear picture of the house and its surroundings, the next task is to talk to the users to discover their particular problems and what each of them requires from the new extension. Inevitably, what the architect is told at this stage will not be a specific set of requirements that can be agreed by all parties. Members of the family may not be clear in their own minds what exactly they want from the extension, or requirements of different family members may conflict with each other. The parents, for example, may view the extension as primarily for the grandmother's use, as she is no longer able to live on her own, but still values a certain amount of independence. The teenage children, however, also want a space of their own to play music and have their friends round (see Figure 4.4).

Figure 4.4 Different views of the new extension

Whatever way the extension is used, it will take space from the garden, leaving less room for the dog to run around in and possibly displeasing the next-door neighbours. Ultimately, these conflicting requirements will have to be resolved by the family, but it is part of the architect's job to identify problems and to help the family to make decisions about the extension. The architect must also be aware of possible requirements for the extension that do not come from the clients or users; these will include neighbours' rights to privacy, light and access, and the building regulations which are in force in the area.

After collecting as much relevant information as possible, the architect produces an initial model of the proposed extension; the model at this stage generally consists of an artist's impression of how the extension might look and draft plans of the internal layout. Part of a typical plan can be seen in Figure 4.5.

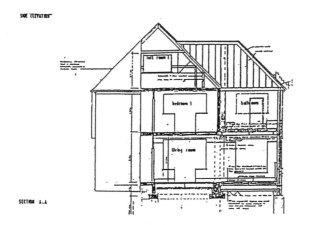

Figure 4.5 Draft plan of the extension

The drawing and plans are then discussed with the family and modified in the light of their comments. The cycle of discussion and modification of the plans continues until the family are satisfied that the model accurately expresses the requirements for the new extension. At this point planning permission is applied for from the local council, which may lead to more modifications to the plans to meet objections from neighbours and comply with building regulations. The whole process of establishing, modelling and agreeing the requirements for the extension may take several months, but only after this is complete can building begin. However, the architect's job does not end there. Inevitably, as building progresses, members of the family will find that they change their minds about certain aspects of the extension (perhaps they want an extra window, or a door in a different position). Alternatively, the family's circumstances may change and their original requirements are no longer appropriate (see Figure 4.6). All new requirements and changes to old ones have to be established, modelled and agreed in the same way as the original requirements.

Figure 4.6 Changes in circumstances will mean changes in requirements

The role of the requirements engineer in a system development project is very similar to the role of the architect, as we have described it here. However, there is one important difference, which makes the requirements engineer's job even more difficult than that of the architect. A building project, such as an extension to a house, is dealing with a physical entity; components of the architect's plans, such as rectangles and parallel lines, clearly represent elements of the extension, such as rooms and stairs. In a system development project, however, what is being built is an abstract entity; we cannot see, feel or hear a software system, only the external results of its internal processes. This is an extra complication for the requirements engineer, particularly when constructing models of requirements; an architect can represent elements of a building simply by drawing their shapes, but how can a requirements engineer represent a process or a collection of data? We shall return to this point later when we discuss modelling; our aim here is simply to introduce you to the job of the requirements engineer and the part he or she plays in the software development process.

4.2 The requirements engineering process

The term requirements engineering refers to the collection of tasks that identify, record and validate the requirements for the system. Each requirement is a statement, originating from a client, user or other stakeholder, that defines some desired feature of the system. Requirements are frequently described as stating WHAT the system will do, rather than

HOW it will do it, but this distinction is often not very helpful. For example, in a marketing system, a client may ask for the facility to send information to everyone on a mailing list; it is not clear (and not important) whether the mailing requirement is what the system is to do or how the marketing is to be carried out.

A further distinction that is frequently made today is between functional and non-functional requirements. In the past, requirements engineering meant defining functional requirements: what the system was to do, what its inputs and outputs were and how these were linked. Correct functional requirements are still considered essential for successful software development today, but in recent years developers have also come to realise the importance of non-functional requirements. These can be defined as the attributes of the system as it performs its job and can be divided into non-functional requirements of the system and non-functional requirements arising from external sources.

Non-functional requirements of the system will include issues such as usability, performance, reliability and security. Requirements relating to usability address questions such as how the system can attract its intended users, the right level of help to provide and whether the system will fit in with the users' preferred way of working. Performance requirements specify aspects of the system such as how quickly it must respond to satisfy the users' needs and the volume of transactions that it will be expected to deal with. Reliability requirements relate to the confidence that the clients and users should have that the system will behave consistently as expected, and security addresses the question of how to prevent unauthorized access to the system and modification of confidential data.

Non-functional requirements that arise from external sources include methods of operation, such as the client's existing procedures; physical constraints, such as the layout of the accommodation available; international quality control standards, such as ISO 9001, and constraints relating to costs or the system delivery date.

The goal of the requirements engineering process is to produce an agreed specification of the behaviour of the intended system. The specification is a cornerstone of a system development project, since it encapsulates the shared understanding and intentions of all the stakeholders. The specification may be used as a vehicle for communication between developers, users and other stakeholders; it may also form the basis of a legal contract between developer and client, and it is the document that guides the programmers in their implementation of the system.

Evidence suggests that errors in requirements may account for approximately 50% of the total cost of debugging a software system, yet it is only relatively recently that serious research has been carried out on the subject of requirements engineering. In general, traditional system development methodologies, most of which are underpinned by a standard life cycle model (see Chapter 3), merely pay lip service to the problems of identifying, describing and validating the requirements for the system. In the past it was frequently the case that the initial informal problem description was agreed and signed off by the client, who would then have little more to do with the development process until delivery and installation of the final system. Needless to say, this method of development often led to unsatisfactory systems and unhappy clients.

Today, requirements engineering is recognized as a crucial stage in the development of software. Each year more and more requirements methods become available, often as expensive commercial products, involving computer-based tools, training programmes and extensive documentation. However, since research into requirements engineering is still in its early stages, we have, as yet, little reliable information about the relative effectiveness of the various methods.

Although there is a huge variation in the ways in which requirements engineering is carried out, virtually all approaches can be divided into three main stages. The first of these is requirements elicitation, which aims to gather as much information as possible about the problem domain, the clients' and users' current difficulties and what they would like the intended system to do for them. The second stage is requirements specification, during which the information from the elicitation process is analysed and recorded using textual and diagrammatic modelling techniques to represent the problem and the proposed solution. The final stage is requirements validation which checks that the recorded requirements correspond to the intentions of the stakeholders about the system. Each of these stages of requirements engineering is discussed in more detail in the following sections.

4.3 Requirements elicitation

Requirements engineering begins with the task of finding out as much as possible about the clients' organization, their current problems and what they would like the new system to do for them. This is deceptively simple, since it involves sifting through large amounts of information and deciding what exactly is relevant. It is also extremely difficult for the requirements engineer to be sure that he or she has a complete and accurate understanding of what the clients want. Good communication skills, both oral and written, are essential for requirements elicitation, since nearly all methods of fact-finding depend on communication with clients and users.

4.3.1 Requirements elicitation methods

Requirements elicitation covers several different types of activity, such as observation of the users at work, study of relevant documents, formal meetings with stakeholders and user questionnaires, but often the most effective way of getting information is simply to talk to the people involved in the system.

Interviews

A useful interview is one that has been prepared thoroughly. Interviews may take place for a variety of reasons, such as obtaining information about the client organization or checking the requirements engineer's understanding of specific requirements. Later on in the development project, interviews may be used to explain details of the new system to clients and users and to obtain feedback on what has been proposed.

Whatever the purpose of the interview, it is important that both the requirements engineer and the interviewee should be clear about it and what they each want to get out of the interview. A plan for the interview should be prepared in advance by the requirements engineer, identifying the purpose of the interview, any documents that are to be made available and setting out a draft agenda. A plan for the initial interview with Sue and Harry Preston of *Just a Line* is shown in Figure 4.7 below.

D&B Systems – Interview Plan

System: *Just a Line*	**Project reference:** JaL/MB/00

Participants:
Sue Preston (*Just a Line*)
Harry Preston (*Just a Line*)
Mark Barnes (D&B)

Date: 10/4/00	**Time:** 14.30	**Duration:** 45 minutes	**Place:** Sue's office

Purpose of interview:
Preliminary meeting to identify problems and requirements regarding security at the *Just a Line* site.

Agenda:
- problems with security and any other concerns
- current security procedures
- initial ideas
- follow-up actions

Documents to be brought to interview:
- rough plan of building and site
- any documents relating to current security procedures

Figure 4.7 Plan for the first interview with Sue and Harry from *Just a Line*

Before the interview, the requirements engineer should have established relevant details about the interviewee, such as his or her background, position in the organization, length of time with the company and special skills, such as level of computer expertise. It is part of the requirements engineer's job to put the interviewee at ease, particularly if the interview takes place away from the interviewee's place of work. It is worth spending some time chatting in general terms and very important to listen carefully to what the interviewee has to say, even if it does not appear to be directly relevant. The ability to listen attentively and identify important and relevant information is one of the essential skills for a requirements engineer. Although direct questions are needed to control the interview, a lot of information can also be discovered by smiling, nodding encouragingly and making the interviewee feel that what they are saying is important. The requirements engineer should direct the interview, but must not dominate it.

A useful interview will be a source of several different kinds of information for the requirements engineer. Some of these are listed below:

- information that is already structured in lists, forms, company guidelines or policies;
- information about company procedures: how certain tasks are carried out at present;
- measurements such as the number of customers or the average size of an order;
- problems that the client has identified in the current system;
- initial requirements and wishes for the new system;
- information that is not stated directly, but where there are definite vibes. An example of this might be where the clients complain that their supplier always delivers late and they are always rushed when the order comes in, whereas what is actually happening is that their normal procedures cannot cope with the extra workload.

Figure 4.8, below, shows the initial interview of Sue and Harry Preston of *Just a Line* by Mark Barnes of D&B Systems.

Sue: Hello, Mark, good to see you. Come and sit down.

Harry: Hello again. It must be quite a while since we last met; I expect you'll notice a few changes.

Mark: Hello there. Yes this is certainly different from your other place; you've come a long way. Mind you, I'm not surprised, I see your cards all over the place nowadays.

Harry: Excellent—we've been trying really hard to increase our market share and I think we're doing OK at the moment. Of course, the hard thing is to keep one step ahead all the time. You get a winning idea—like those edible cards for example, they've been brilliant – but then you have to think up something else that's just as good, if not better. You can't relax for a minute.

Sue: Yes, you can see why it was such a blow when *Global Greetings* produced their card sculptures just weeks before ours were due to come out. And they are so similar; it's absolutely sickening. Harry and his group worked incredibly hard for months on that line and we were counting on them being something really different when they hit the market.

Harry: Well, I can't believe it's a coincidence. I mean, just look at this site; anyone can wander in and out at any time more or less as they please. Of course, we know our own employees, and we do get a lot of bona fide visitors, but you are always seeing people around that you don't recognize, and really, it could be anyone. We even get locals using our car park, just because it's free and convenient for the new shopping centre opposite.

Mark: I think that's what you wanted to talk to me about, isn't it—security on the site, I mean?

Sue: Well, basically yes, we do need to tighten up on security, but at the same time I really think it's very important that we don't antagonize the staff, or make them think that we don't trust them. We don't know how *Global Greetings* got wind of our card sculptures, but I honestly can't believe any of our staff would have told them.

Harry: Most people here have been with us for quite a while, we have a friendly, informal, hard-working atmosphere and we don't want to spoil that, by bringing in draconian measures that will just get up people's noses.

Mark: Yes, I can see that; it's a bit of a problem, but I'm sure we can work round it. Can you just give me a brief idea of what security procedures you have at the moment?

Sue: Well, not a lot really. There's Jane on reception—that's on the left as you come in. But the site's a funny sort of shape, with the building on a corner, then the delivery area next to it and the car park off to the side opposite the shopping precinct. Look I've drawn it for you.

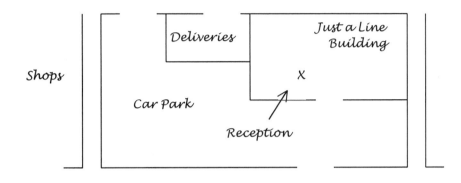

Mark: OK, I see. Can you give me some idea of how many of your employees use their cars to get to work?

Harry: Well most of them I should think, but I'm afraid I couldn't give you an exact number at the moment. We've got ninety-six people on the staff here if that's any help to you.

Mark: Right, and can people drive in and out of both the car park entrances, or is it one way?

Sue: No, you can come in and out of either entrance and park wherever you can find a space. It's all pretty casual.

Harry: That's another problem we've got. Staff come and go quite a bit during an average day, going to see customers, meetings off site etc. Then, when they get back here, they often can't find a space because the car park's full of shoppers. It's extra irritating because the car park is an odd sort of L-shape, so you have to drive right round it just in case there's a space you've missed. It's a terrible waste of time.

Mark: Does anyone check the cars that are parked on site during the day?

Sue: Jane on reception has a list of employees' cars. Here's a copy for you. She's supposed to go out two or three times during the day to make sure that only our staff cars are in the car park and slap a notice on any that are nothing to do with *Just a Line*. Trouble is, that doesn't really have much effect and we haven't thought about what to do when we find cars that aren't part of the company, but that keep using our car park. And that's when Jane actually goes out and checks—I'm sure she spends most of the day on the phone to that dopey boyfriend in marketing.

Harry: Now, that's not really fair, Sue. Jane's quite an asset. A lot of our customers like the image she projects.

Sue: A lot of our customers like . . . . sorry, Mark, we seem to be wandering from the point rather.

Mark: What about Jane's other duties? You said she's on reception, so does that mean that she checks people coming in and out of the building?

Sue: Well she knows our staff, and visitors are supposed to report to her when they arrive. You can see from the diagram, though, where she sits is a bit out of the way and she is on the main switchboard as well, so really it would be dead easy for someone to walk in and she wouldn't notice. Actually, it would be dead easy for someone to be standing right in front of her and she wouldn't notice!

Mark: So, let's see. It looks as if you've got two problems: you've got to tighten up a bit on security, though you have to be careful that you don't offend your staff, and you want to keep outsiders from using your car park.

Sue: Yes, that's pretty much it, except that, of course, it would be nice to have something in place as soon as possible. I expect you're used to clients saying that, aren't you, but I am a bit worried about things. It's not just the security side. What about our legal liability if someone gets injured in our car park, even if they're not supposed to be there?

Mark: Well, I think there are a couple of things that you can do straight away. First of all, why don't you move Jane's desk out into the foyer, facing the main entrance? It would look more welcoming and give her a much better view of who is coming and going. Then, look at the car park; at the moment people can drive in and out of either entrance, which isn't a good idea. There's no reason why you can't make one of the car park entrances for coming in only and the other for exits. The entrance would be the one near the front of the building and the exit the one in the far corner. That would make it impossible for shoppers to pop in and out the back way. Look I'll show you what I mean on the drawing you did for me.

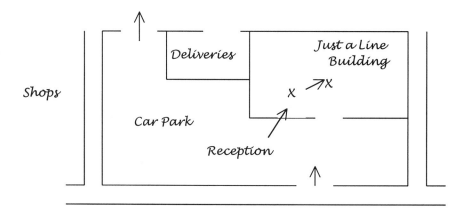

Sue: Yes, I see. I think that would help. It would take a lot more brass neck to drive into the car park through the main entrance than to slip in and out at the back where nobody can see you.

Harry: And I like the idea of putting Jane in a more central position. I think she'd enjoy it and it would certainly be harder for casual visitors to wander around the building.

Sue: And it would be easier for us to see what she gets up to all day. Those ideas are both fine for now, they'll be an improvement, but, on the other hand, I don't think they'll solve our problems in the long term.

Mark: No, you will have to do more than move Jane's desk and put up a few notices in the car park, but I'd like a bit of time to think about the best way to approach this.

Obviously you could go for a sophisticated system with swipe cards for employees that allow entry into different parts of the building, but my gut feeling is that that would be overkill in your case. I think the answer is to start by seeing what we can do with the car park. Keeping your staff happy is a very important issue, so I'd like to arrange to talk to one or two of your employees, you know, chat to them about how they would feel about added security on site and also whether they have problems with car parking.

Sue: Yes, of course, that's no problem. I should think Annie Raines would be a good person to start with. She's been doing the accounts for us since shortly after we started *Just a Line* and she's definitely someone that I want to keep on side. I'll have a word with her and tell her you'll be contacting in the next few days.

Mark: Thanks, and there's another thing. I need to get a much more accurate idea of how many of your employees use their cars for work and how the car park is actually used during the day. Would it be OK with you if I circulate a simple questionnaire to all staff? It wouldn't take them any time to fill it in and it would give them the feeling that they are being consulted.

Sue: Of course, we can get Jane to give them out and collect in the replies if you like. I think she can just about manage that.

Mark: So finally, could we fix up another meeting to talk about the next stage when I've had a chat to Annie and got the questionnaire information—say in about 10 days time?

Harry: Yes, good idea. Sue'll fix that up for you and in the meantime come along and I'll introduce you to Jane.

Figure 4.8 Interview of the Prestons of *Just a Line* by Mark Barnes of D&B Systems

Questionnaires

Apart from interviews with clients and users, the most useful form of requirements elicitation is often a questionnaire. This is particularly effective when a small, well-defined amount of information is needed from a large number of people, especially if they are widely scattered. A questionnaire could be used, for example, in the *Just a Line* case study to establish how employees use the company car park and what problems they are experiencing with the current parking system.

As with interviews, it is essential to prepare questionnaires thoroughly, including testing on a small sample of people to ensure that the questionnaire is easy to understand, simple to fill in and that it will produce useful results. It is the responsibility of the requirements engineer to make sure that people who fill in the questionnaire are aware of its purpose and how their answers will be used.

A variety of question types may be used, including multiple choice, short answer and extended answer questions, but the main priority must be to ensure that all questions are as clear and straightforward as possible. If a question does not contain enough information, the person filling in the questionnaire will not understand what is required but if it contains too much information, nobody will bother to read it.

Figure 4.9 shows a questionnaire on use of the car park at the *Just a Line* site. Its purpose is to help the requirements engineer find out how the car park is used at present and what problems employees are experiencing with the way it is operated.

D&B Systems – Car park survey for *Just a Line*

We have commissioned D&B Systems to investigate use of the company car park and current problems, so that the present system can be improved. This is your car park and we would like your opinion on how it should be organized. Please spare a few minutes to answer the questions below and return the form to Jane in reception by Friday 14th April.

Please circle your answers to the following questions:

1. How many times a week do you use your car to get to and from work?
    never / once or twice / two or three times / every day / no regular pattern

2. Which car park entrance do you normally use to come into the car park?
    main entrance / back entrance / either

3. Which car park entrance do you normally use to leave the car park?
    main entrance / back entrance / either

4. How often do you need to use your car for work during the day?
    never / rarely / about once a day / two or three times a day / no regular pattern

5. Do you have problems finding a space in the car park?
    never / sometimes / frequently / always

6. If you have problems finding a space, when does this usually happen?
    at the start of work / during the morning / lunchtime / during the afternoon /
    at the end of the day / no regular pattern

7. Would you like to see more security in the car park?
    yes / no / don't mind

8. Please note below any comments you have on the current car parking system.
    _____
    _____
    _____

9. Please note below any suggestions for improving the car parking at *Just a Line*.
    _____
    _____
    _____

Your name: _____

Your department: _____

Thank you for completing this questionnaire.

Figure 4.9 Questionnaire to investigate use of the car park at *Just a Line*

Structured meetings

In the case of large, complex systems, successful requirements elicitation is often carried out by means of structured meetings with stakeholders who may include not only clients and users, but also user managers, marketing staff, project managers and software trainers. Such meetings often take up the time of many people and so must be carefully planned with a well-defined purpose and clear agenda. Effective management during the meeting is also important in order to avoid unnecessary conflict or deviation from the main purpose.

One particular type of structured meeting, which originated in Scandinavia, is known as the future workshop. Future workshops come from a development approach called Participatory Design which views users of the system as experts in the problem domain and aims to include them as active collaborators in the development process. A future workshop is generally organized and run by two facilitators who spend some time beforehand familiarizing themselves with the client organization, its processes and any existing hardware and software.

The workshop itself is divided into three separate stages: critique, fantasy and implementation. During the critique stage participants in the workshop focus on current problems in the organization; brainstorming rules apply, so speaking time is limited, statements do not have to be justified and criticisms of them are not allowed. The aim of the fantasy stage is to imagine the perfect future system, without considering any constraints. This, again, is carried out using brainstorming to generate statements about the future system; at the end of this part of the workshop, participants vote to rank the statements, in order to identify those that have most support. In the final part of the workshop, the implementation stage, participants discuss ways in which the fantasy view may be realized, taking recognized constraints into account. After the workshop the facilitators develop part of the proposed implementation as a prototype in order to validate and refine the system requirements.

Scenarios

One of the most successful ways of eliciting requirements is to use scenarios. A scenario is a description in natural language of a particular sequence of interactions between the user and the system. Scenarios have been around for some time, but in recent years they have become a major part of object-oriented system development. Scenarios are discussed in detail in Chapter 6.

Prototyping

Prototyping has already been introduced in Chapter 3 as a way of developing software systems. It is a technique that is useful at all stages of requirements engineering and is discussed in this chapter under each of the headings of elicitation, specification and validation.

Prototyping is particularly effective as a means of requirements elicitation if clients are unsure of what they want. Initial ideas can be represented in a skeleton prototype, which clients can then relate to their own experience. It is often much easier to make constructive comments about something that exists, even in a very elementary form, than to think about problems and requirements in the abstract. In the case of *Just a Line,* for example, the requirements engineer might produce a prototype identity card (see Figure 4.10, below) and show it to members of staff during interviews for feedback and comments.

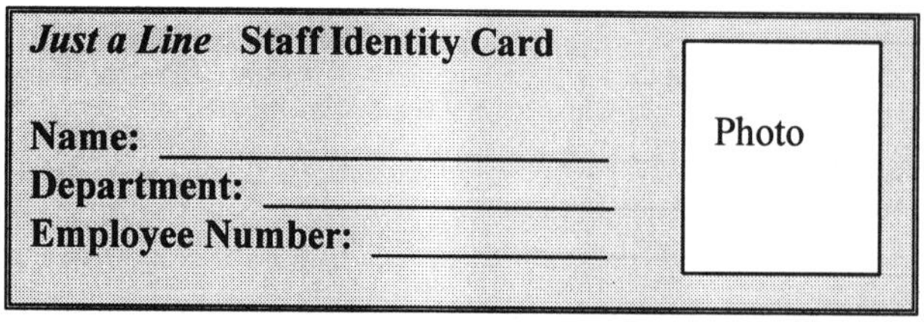

Figure 4.10 Prototype identity card for *Just a Line* staff

Considering all sources of requirements

Although the vast majority of requirements for a software system will come from clients and users, it is important for the requirements engineer to remember other useful sources. These may include literature about the problem domain (such as newspaper articles or market surveys), information from the World Wide Web, similar systems that already exist in the domain, and relevant laws and industry standards. Successful requirements elicitation must take full account of how the new system will affect and be affected by its environment and this can only be achieved by a comprehensive investigation and sound understanding of the problem domain.

4.4 Requirements specification

Whereas requirements elicitation involves an expansion of the developer's knowledge about the problem domain and the clients' wishes, requirements specification involves sifting through the information to pick out the important and relevant issues. It is during specification that information gathered during elicitation is analysed, interpreted and recorded in an appropriate form. The medium for specification may be narrative English, diagrams, or a notation that combines graphics and text. In Chapters 5 and 6 we discuss specification techniques that are widely used ways of recording requirements based on an object-oriented approach.

Formal specification languages

In safety-critical or security-critical systems, where the consequences of failure would be extremely serious, requirements are often described using a formal specification language, based on maths or logic. Formal specification brings many benefits to system development, and has been an important area of research for a number of years. Some object-oriented methodologies, such as Syntropy and Fusion, include specification using a formal language. However, there are, as yet, no formal specification languages that are themselves object-oriented and that are generally accepted in industry.

Prototyping

One of the most effective ways of recording requirements is prototyping, where the developer builds an unpolished version of all or part of the system. The working model facilitates communication and, at the same time, clients and users can get a feel for what the new system will be able to do and what it will look like. As well as improved communication, a live model offers other advantages to the requirements engineer. Paper-based models, whether textual or diagrammatic, tend to be inflexible and difficult to change. Yet, in developing systems, change is the norm and prototypes are built to accommodate it. Even in situations where prototyping is not feasible as the main specification technique, it should still be used to specify the user interface. This is the area which, more than any other, benefits from a prototyping approach and increased user involvement, since it is the way the interface is developed that determines how the system will appear to its users.

Content and quality of the requirements specification

Whatever language or method is chosen for the specification of requirements, certain information must be provided and the requirements specification itself must have certain qualities. For each separate requirement the following information should be included:

- a number or code that uniquely identifies the requirement;
- the source of the requirement;
- the date this version of the requirement was suggested;
- a brief, natural language description of the requirement;
- priority of the requirement (essential (E), desirable (D) or optional (O));
- a list of related requirements;
- alternatives to the requirement, if any;
- related documents, diagrams or tables;
- if the new requirement involves a change to a previous one, then this must be fully documented, together with the reasons for the change and the effects it will have on other system requirements.

Figure 4.11 shows a requirement from the *Just a Line* system in tabular form.

No.	Source	Date	Description	Priority	Related Reqs.	Alternative Reqs.	Related Docs.	Change Details
4.4	Meeting with Sue & Harry Preston	10/4/00	Ensure that only staff and visitors are able to use the car park.	E	2.9 4.6		List of staff car nos.	

Figure 4.11 Specification of a requirement from the *Just a Line* system

Much has been written about the qualities of the requirements specification. One of the most useful sources is the IEEE Recommended Practice for Software Requirements Specifications from the IEEE Standard 830-1993. The following list describes the qualities that most authors regard as essential in a requirements specification document:

- correct: the specification should not contain statements that are false;
- consistent: the specification should not contain statements that are contradictory;
- unambiguous: statements in the specification should have only one possible interpretation;
- traceable: the development of a requirement should be clearly visible from its original source through to the final software system;
- verifiable: it should be possible to check that the system meets the requirements. This can only be achieved where a requirement is expressed in a way that allows it to be measured. Requirements that contain expressions such as "easy to use", "quickly" or "most of the time" cannot be rigorously tested. A requirement that states that "the system shall respond to queries in not more than 3 seconds" is verifiable;
- understandable: the specification should be intelligible to non-computer specialists;
- modifiable: it should be easy to make alterations to the specification;
- comprehensive: although it is not feasible to cover every possible eventuality, there should be no obvious gaps in the specification.

One of the most important factors in producing a requirements specification that fulfils these criteria is the modelling technique that is used. An effective modelling technique helps the requirements engineer to impose some order on the jumble of informal spoken specification. It forces him or her to ask questions and encourages reasoning about the problem area and the early stages of the system. The right technique allows both requirements engineer and client to concentrate on the problem in hand rather than worrying about understanding and manipulating the technique itself. As an example, we only need to think how much easier it is to perform multiplication and division with Arabic rather than with Roman numerals.

The role of models in software system development and the techniques used in object-oriented modelling are discussed in Chapters 5 and 6.

4.5 Requirements validation

The purpose of requirements validation is to establish whether the requirements as specified are those that the stakeholders intend. Models of the problem and the proposed solution are checked to ensure that they are an accurate, consistent and relevant representation of the stakeholders' needs and wishes regarding the system.

Although it is a time-consuming process to check that a requirements specification has all the qualities listed in Section 4.4 above, it is certainly feasible for the system developer to feel satisfied that the requirements specification document is of the desired quality. What is much more difficult to ascertain is whether the requirements expressed in the specification are really what the client wants and needs. The situation is further complicated by the fact that the client may not know what he or she wants, or that what they want may be different from what they need. The process of checking that the requirements as specified are a true representation of the clients' needs and wishes is known as requirements validation.

4.5.1 Requirements validation methods

There are many different approaches that can be used to validate requirements for a software system; some of the most widely used of these are discussed below.

Interviews

In Section 4.3.1 of this chapter, we described how interviews are used to elicit requirements for the system from clients and users. Interviews are also a useful validation technique to ensure that the requirements engineer fully understands what is wanted. During interviews with clients and users there should be constant feedback to ensure that the developer has fully understood what is being said. This is also useful in that it helps the interviewee to feel that what he or she is saying is helpful and relevant. Validation is also carried out by taking notes during the interview and, later, producing a written summary for the interviewee. The developer should always ask permission to take notes and be prepared to show the interviewee what is in them. Shortly after the interview, the developer should produce a written summary, so that the interviewee can check that the important points have been understood. A summary of the initial interview with Sue and Harry Preston of *Just a Line* can be found in Figure 4.12.

Combining techniques from elicitation

Different elicitation methods can be used in combination to validate requirements. This may be carried out by comparing answers on a particular topic from a questionnaire with comments on the same topic obtained during interviews with clients and users. A client's account of certain business procedures may be checked by studying relevant documentation or by observing how the procedures are actually carried out in practice.

Fagan Inspections

Fagan inspections aim to uncover defects in the output from any stage in the software development process; they are a systematic and structured way of checking documentation that is produced, such as the requirements specification. Each inspection usually concentrates on a small component of the documentation and lasts up to two hours. Inspections are carried out by small teams of people consisting of a moderator or chair, a note-taker, the person who produced the component and one or more people to inspect it. A typical Fagan inspection has six separate stages:

- planning, when the team is selected;
- overview when the component is presented to the team;
- preparation, when each team member studies the component individually;
- meeting, when the team reviews the component together;
- rework, to remedy the defects that have been identified and agreed by the team;
- re-inspection, which may be carried out by the chair, rather than by the whole team.

D&B Systems – Interview Summary	

System: *Just a Line*	Project reference: JaL/MB/00

Participants:	Sue Preston (*Just a Line*) Harry Preston (*Just a Line*) Mark Barnes (D&B)

Date: 10/4/00	Time: 14.30	Duration: 45 minutes	Place: Sue's office

Purpose of interview:
Preliminary meeting to identify problems and requirements regarding security at the *Just a Line* site.

No.	Item	Action
1	Very little security at present, both in building and on site.	
2	Lack of security on site appears to have allowed leaks about designs.	
3	Any new security measures must not offend staff.	Interview some staff members (start with Annie Raines).
4	Receptionist not in central position in entrance to building.	Move receptionist's desk to foyer, facing main entrance.
5	Staff often need to use cars during the day; problem finding a space when they get back.	
6	Not clear exactly how staff use car park.	Ask staff to fill in questionnaire on car park usage.
7	Car park frequently used by people not connected to company (close to shopping centre and no charge).	
8	Two entrances to car park (one opposite shopping centre). No route system in car park.	Introduce one-way system; entrance to car park via front only.
9	No penalty for unauthorized parking.	
10	Impossible to tell if car park is full without driving round it.	
11	Further discussions needed when more info. available.	Arrange follow-up meeting with Sue and Harry (in about 10 days' time).

Figure 4.12 Summary of the initial interview with Sue and Harry Preston of *Just a Line*

Prototyping

Prototyping has already been discussed as a way of developing software systems and as a useful technique for eliciting and specifying requirements (see Chapter 3 and Sections 4.3.1 and 4.4 of this chapter). When used for requirements validation, a prototype allows the client and users to get some feeling for how their requirements will work once implemented in a computer system. Prototyping can uncover misunderstandings between users and the requirements engineer and identify gaps in the stated requirements. Experimenting with a prototype allows users to see what their ideas will be like in practice and how they will fit into their current ways of working. Prototyping will involve the clients and users, not merely in discussions about the system, but also in realistic simulations of work situations. It is possible to see how the system will perform in relation to tasks in the organization. If, for example, a particular report is required at the end of each month, the client can see from the prototype how the data for the report is collected, entered, selected, ordered, formatted and finally printed. If the layout of the final report is not exactly what is wanted, it can be changed with relatively little effort. Examining and playing with a prototype is a very effective way to establish how well the requirements engineer understands the requirements of clients and users.

Although it is never possible to prove conclusively that a requirements specification describes exactly what the client wants and needs, it is essential that both the system developer and the client are happy that the requirements as stated have been thoroughly validated. The validation process can be regarded as the application of quality assurance to the requirements specification, leading to a well-founded belief on all sides that the specification is an accurate description of the stakeholders' requirements for the system.

4.6 The difficulties of requirements engineering

Requirements engineering is widely recognised as one of the most important, yet most problematic, activities in the development of a software system. It is important because the information collected and recorded during the requirements engineering process underpins the whole of the development of the system. It is problematic for several reasons. First, clients and users may have very little knowledge of the capabilities and limitations of computer systems; it is hard for them to grasp exactly which of their problems can be solved by a computer and which have to be resolved by some other means.

It is no surprise to requirements engineers that clients and users may not be familiar with software systems, but what often comes as a shock is the fact that users frequently have only a limited understanding of their own problems and requirements. They often express these in a way that is vague, ambiguous and inconsistent, and repeatedly change their minds about what they want the intended system to do for them. Even when a stakeholder has a very clear view of the problems and requirements, this may be in direct conflict with the views of other stakeholders.

The problems of requirements engineering do not all stem from the clients and users. Traditionally, it was not considered necessary for a requirements engineer to be familiar in advance with the problem domain; the view was that, as an objective outsider, he or she would be able to acquire information without pre-existing bias. Increasingly, however, it has come to be recognized that a requirements engineer who has no knowledge or experience of the problem domain will not be in a position to identify all the relevant and useful information.

Knowledge of the domain and the jargon associated with it also reduces the difficulty of developers and users expressing ideas about the system in completely different languages. However, the problem of how to be sure that all stakeholders have a common understanding remains one of the most intractable in software systems development.

Another major problem is the fact that requirements are not fixed, but tend to evolve as development of the system progresses. Modern approaches to requirements engineering differ significantly from traditional methodologies in that they do not assume that a requirements specification document is agreed by the client and then remains cast in stone for the duration of the software development project. System developers today are fully aware that requirements are dynamic and evolve constantly during development of a software system. Organizations themselves are constantly changing; even though the basic business remains the same, the organization's scope and objectives will change and this will influence what is required of the software system. Moreover, development of the software system itself has an effect on the organization; in-depth discussions about current practices and problems often lead to fresh ideas and to new ways of working which will, in turn, have an affect on the original system requirements.

In comparing the job of the requirements engineer to that of an architect, in Section 4.1 above, we saw that the abstract nature of software makes it difficult to identify and describe requirements for it. At the same time, the software that is to be specified is highly technical, yet has to operate in a human environment. The combination of the abstract, yet technical nature of software and the non-technical, human environment often makes it difficult for clients and users to express exactly what they want the system to do for them.

Trends in the way software development projects are organized also complicate the requirements engineering process. Issues, such as the need for co-operative working, or the organizational context in which tasks are to be carried out, add extra complexity to the basic problem of specifying the software system. Increasingly, projects today involve more than one client, many different user groups and large teams of developers, possibly with widely differing backgrounds and training. Any or all of these groups of stakeholders may be geographically distributed, so that requirements engineering may have to take place at a distance, using technology such as video conferencing and the internet.

Given all the difficulties of carrying out requirements engineering, we may be tempted to ask if it is worth the effort. The answer is an unqualified Yes, for a whole variety of reasons. We can see why requirements engineering is so important if we turn the question on its head and think about what would happen if we didn't bother with it. First, there would be no agreed specification to record the decisions that have been taken about the intended system or to act as the basis for communication between stakeholders. Any contract between clients and developers would not be worth the paper it was written on, since there would be no recorded agreement as to what was to be developed. Testing the completed system would be difficult, if not impossible, since black-box testing of the system's observable behaviour is generally based on the requirements specification (see Chapter 10). Finally, time and money would be wasted correcting errors and misunderstandings that should have been sorted out during the requirements engineering stage of the development project.

Exercises

4.1   Find an example from the interview between Mark Barnes and Sue and Harry Preston (see Figure 4.8) of each of the different types of information listed in Section 4.3.1 of this chapter.

4.2   What other questions could Mark Barnes usefully have asked Sue and Harry during the interview?

4.3   Jane, the *Just a Line* receptionist, has produced a questionnaire to collect information about people who visit the company (see Figure 4.13, below). Unfortunately, there are a few problems with Jane's effort. Make a list of those you can identify.

Just a Line **Visitor's survey**

Are you visiting *Just a Line?*
Please answer the questions below and return this form to Jane.

- Is this your first visit to *Just a Line?*
  yes / no

- Are you a regular visitor?
  yes / no

- Do you always report to reception when you visit *Just a Line?*
  yes / no / sometimes

- Who do you usually visit at *Just a Line?*
  _____

- What transport do you usually use?
  own car / taxi / bus / bike / walk / other

- Do you think there should be more security at *Just a Line?*
  yes / no / maybe / don't know

- Any other comments
  _____
  _____
  _____

Your name: _____
Your company: _____

Figure 4.13 Jane's visitors' questionnaire

4.4   Design a questionnaire to collect customer comments on a system that you know something about (e.g. the lending and reservation system at a video shop, or a doctor's appointment system).

4.5   Draw up a list of criteria that you consider important for a good requirements modelling technique.
N.B. These will be similar to, but not the same as, the criteria for a good requirements specification (see Section 4.4).

4.6   One of the difficult problems in recording requirements is to write clearly and unambiguously. Write a set of requirements for a simple system, with which you are familiar, for example a set of traffic lights or a cash machine. A book that will help you with this is *The Complete Plain Words* (see reference below).

4.7   Organize a future workshop with a small group of people to identify initial requirements for one or more of the following systems:

- a public information system for your local area;
- a personal organizer;
- a system to monitor heart patients in hospital;
- a system to handle orders from a charity's Christmas catalogue;
- a system to control traffic lights at the junction near a village school.

The workshop should cover the three stages of critique, fantasy and implementation. Details about future workshops can be found in Section 4.3.1.

References and further reading

Davis, A.M. *Software Requirements: Objects, Functions and States,* Englewood Cliffs, N.J.: Prentice-Hall, 1993.

Department for Trade and Industry and National Computing Centre *The STARTS guide,* 2nd edn, Volume 1, NCC Publications, 1987.

Gowers, E. *The Complete Plain Words,* London: Penguin, 1987.

The Institute of Electrical and Electronics Engineers, Inc., *IEEE Recommended Practice for Software Requirements Specifications,* New York: IEEE, 1994.

Jackson, M. *Software Requirements & Specifications : A Lexicon of Practice, Principles, and Prejudices,* Wokingham: Addison-Wesley, 1995.

Kotonya, G. and Sommerville, I. *Requirements Engineering: Processes and Techniques,* Chichester: Wiley, 1998.

Loucopulos, P. and Karakostas, V. *System Requirements Engineering,* Maidenhead: McGraw-Hill, 1995.

Macaulay, L. *Requirements Engineering,* London: Springer-Verlag, 1996.

Skidmore, S. *Introducing System Analysis,* 2nd edn, Oxford: NCC Blackwell, 1994.

Sommerville, I. and Sawyer, P. *Requirements Engineering: A Good Practice Guide,* Chichester: Wiley, 1997.

Wieringa, R.J. *Requirements Engineering,* Chichester: Wiley, 1996.

5

Object Modelling

In order to understand how modelling is carried out in object-oriented system development, we need first to appreciate what is meant by the term 'modelling' and how models are used in the development of software systems. This chapter begins with a discussion of modelling in general and its role in systems development. We then discuss each of the stages in building the class diagram, which is the model that is central to object-oriented development of systems. In the final section of the chapter, we introduce a standard notation for constructing a data dictionary.

5.1 Modelling

We saw, in Chapter 4, that requirements engineering is divided into three separate stages: elicitation, specification and validation. The central activity of the requirements specification stage is producing models of the problem in order to record, analyse and interpret the information that has been collected during elicitation. We begin this chapter by discussing how the term 'model' is used in this context and explaining how models can improve communication and help developers to deal with complexity at all stages of the system development process.

5.1.1 What is a model?

Modelling is used extensively in software systems development. For this reason it is important to understand what system developers mean by the term. A model of a system represents a part of the real world. The model differs from reality in that it concentrates on certain aspects while ignoring others—it is an abstraction. Modelling is the process of abstracting and organizing significant features of part of the real world, or how we would like it to be. A good model will represent only those features of reality that are useful for the purpose in hand and ignore currently irrelevant details.

In Chapter 4, we mentioned some of the similarities between the role of the requirements engineer in the development of a software system, and that of the architect in a building project (see Section 4.1). The architect uses different models from those of the requirements engineer, but the purpose of the models and the way they are used are very much the same. Both the architect and the requirements engineer use models to help them record information, communicate with clients and manage the complexity of the problem. The architect is modelling when he or she draws a rough sketch of a building to show clients approximately what the building will look like. This model is different from, and serves a different purpose from, a scaled drawing of the same building which might be drawn to show planners how it will fit in with its surroundings. Each of the models that the architect uses says something about the subject, but not everything. In Figure 5.1 we can see three different models of a planned extension to a house: a drawing, a map and a diagram. Each of these is a particular view of the extension and gives us certain information about it. Different types of model illustrate different things.

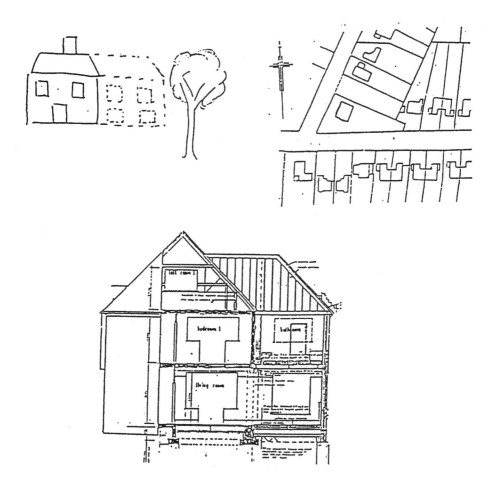

Figure 5.1 Different types of model illustrate different things

All of these models, however, are two-dimensional and drawn with pen and paper. When the design is at a more advanced stage, the architect might construct a three-dimensional model of the building to give the clients a clearer understanding of the design, of how the building will look from all angles and how the rooms relate to each other. Plans will also have to be drawn to serve as working documents for the builders and site engineers: blueprints drawn to scale with precise measurements of widths, depths, materials and loadings specified. Each model is a partial representation of the building the architect is designing; each model says something about the building, but not everything. Each is used for a particular purpose and makes a different contribution to the development of the building.

5.1.2 Using models for communication

It is no accident that software systems development has introduced the extensive use of modelling, particularly graphical modelling. Earlier attempts to produce a document expressing the client requirements of the system were conspicuously unsuccessful. This document was typically an enormously thick and indigestible text with little or no use of graphics to leaven the lump. Clients were supposed to 'agree' and sign it. Frequently, it was unread both by the clients, who therefore failed to pick up any errors, and by the programmers, whose job it was to translate clients' and users' requirements into a piece of software.

Many of the models used by requirements engineers today make use of graphics. A graphical representation of the system has several advantages over a purely narrative document. Diagrams tend to appear more user-friendly than text and to be more readily understood by both clients and system developers. Diagrams can express certain ideas more concisely, which makes the size of the documentation less daunting.

Models, whether graphical, textual, or a mixture of both, have many benefits for software system development. They impose structure on the jumble of facts and opinions gathered during requirements elicitation. They are useful both to record facts and to sort them into some kind of order. The requirements engineer models the system as he or she currently understands it. Discussion of these models with the other stakeholders, including the client, will identify gaps, inconsistencies and misunderstandings. Having a model on which to centre discussions makes this process easier and produces more useful feedback. In object-oriented system development the same modelling techniques are used to describe the existing system and the new, required system. Clients may find some effort is required initially to understand the models, but the effort will be worthwhile, as the understanding gained can be applied to models at all stages of the system development process. During the construction of the models the requirements engineer becomes aware of questions that need to be asked, details that have been left out and contradictions in his or her understanding of the system. Producing the model highlights the shortcomings; discussing the model with clients will help to resolve them. Finally, once modelling of the new system is complete, the requirements engineer can test the model and check it for consistency and completeness. It can be evaluated informally and provide a fairly good idea at an early stage in development whether or not the intended system will satisfy the specified client requirements. This sort of checking would be almost impossible to carry out using a purely narrative document, because of its unwieldy nature.

5.1.3 Using models to tackle complexity

Models help the requirements engineer to communicate with the client and help the client to understand the new system. They are also useful to system developers when tackling the complexity of large systems. Computer scientists have commonly used two main intellectual techniques to cope with complexity:

- Decomposition—dividing the problem into 'brain-sized' chunks;
- Abstraction—concentrating on the most important elements while ignoring currently irrelevant details.

The models used in software system development make use of both these techniques. The first, decomposition, takes a divide and conquer approach. A large and complex problem will be made up of lots of smaller problems. The developer will keep splitting the problem into smaller and smaller sub-problems, until a brain-sized problem is left, one that is small enough to be held in the developer's head.

The second technique, abstraction, allows a developer to concentrate on one aspect of a problem at a time. In designing a house, the architect can safely ignore, for example, consideration of the precise type of brick to be used, when deciding how many bedrooms the house will have. In the same way the system developer can safely ignore consideration of precisely how data will be stored in the system, when deciding what the user interface will look like. Decomposition and abstraction both help the system developers to reduce the size of the problem to be thought about at any one time, without loss of detail. They allow parts of the problem that are not currently relevant to be shelved and considered later in the development process. To model large and complex systems, system developers first need different kinds of models to highlight different aspects of the system, that is, to model it from different perspectives. Secondly, they need modelling techniques with the ability to partition a problem, to allow the developers to concentrate on one sub-section at a time, independently from the rest of the problem. We shall see that the modelling techniques used in object-oriented systems development support both abstraction and decomposition. They support the developer's need to concentrate on one aspect of the problem at a time in that each technique has its own view of the system; its own perspective on the problem.

5.1.4 Different stages of development

During the development of a software system the same technique may be used to model the system at different stages. Like the architect's models, the models in the early stages of system design are non-technical. Later on in the project, a more precise version of these early sketches may be used as the basis for a technical design. For example, the central model in object-oriented development, the class diagram, may be sketched during the early stages of requirements specification and used as a basis for describing the existing system and outlining ideas for the required system. In this form it is a non-technical diagram and can be used as a vehicle for discussions with clients. Later in the development process, details are added to the class diagram to take account of technical considerations and constraints arising from the implementation environment. Eventually, the diagram, complete with technical details, will provide the basis for the design of the system structure and program specifications.

5.2 The class diagram

The starting point for object-oriented system development is the object, but the concept that is central to development is the class, and the principal modelling technique at each stage is the class diagram. The class diagram models the data elements in the system, the ways in which these may be grouped together, and the relationships between them. For each class, the diagram identifies the attributes and operations associated with it.

The structure of the system, as modelled in the class diagram, is based on data. Systems that have a foundation in data tend to be more stable than those based on process, since data is, in general, less volatile than functionality. If we consider a mail-order system, for example, we can imagine that the processing that is required will change during the lifetime of the system: orders may be taken in a different way, or more sophisticated methods of payment may be introduced. However, the data that is the subject of the processing, such as the customers, orders and invoices, will remain the same. The class diagram is a modelling technique that can be used at different stages of system development and its strong, data-based structure provides a firm foundation for the system under construction.

5.2.1 Stages in building a class diagram

The stages in building a class diagram are listed below and discussed in detail in the following sections. Although the list implies ordering of the stages, this is an iterative, not a sequential process. Activities are often carried out in parallel and early stages are frequently revisited.

- Identify objects and derive classes from them.
- Identify attributes of classes.
- Begin to construct a data dictionary.
- Identify operations on classes.
- Use the CRC card technique to uncover responsibilities and collaborations.
- Identify relationships between classes, using association, aggregation and inheritance.
- Iterate and refine the model.

In constructing the class diagram, we use many of the object-oriented concepts, including those that were introduced in Chapter 2. We do not explain those concepts in detail again here, but refer to relevant sections of Chapter 2 where appropriate.

Identify objects and derive classes from them

The first step in constructing a class diagram is to identify objects in the problem domain. These may be physical objects, such as people or documents; organizational entities, such as companies or departments; transactions, such as orders or loans; or concepts, such as schedules or structures. All the objects identified at this stage should be understandable as part of the problem domain.

One useful source of objects is the initial problem brief, which is a short, high-level statement of the problem area and the intended system. Every noun in this statement should be noted as an object, which may later be generalized into a class; it is easier to discard irrelevant objects at a later stage than to try to remember objects that should not have been rejected in the first place.

Returning to the problems at *Just a Line* (see Chapter 4, Section 4.3.1), we find that Sue and Harry have decided to start tightening up security by restricting access to the car park to company staff and bona fide visitors. Figure 5.2 gives a brief description of the *Just a Line* car park problem, with the nouns underlined. At this early stage, all these nouns are identified as potentially useful objects.

Just a Line management wishes to increase security, both in their building and on site, without antagonizing their employees. They would also like to prevent people who are not part of the company from using the *Just a Line* car park.

It has been decided to issue identity cards to all employees, which they are expected to wear while on the *Just a Line* site. The cards record the name, department and number of the member of staff, and permit access to the *Just a line* car park.

A barrier and a card reader are placed at the entrance to the car park. The driver of an approaching car inserts his or her numbered card in the card reader, which then checks that the card number is known to the *Just a Line* system. If the card is recognised, the reader sends a signal to raise the barrier and the car is able to enter the car park.

At the exit, there is also a barrier, which is raised when a car wishes to leave the car park.

When there are no spaces in the car park a sign at the entrance displays "Full" and is only switched off when a car leaves.

Special visitors' cards, which record a number and the current date, also permit access to the car park. Visitors' cards may be sent out in advance, or collected from reception. All visitors' cards must be returned to reception when the visitor leaves *Just a Line.*

Figure 5.2 A brief description of the *Just a Line* car park problem

The purpose of identifying objects in the problem domain is to derive useful classes. Classes are discussed in detail in Section 2.3 of Chapter 2. The problem brief is a good starting point, but should not be relied on to produce a definitive list of classes. On the one hand, not every object mentioned will yield a class, and on the other hand, there may well be objects that will form the basis of classes that are not included in the problem brief. As we shall see in Chapter 6, scenarios are another effective way of identifying classes.

The objects that can be picked out from the *Just a Line* problem brief are shown in Figure 5.3.

Just a Line	management	security	building
site	employee	people	company
car park	card	name	department
number	member of staff	access	barrier
card reader	entrance	driver	car
system	signal	exit	space
sign	visitor	reception	

Figure 5.3 Objects in the *Just a Line* problem brief

The next step in constructing a class diagram is to study the list of objects and reject those that are unsuitable for use as the basis for classes. Objects should be rejected if they are:

- *duplicates*: if two or more objects are simply different names for the same thing, then only one of these should be used as the basis for a class. Examples from the list above are employee/ member of staff, and company/*Just a Line*;
- *irrelevant*: objects which exist in the problem domain, but which are not part of the intended system should also be discarded. Examples here are management, building, site, company, visitor and reception. The new car park system will not require details of any of these objects, so they can safely be rejected at this point;
- *vague*: when considering words carefully it sometimes becomes clear that they do not have a precise meaning and cannot be the basis of a useful class in the system. Examples here are security and people;
- *general*: some words, such as system, are unlikely to make useful classes, as their meaning is too broad. We are trying to decompose the problem, not treat it as one single class;
- *attributes*: one of the best tests for a class is to consider what we need to know about it. We sometimes discover, with words such as department, for example, that we are only interested in the department as part of some other class, such as card. In this case department would be an attribute of the class card, not a class itself; the same applies to name, number and date. Another good test is to think about how the potential class would behave. If the only operations we can identify are those to set and get data, then this is not worth modelling as a class;
- *associations*: sometimes words, such as access in this example, appear to be objects themselves, but actually represent relationships between objects. These should be represented as associations, not classes;
- *roles*: sometimes objects may be referred to by the role they play in a particular part of the system. When potential classes, we must be careful to pick the name that corresponds to the basic identity of the class, such as employee, and not names of roles that it may play at different times, such as driver;
- *implementation constructs*: classes relating to how the system may be implemented are not part of the class diagram at this early stage, although they may be added later during design. We would therefore not include words such as signal in the initial class list.

We also need to consider whether any classes have been missed out at this stage. Some of the important sources of objects and classes are expert knowledge of the problem domain, general knowledge of the environment in which the system will operate, and common sense.

In the case of *Just a Line,* knowledge about how car parks operate and our common sense should tell us that we will have to include sensors in the system, one for each barrier. The sensors will detect when a car arrives at the barrier, and when the car is no longer present and the barrier can be lowered.

Figure 5.4 shows the nouns that are left as potential classes, after discarding unsuitable candidates for the reasons shown above and considering the problem domain. In addition, we have chosen to distinguish between the two types of card by referring to them as Staff Card and Visitor's Card.

Identify attributes of classes

We have already mentioned in the previous section that one of the best ways of identifying a useful class is to consider what we need to know about it, what features or attributes of the class will need to be recorded. You can find more information about attributes in Section 2.3 of Chapter 2. The problem brief is often a useful source of attributes; they can be identified from phrases, such as "the number of the member of staff", and from adjectival phrases, such as "numbered card". Knowledge of the problem domain is another important source.

Car Park	**Staff Card**	**Visitor's Card**	**Employee**
Entrance	**Exit**	**Card Reader**	**Barrier**
Full Sign	**Space**	**Sensor**	**Car**

Figure 5.4 Potential classes in the *Just a Line* car park system

Attributes that are not relevant to the specific problem in hand should be avoided; for example, we would not hold information on the cost of a card, as this is not needed in this system. We should also avoid storing information unnecessarily. This means that we should reject attributes that can be derived from others; for example if we decided to record the time of entry and the time of exit of a car, we should not also record the car's time in the car park. At this stage of development, we should avoid attributes that relate to implementation, such as pointers to other classes; these will be added later on.

When thinking about attributes, we often discover that we are recording the same details for two different classes; this indicates that one of the classes is superfluous. In our example, above, we record the name, department and employee number for both the Staff Card and Employee classes, so we shall drop the Employee class, since it does not add any extra information. We may also discover that there are some potential classes in our original list about which we do not need to record any details, or which do not perform any function in the system. Examples here are Entrance, Exit, Car and Space, so we will discard these as classes in the system.

Each object in a class will have the structure specified by the class, but will have its own particular data values. In the diagrams below, Figure 5.5(a) shows the class Staff Card in the *Just a Line* car park system, with attributes number, name and department. Figure 5.5(b) shows three Staff Card objects, with specific values for each of the three attributes.

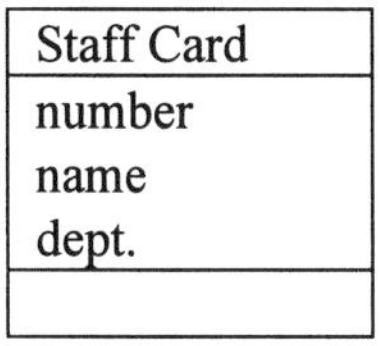

Staff Card
number
name
dept.

Figure 5.5(a) Staff Card class with three attributes

: Staff Card	: Staff Card	: Staff Card
number = JL437	number = JL722	number = JL209
name = Sam Parker	name = Mira Patel	name = Chris Doolan
dept. = Marketing	dept. = Marketing	dept. = Design

Figure 5.5(b) Three objects of class Staff Card, with specific values

Begin to construct a data dictionary

As soon as we begin to fill in details of classes, it is helpful to have some standard way to describe both the classes and their features. This may be informal, such as a brief paragraph indicating the name, scope, role and attributes of the class, or more structured, using a type of data dictionary notation. Object-oriented development does not prescribe any particular method of describing the data in the system, but it is, nonetheless, useful to have an agreed way of doing this. Figure 5.6 gives informal descriptions of some of the classes in the *Just a Line* car park problem and, in Section 5.3 of this chapter, we have included information on a more formal way of constructing a data dictionary.

Car Park: represents the physical car park and keeps count of the number of spaces available.

Staff Card: a card, issued to a member of the *Just a Line* staff, that records the staff member's number, name and department. The number uniquely identifies the member of staff within *Just a Line*. The card also permits access to the *Just a Line* car park.

Visitor's Card: a card, which permits access to the *Just a Line* car park, given to someone visiting the company. The card records a number and the current date. Visitors' cards may be sent out in advance or collected from reception, and all cards must be returned to reception when the visitor leaves *Just a Line*.

Card Reader: a machine that reads a card that is input and checks the card number against a list of valid numbers. If the card is valid, the reader sends a signal to raise the barrier.

Barrier: a bar, which raises or lowers itself according to signals received from either one of its associated sensors, or from the card reader.

Sensor: a device for detecting the presence of a car

Figure 5.6 Informal descriptions of some of the classes in the *Just a Line* car park problem

Identify operations on classes

As we have seen already, the object-oriented approach to developing software systems is based on the data in the problem domain. This does not mean, however, that object-orientation ignores specification of behaviour. Classes are not only defined in terms of their attributes, but also in terms of operations that affect instances of the class. Operations are introduced in Section 2.3 of Chapter 2. The attributes and operations together are referred to as the features of the class. An operation is defined by its name and, in the later stages of development, by a list of arguments and type of result; however, this amount of detail is not considered essential in the early stages of analysis.

Figure 5.7, below, shows the Car Park class with attributes 'capacity' and 'spaces' and three operations. The first two operations increment and decrement the number of spaces in the car park as cars leave and arrive. The third operation returns the number of spaces currently available in the car park.

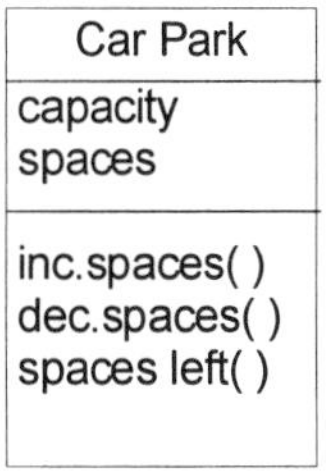

```
┌─────────────────┐
│    Car Park     │
├─────────────────┤
│ capacity        │
│ spaces          │
├─────────────────┤
│ inc.spaces( )   │
│ dec.spaces( )   │
│ spaces left( )  │
│                 │
└─────────────────┘
```

Figure 5.7 The Car Park class, with attributes and operations

Operations may be identified from verb phrases in the problem description, such as 'check card', or from the presence of an attribute that needs to be updated or read. For example the attribute 'spaces' in the Car Park class (see Figure 5.7) is obviously not a constant value and therefore needs operations to change it as required. A very effective way of identifying operations is to use scenarios, which are descriptions of particular sequences of interactions between the user and the system. Scenarios are one of the main techniques for dynamic modelling in object-oriented development and are discussed in detail in Chapter 6.

Use the CRC card technique to uncover responsibilities and collaborations

As well as considering attributes and operations, it is also useful to think, at a higher level, about the purpose of a class. Common sense and analysis of objects from the problem brief give us an idea of what classes we want and the data that we want them to store, but we also need to sort out the functionality of the classes, in other words, what we want them to do. The most effective way of doing this is to use class-responsibility-collaboration (CRC) cards. CRC cards are part of a development approach called Responsibility Driven Design, which we mentioned earlier in Section 3.2.3 of Chapter 3. The aim of Responsibility Driven Design is to look at the overall functionality of the system and to divide this functionality up between classes. Responsibility Driven Design considers the purpose or functionality of a class in terms of its responsibilities to provide services to other classes. A responsibility of a class describes something that the class can do. The class is able to fulfil the responsibility because it has relevant information, either stored in its attributes, or accessible through collaboration with other classes. Considering a responsibility leads us to identify the operation, or operations, needed to fulfil it.

In the car park system, for example, the Car Park class has a responsibility to monitor the number of spaces left in the car park each time a car arrives or leaves. To do this, the car park class has operations to increment and decrement the number of spaces in the car park. As another example, the Full Sign class has a responsibility to light up when there are no spaces left in the car park, and to turn off when a space becomes available. To carry out these responsibilities, this class has operations to switch on and off (see Figure 5.8).

Figure 5.8 The Full Sign class with attribute and operations

A class may sometimes act as a server, providing a service to another class, and sometimes act as a client, receiving a service from another class. The Car Park class is responsible to the Full Sign class for indicating that there are no free spaces and the sign should switch on. However, in order to fulfil this responsibility, the Car Park class must know when there are no spaces left in the car park. It receives this information from the barrier at the entrance. This means that the Barrier class has a responsibility to the Car Park class to provide information each time that a car enters the car park. The Car Park class, in turn, has a responsibility to tell the Full Sign class when to switch on. The Car Park class therefore acts as client to the Barrier class and as server to the Full Sign class. Figure 5.9 shows a fragment of the class diagram for the car park that illustrates this.

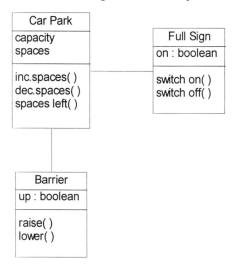

Figure 5.9 The Car Park class acts as client to the Barrier class and as server to the Full Sign class

Another way of looking at this is to consider collaborations between classes. Sometimes a class has been designed in such a way that it needs help from other classes to fulfil a responsibility. These classes are called the collaborators of the original class. Considering which collaborators are required to fulfil a responsibility is a useful way of identifying connections between classes and building up the class diagram. The Barrier class has responsibilities to raise the exit barrier if a car wishes to leave the car park, and to lower it when the car is through. In order to do this, the Barrier class has to receive information from a sensor, which detects the presence or absence of a car; in other words, it has to collaborate with the Sensor class to fulfil its responsibilities.

The most practical and effective way of identifying responsibilities and collaborations is to use CRC (class-responsibility-collaboration) cards. Each class is represented on an index card, 10 × 15 cms. The size is important because it restricts the amount that can be written on it. Usually a high level description of the class is written on the back of the card, and the front looks as shown in Figure 5.10 with the class name, its responsibilities and its collaborators, if any. Figure 5.10 shows a CRC card, which records the Barrier class with its responsibilities and collaborations.

Barrier	
Responsibility	Collaborator
raise	Sensor
lower	Sensor

Figure 5.10 An example of a CRC card with responsibilities and collaborations

Figure 5.11 shows another example of a CRC card, in this case, an incomplete card for the Card Reader class.

Card Reader	
Responsibility	Collaborator
read card	
validate card	

Figure 5.11 Incomplete card for the Card Reader class

This CRC card illustrates an interesting problem: in order to validate a card, the card reader must have access to the list of card numbers that are known to the *Just a Line* system, but it is not clear where this list of known cards should be held. One option is to store the set of known cards in the Card Reader class. This is illustrated in Figure 5.12.

Figure 5.12 Card Reader class with list of card numbers known to the *Just a Line* system

Storing the known cards in the Card Reader class is fine for the current *Just a Line* system, since there is only going to be one card reader. However, a problem arises if Sue and Harry decide that they want more than one entrance to the car park (and therefore more than one card reader). Each new card reader would have to store the list of known card numbers, which would be both inefficient and a potential source of confusion if the lists in different readers were updated separately. A more flexible solution is to create a new class, Valid Cards, which is responsible for storing a single set of known card numbers. This means that any card reader in the car park system can collaborate with the Valid Cards class to access the list of card numbers that are known to *Just a Line*. The Card Reader and the new Valid Cards class are shown in Figure 5.13.

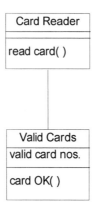

Figure 5.13 Card Reader and new Valid Cards class

Three points of interest arise out of considering where to store the list of cards that are known to the system. First, we have already said, at the beginning of Section 5.2.1, that building a class diagram is an iterative process and early stages will frequently be revisited. This is one example of how a new class may be identified during the later stages of constructing the diagram. The second point is that separating the known card list from the card reader allows greater flexibility and offers more potential for reuse than storing the known cards in the reader. Reuse is one of the main concerns of object-oriented development and this is a good example of how potential reuse can be achieved. Finally, dividing functionality between separate classes in this way is in line with the object-oriented philosophy of creating classes that are internally cohesive, incorporating a set of logically connected ideas.

Many advantages are claimed for CRC cards. Some of these are technical, including the assertions that the cards are a powerful way of establishing class operations and identifying links between classes, and that they make it easy to trace responsibilities from card to card and identify gaps. In terms of project management and team building, CRC cards are popular with developers and have proved to be a good way of promoting ideas and useful discussions. Finally, CRC cards are a particularly effective technique to use in conjunction with use cases and scenarios; these are discussed in full in Chapter 6.

Identify relationships between classes, using association, aggregation and inheritance

Objects are the basic building blocks of O-O software but, for the software system to do what the user requires, these objects must collaborate with each other. In the class diagram we start to specify how the objects must be related so that this collaboration can be achieved. In the class diagram we are specifying the static relationships between classes. If we model a relationship between two classes, A and B, we are saying that all objects of class A potentially have a relationship with one or more objects of class B. The relationships that we model on a class diagram are those of association, aggregation and inheritance.

Association. Modelling an association between two classes means that there is some sort of relationship between objects of those classes, such as that a student studies a course. This relationship is illustrated in Figure 5.14 below. The association between the classes is shown by the line joining them. The association can be named, as shown here, but this is frequently omitted in order to reduce clutter on the diagram.

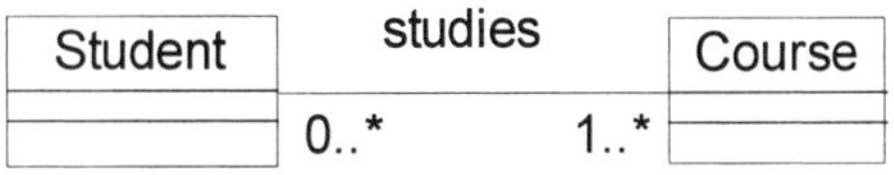

Figure 5.14 Association relationship between classes Student and Course

The numbers and asterisks on the line indicate the multiplicity of the association: the numbers of objects of each class that may be connected in this way. The diagram in Figure 5.14 states that a student may study one or more courses; whereas a course may exist without any students, or be studied by any number. Notations used to specify different multiplicities in associations are as follows:

Zero or one	0..1
Exactly one	1 (or may be omitted
Zero, one or many	*, or 0..*
One or more	1..*
An exact number	e.g. 2, 3, 24
A range	e.g. 2..4, 8..*

Associations between classes can often be identified from collaborations between classes (see previous description of CRC cards) or from the problem brief. If we look at the extract from the *Just a Line* problem brief shown in Figure 5.15, we can see that the card number is checked as one that is recognised by the *Just a Line* system. In order for the system to be able to perform this check, there must be a relationship between the Card Reader and Valid Cards classes.

> The driver of an approaching car inserts his or her numbered card in the card reader, which then checks that the card number is known to the *Just a Line* system.

Figure 5.15 Extract from the *Just a Line* problem brief, indicating an association between the Card Reader and Valid Cards classes

This relationship is illustrated in the extract from the class diagram for the *Just a Line* Car Park system, shown below in Figure 5.16. The multiplicity of the association (1..* : 1) indicates that one or more card readers can access a single set of valid cards.

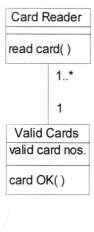

Figure 5.16 The association relationship between the Card Reader and Valid Cards classes showing that one or more card readers can access one set of valid cards.

Aggregation. When constructing a class diagram, it is often difficult to decide whether classes are related through an association or an aggregation relationship. However, the distinction between the two types of relationship is rarely crucial to the success of the final system; it is worth thinking about, but not worth agonizing over.

Aggregation expresses the relationship that occurs when one class is made up of several others, or when one class is made up of more than one occurrence of another class. Clues to aggregation can be found in phrases such as 'part of', 'consists of' or 'is made up of' in the problem brief, but even if it is not explicitly expressed in the brief, aggregation may still be present. Aggregation is represented as a diamond in the class diagram (see Figure 5.17).

In the *Just a Line* Car park system there are several relationships that we have decided to model as aggregations in the class diagram. At this stage, we view the *Just a Line* car park as made up of two or more barriers (one at each entrance and exit), two or more sensors (one for each barrier), one card reader and one or more 'Full' signs. This is shown in Figure 5.17.

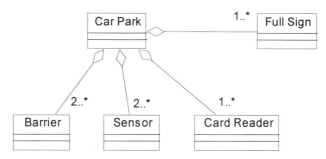

Figure 5.17 Some of the aggregation relationships in the *Just a Line* car park system

Inheritance. When one class is a specialization of another the relationship between the classes is called inheritance. We can see an example of this in the *Just a Line* car park system when we look at the different types of cards that are needed. The problem brief mentions cards and visitor's cards; in order to make the distinction between these clear, we refer to staff cards and visitor's cards. A user of the car park will have either a staff card or a visitor's card; these are different types of card, but, nonetheless, they have many features in common. When we come to model the cards in the *Just a Line* system, we want to represent both the differences and the similarities between them; for this we use inheritance, as shown in Figure 5.18.

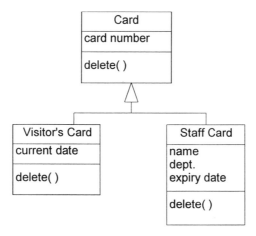

Figure 5.18 An example of inheritance from the *Just a Line* car park system

In this diagram, we can see a new class, Card, which has the attribute card number and the operation delete. Card is a super-class and has been added at this stage to model the features that Staff Card and Visitor's Card have in common. These are now modelled as sub-classes of class Card. The sub-class Staff Card inherits the card number attribute from class Card and has the extra attributes name, dept. and expiry date; an object of this class will therefore have the attributes card number, name, dept. and expiry date. The sub-class Visitor's Card also inherits the card number attribute from class Card and has the extra attribute current date; an object of this class will have the attributes card number and current date.

Since every card object in the system will be either a Staff Card or a Visitor's Card, it may seem rather pointless to include a general Card class. Card is an abstract class, it does not have any objects in the system, but it is useful as a way of modelling attributes and operations that are common to Staff Card and Visitor's Card. This is important for future modification and reuse. If, for example, we later want to modify the way that card numbers are implemented in the system, it is much tidier and more efficient to do this once in the Card class, than in both the Staff Card and Visitor's Card classes.

You will see, in Figure 5.18, that all three classes have a delete operation. This occurs as a generic operation in class card, and is then refined in different ways by each of the sub-classes. The delete operations in the Staff Card and Visitor's Card classes override the delete operation in class Card. This means that they will be implemented in different ways, but, as they will have the same names, arguments and result, these differences will not be visible externally.

If you compare Figure 5.18 with the Staff Card class in Figure 5.5(a), you can see how our ideas about cards in the system have developed during the course of modelling the system. The benefit of modelling is not only the final product, which can be used as the basis for design and implementation of the system, but also the increased understanding on the part of the developer of the problem and how the proposed system will solve it.

Figure 5.19 shows our version of the class diagram for the analysis stage of the *Just a Line* car park system; in order to emphasize the relationships between the classes, we have omitted attributes and operations from this diagram.

As a final note, we should say that this is only one possible class diagram for this system. Modelling is a creative process and it is very unlikely that any two people will produce exactly the same model for even a simple system.

5.3 Data dictionary

In Section 5.2.1, in the sub-section on beginning to construct a data dictionary, we talked about the importance of having an agreed notation to describe elements of the system. Informal descriptions, such as those in Figure 5.6, are adequate in the early stages of requirements engineering but, as development progresses, we need to adopt a more structured, standardized approach.

It is important to remember that all models incorporate some element of natural language and that no software development can take place without a basic reliance on spoken language and extensive use of its written form. Natural language has frequently been derided as a notation by computer scientists, who claim that it is imprecise, ambiguous, inconsistent and verbose, yet there is nothing inherently ambiguous, inconsistent or imprecise about English or any other natural language. Anyone who is old enough to remember learning grammar and parsing at school is well aware of the detailed structure of English sentences and the exact shades of meaning that can be achieved. For those who wish to see how precise, unambiguous and expressive written English can be, Gower's *The Complete Plain Words* provides numerous examples.

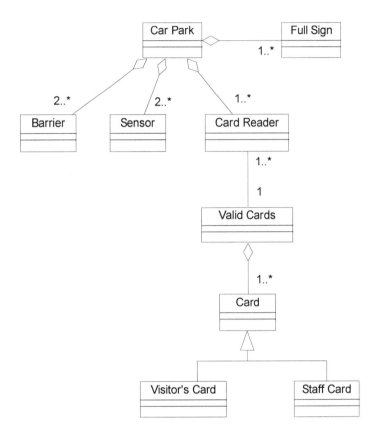

Figure 5.19 Class diagram for the *Just a Line* car park system

A class diagram, such as the one in Figure 5.19, gives us an overview of the different classes in the system and the relationships between them. If attributes and operations are included, they will have the minimum of detail, in order to keep the overall picture clear and uncluttered. This level of detail is sufficient for the purposes of the class diagram, but it only gives a partial picture of the classes and their features. For a more complete understanding, the developer and the client need detailed descriptions. This is recorded in the data dictionary. A data dictionary provides a central store of data about data. It allows the developer to describe classes and attributes by simple names, keeping the class diagram readable and uncluttered. A data dictionary solves many communication problems, since everyone working on the same project knows the agreed meaning of the words and terms used.

A data dictionary can be recorded manually, on paper, or it can be automated. This section describes a notation and approach suitable for a manually recorded data dictionary. The precise content and layout of the data dictionary will vary from one methodology to another. The data dictionary technique described here is suitable for describing a small system, such as the one for the *Just a Line* car park.

5.3.1 Value of a data dictionary

Whether automated or manual, the data dictionary is an invaluable tool. Data dictionary descriptions are used throughout the analysis and design stages of system development. The amount of detail required changes as the project progresses; normally it is inappropriate to attempt to describe the data with too much low-level detail in the early stages. The data dictionary provides an unambiguous and concise way of recording data about data. It forms a central store of data which supports the information given in other models of the system, not only the class diagram, but also the interaction and state diagrams (see Chapter 6). One of the advantages of this is that these models of the system can use short simple labels to describe data items, attributes and operations. The models are kept uncluttered and readable with no loss of precision, as all the labels are cross-referenced to descriptions in the data dictionary.

Another advantage of using a data dictionary common to all system models is that it encourages consistency; if the same name is used in two models it means the same. Wherever the reader of the model requires more information about a label, it can be looked up in the data dictionary. For example, the Staff Card class in Figure 5.18 has simple labels for the attributes name, dept. and expiry date. Each of these will have an entry in the data dictionary, where a detailed description will be given. To ensure that all labels are properly documented, the data dictionary should be built up as the class diagram and other models are created.

A well-maintained data dictionary avoids ambiguity about the terms used on a project and ensures that everyone working on the project is using terms consistently. It also resolves problems of aliases where different people or departments use different names for the same data item. Both names are entered in the data dictionary and shown to be equivalent.

5.3.2 Data dictionary notation

A data dictionary notation must document accurately the attributes that make up the data items in the system, and the way in which these attributes are combined. It must be able to express:

- the sequence in which attributes occur;
- attributes or groups of attributes which repeat;
- attributes that are optional;
- that one of several possible attributes must be selected;

- the possible set of values for an attribute;
- comments about the entries in the dictionary.

An example notation

There are several different notations for recording data dictionaries. The one shown in Figure 5.20 is simple, but capable of describing the basic configurations in which data items can occur. This notation is concerned specifically with definitions of data items and their attributes; it does not cover descriptions of operations, which we discuss later in this section.

SYMBOL	MEANING	DESCRIPTION
=	consists of	indicates the start of a definition of a data item
+	and	joins components of the definition in sequence
{ }	one or more	attribute may be repeated
( )	zero or one	attribute is optional
[ ]	alternatives	selection is indicated by enclosing the alternative attributes in square brackets, [ ]
|	either.. or	alternatives in [ ] are separated by a vertical bar
" "	specific value	indicates specific values e.g. [" Y" | "N"]
...	comment	comments are enclosed between asterisks

Figure 5.20 Notation for a data dictionary

The label on a class names a collection of objects in the system that all have common features. For example, if we were developing a large security system for *Just a Line*, we would include a class Employee. Objects of the Employee class could have the attributes number, title (optional), first name or names, last name, address, phone number and department. An example of a specific object of the Employee class is shown in Figure 5.21, below.

```
: Employee
number = JL104
title = Mrs.
first names = Anne, Christine
last name = Raines
address = 46, Ferry Road,
            Littleburgh, PT6 0JQ
phone number = 01234 56789
dept. = Accounts
```

Figure 5.21 An example of an Employee object

Using the notation from Figure 5.20, the Employee class could be described in the data dictionary as:

Employee   =   number + (title) + {first name} + last name + address + phone number
              + dept.

In the data dictionary description of Employee, the parentheses ( ) indicate that the title is optional, some employees may not wish to record whether they are Mr., Mrs., Ms. or Dr. The curly brackets { } indicate that an employee may have one or more first names. If, as analysis proceeds, it is discovered that some employees record all their first names in full, while others only give their initials, the entry in the data dictionary can be updated to reflect this by using square brackets. In the example below the square brackets, [ ], indicate selection, and the vertical bar, |, separates the alternatives. We may also wish to restrict records of first names or initials to a maximum of three; to do this, we add numbers before and after the curly brackets.

Employee   =   number + (title) + $_1${[first name | initial]}$_3$ + last name + address + phone
              number + dept.

In order to be more precise, we may wish to describe the possible values of dept. with a separate entry in the data dictionary, with the alternative values enclosed in inverted commas:

dept. = [" Accounts " | " Design " | " Marketing " | " Administration "]

Describing documents

During the interview with Mark Barnes of D&B Systems (see Section 4.3.1), Sue Preston mentioned that Jane, the *Just a Line* receptionist, has a list of employees' cars, so that she can check that only company cars are in the car park. Figure 5.22 shows part of this list for April 2000.

Just a Line Car Park List						April 2000
Name	**Dept.**	**Ext.**	**Car make**	**Model**	**Number**	**Colour**
Sue Preston		361	Renault	Clio	P409 JPG	red
Harry Preston		360	Porsche	Carrera	JAL 1	silver
Annie Raines	Accounts	579	Volvo	340	H53 KJN	white
Chris Doolan	Design	488	VW	Golf	R401 CDV	grey
Chris Doolan	Design	488	Renault	Espace	L43 JKB	green
Sam Parker	Marketing	640	Peugeot	406	R339 BJS	blue
Mira Patel	Marketing	636	Ford	Mondeo	T324 TSS	red
……….	……….	….	……….	……….	……….	………
……….	……….	….	……….	……….	……….	………

Figure 5.22 Part of the *Just a Line* car park list for April 2000

If we want to store these details in the new system, we need to describe the current list in data dictionary notation. A first data dictionary definition for the list might be as shown below:

Car Park List   =   month + year + {employee name + (dept.) + extension + $_1${car make + car
model + car number + colour}$_2$}

We can see from this definition that the car park list consists of a month, a year and many entries, each of which records an employee's name, department (which is optional), extension number and car details. Note that the department does not have to be recorded; Sue and Harry Preston, for example, own the company and do not work for any particular department. The definition also tells us that an employee can register up to two cars; we can see from Figure 5.22 that Chris Doolan uses either a VW Golf or a Renault Espace. However, this description is rather long, difficult to read and may be difficult to reproduce without introducing transcription errors. The list can be described more elegantly as:

Car Park List = date + {entry}
date = month + year
entry = employee + {car}$_2$
employee = name + (dept.) + extension
dept. = [" Accounts " | " Design " | " Marketing " | " Administration"]
car = make + model + number + colour

This description tells us that the car park list consists of a date and one or more entries. Date is defined as a month and a year, and entry as an employee and one or two cars. Employee and car both have a separate description in the dictionary. Notice that in one respect the data dictionary can be used like a normal English dictionary; terms that are used in the description of one entry may themselves be entries in the dictionary. Thus, entry is used to describe Car Park List and can itself be looked up in the data dictionary. Entry is an example of a data structure, a group of data attributes referred to by a label. Data structures are used for convenience in the data dictionary in that a long string of attributes can be replaced with a label that describes them. This technique keeps descriptions concise and more readable, avoids repetition of long strings of attributes and helps prevent transcription errors creeping in.

All the essential information recorded on the car park list currently used by *Just a Line* has been captured in this data dictionary description. The information content of the car park list has been abstracted from the physical document on which it is recorded. The process of describing the list in data dictionary notation results in the separation of what the system records from how it records it. The information content of the list, what the system records, will be carried forward to be used in the implementation of the new system.

Appropriate level of detail

The amount of detail appropriate for a data dictionary depends on how the data dictionary will be used. The data dictionary during analysis, for example, will normally go into less detail than at the detailed design stage. If the data dictionary is to be used simply to document the system developer's understanding of the current system and to support discussions with the client, labels such as 'extension' or 'number' will be self-explanatory;

no more detail is required. At the detailed design stage, however, the developer is thinking ahead to the detail required in an automated system. Decisions have to be made that were unnecessary earlier; decisions, for example, about input and output formats for dates and how they are going to be represented internally. Will the system, for instance, use '20/10/20xx' as input format, and '20th October 20xx' as output format? Will dates be stored internally as 3 integers, or a string of 8 numeric characters? Decisions must be made about the format or 'picture' of each data element and about its permissible range of values. This information will be required when input documents or screens are being designed and when input validation checks are devised.

Describing operations

The data dictionary notation shown above provides a clear and precise way of describing classes and their attributes, but does not cover operations. In the early stages of development we are not concerned with how an operation is to be implemented; we require only a brief description of what it does. We can, for example, describe the decrement spaces operation in the Car Park class as follows:

> This operation checks that the value of the attribute 'spaces' in the car park is greater than 0. If this is the case, the value of 'spaces' is decremented by 1. If this results in there being no spaces left, the Full sign is turned on.

Sometimes, it is helpful to use more formal, structured English. Structured English is a limited and structured subset of natural language, with a syntax that is similar to that of a block-structured programming language. Constructs found in structured English typically include the following:

- a sequence construct;
  e.g. the second statement below is executed immediately after the first statement;
     Add 1 to Total
     Divide Total by Count
- two decision constructs;
  e.g. IF Total < 20 THEN add 1 to Total ELSE display error message
     CASE Total < 20: add 1 to Total
- two repetition constructs;
  e.g. WHILE Total < 20 DO ....
     REPEAT .... UNTIL Total =20
- comments enclosed in parentheses;
     (* this is a comment *)

An example of structured English, using the decrement spaces operation, is shown below.
dec. spaces
IF spaces > 0, THEN
   spaces = spaces –1.
   ELSEIF spaces = 0, THEN
   Turn on Full Sign
   ELSE error.

Extract from the data dictionary for the Just a Line *car park system*

Part of a data dictionary to support the class diagram in Figure 5.19 is shown in Figure 5.23. The extract is structured by class in alphabetical order. Attributes that need further definitions, and operations associated with a class, are included directly below the class entry.

Barrier = Barrier type + up

    Barrier type = [" Entrance " | " Exit "]

    up = [" True " | " False "]

    <u>raise</u>: If the barrier is not already raised, this operation takes as argument an object of the Barrier class and returns an object of the same class, with the up attribute set to " True ". If the barrier is already up, the operation returns the error message " Barrier already raised ".

    <u>lower</u>: If the barrier is not already lowered, this operation takes as argument an object of the Barrier class and returns an object of the same class, with the up attribute set to " False ". If the barrier is already down, the operation returns the error message " Barrier already lowered".

Card = number + [Staff Card | Visitor's Card]

    <u>delete</u>: This operation removes the card from the set of cards known to *Just a Line.*

Card Reader = location

    <u>read card</u>: This operation takes a card number as input and checks it against the set of numbers of known cards in the Valid Cards class.

Car Park = capacity + spaces

    capacity = *the total number of parking places in the car park*

    spaces = *the number of currently free spaces in the car park*

    <u>inc. spaces</u>: This operation checks that the car park is not empty (the number of spaces left is not equal to the capacity of the car park). If this is the case, the value of 'spaces' is incremented by 1.

    <u>dec. spaces</u>: This operation checks that the value of the attribute 'spaces' in the car park is greater than 0. If this is the case, the value of 'spaces' is decremented by 1. If this results in there being no spaces left, the Full Sign is turned on.

Full Sign = location + on

    on = [" True " | " False "]

    <u>switch on</u>:

    <u>switch off</u>:

Sensor = car sensed

    car sensed = [" True " | " False "]

    <u>sense car</u>: If a car is detected by the sensor, this operation sets the car sensed attribute to " True ".

Staff Card = name + dept. + expiry date
  name = first name + last name
  dept. = ["Accounts " | "Design " | "Marketing " | "Administration "]
  expiry date = *date after which card is no longer valid*
  delete: If the expiry date on the card has passed, this operation removes the card number from the list of cards known to *Just a Line.*

Valid Cards = known cards *the set of cards whose numbers are recognized by *Just a Line.**

Visitor's Card = current date *date that the card is issued*
  delete: If the date on the card has passed, this operation removes the card number from the list of cards known to *Just a Line.*

Figure 5.23 Part of a data dictionary for the *Just a Line* car park system

Exercises

Modelling is a creative process and it is very unlikely that any two people will produce exactly the same model for even a simple system. In the exercises that follow, do not be discouraged if your answers are not exactly the same as those given; it does not mean that they are wrong. If your answers are very different from the sample answers, you should discuss this with your course tutor.

5.1   Identify some of the classes that you would expect to find in each of the following systems:
a)   a system for a library
b)   a system to manage hotel bookings
c)   a mail-order clothes system
d)   an airline booking system
e)   a system for an X-ray clinic

5.2   Consider the class 'Person'. List the attributes that a person would have in each of the following systems:
a)   a system for a library
b)   a payroll system
c)   a voting registration system
d)   a sports club registration system
e)   a dentist's system

5.3   From each of the following paragraphs, prepare a list of nouns that may be useful as classes. Then go through your list and reject any nouns that will not make useful classes; give a reason for each rejection. List the nouns that you retain as classes.

a)   *On the Move* is a small family firm that hires out cars. A car is bought in new or nearly new from a dealer and is given an initial check. It is then available for hire. Between each separate hiring, the car is given a service and a clean for the next customer. When a car reaches a certain mileage, it is sold.

b)   A credit card company with 6.5 million card holders has arrangements with 500,000 retailers who accept the cards. The retailers include hotels, shops, travel agencies, garages and restaurants. When a card holder wishes to buy something, he or she presents the card to the retailer. If the sale is for more than £50, the retailer then telephones the credit card company to check that the customer has sufficient credit. If the sale is authorized, the transaction is carried out using a 2-part voucher, which records details of the customer, the retailer and the transaction. Details of the transaction are also included on the monthly statement which is sent to the card holder.

5.4   Identify the classes and attributes of the following sets of objects.

a)

Ben Jones	Susan Lee	Joe Davison
Sales	Accounts	Catering
4 Hill Way	17 High Street	42 Forest Road
Anytown	Anytown	Anytown
6/11/77	4/10/71	2/3/63

b)

4929711023541	307749032	4929366009452
Visa	Access	Visa
B.R. Jones	S. J. Lee	J. Davison
4 Hill Way	17 High Street	42 Forest Road
Anytown	Anytown	Anytown
11/02	04/00	05/02

c)

Renault	Volkswagen	Honda
Clio	Passat	Accord
1.4 litre	2.0 litre	1.6 litre
red	blue	white
1991	1996	1997
H48 LPJ	N416 0PK	P16 LBN

d)

Jimbo's Gang Jane B. Carter Penguin 1997 0-14-665761-0	The Big Red Train Peter Hardy Puffin 1996 1-44-298543-6	Sam Goes Home Lee Hunter Penguin 1996 0-14-579342-1

5.5   List some sample attributes for some of the classes that you identified in exercise 5.1.

5.6   List some sample operations for each of the classes in exercise 5.1.

5.7

a)   In Section 2.3 of Chapter 2, we described an example of message passing, which involves a family getting the father's tea. The father, who has a responsibility to satisfy his hunger, tells the mother to get his tea; in order to do this, the mother collaborates with her children, telling them to peel the potatoes, fry the sausages and put the kettle on for tea.
Draw CRC cards for the father, mother and children to illustrate the responsibilities and collaborations in this situation.

b)   A gangland boss is in jail after an unfortunate misunderstanding with the police. On visiting day, he asks his devoted mama for funds so that he can escape. Mama has problems of her own and is rather short of money, so she decides to organize a bank robbery. She selects a team of three gangsters, one to plan the robbery, one to sort out transport and one to organize getting the money to her son. The gangster who is in charge of transport tells his accomplice to steal a fast car that they can use for the getaway.
Draw CRC cards to illustrate the responsibilities and collaborations in this situation.

5.8   Draw diagrams to link the following classes using aggregation, inheritance and multiplicity where appropriate.
a)   Village, Street, House, Shop, Road, Pavement
b)   University Staff, Academic, Administrator, Technician, Domestic
c)   Subscriber, Paying Subscriber, Complimentary Subscriber, Individual Paying Subscriber, Corporate Paying Subscriber
d)   Zoo, Animal, Bird, Mammal, Reptile, Cage, Keeper
e)   Estate, Building, House, Shop Unit, Room, Window, Door, Wall, Floor, Ceiling

5.9   Draw a class diagram, including class attributes, to represent the information given in the paragraph below.

A dental surgery keeps information about its patients, who may be either private or health service. For each patient the surgery records the name, address, phone number, date of birth, and either the health service number or the payment method.

5.10   Write a brief description in English of the information in each of the following class diagrams.

a)

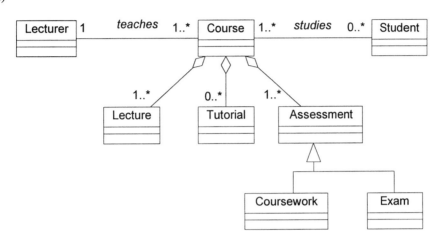

b)

c)

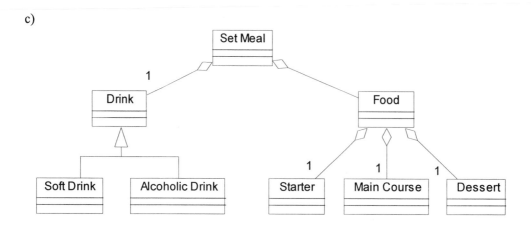

5.11   *Fit for Life* is a chain of health clubs, each with two sections: exercise and beauty. People can join a club as full members or part-time (in which case they are only allowed to use the facilities at certain times). The exercise section of each club has a gym and a swimming pool. Members can use these on a casual basis, but they have to make appointments for treatments in the beauty clinic, such as massage, facial or mud bath. Each club in the *Fit for Life* chain also has a restaurant, which is open to club members and the general public.
Draw a class diagram to represent this information. Where appropriate, your diagram should include association, aggregation, inheritance and multiplicity. You do not need to include attributes or operations.

5.12   Littlesand, Pebblesea and Mudport are three charming resorts on the South Coast which are very popular with tourists, since they score well on beach rating and hours of sunshine for the area. All three resorts have a large number of places to stay, ranging from one-room guest houses to the exclusive Palace Hotel at Pebblesea. The local tourist board wants to set up a central system to deal with room bookings in the area.
Draw a class diagram to represent this information. Where appropriate, your diagram should include association, aggregation, inheritance and multiplicity.
List sample attributes and operations for the class Resort.

5.13   University departments run several courses, each of which is included in at least one degree scheme, run by a Scheme Tutor. A department is headed by a professor and there are also other professors, both permanent and visiting. A student registers on a number of courses and, if successful, is eventually awarded a degree.
Draw a class diagram to represent this information. Where appropriate, your diagram should include association, aggregation, inheritance and multiplicity.
List sample attributes and operations for the class Course.
Write a data dictionary definition for the class Course.

5.14   Littlesand town museum has several rooms with exhibitions of items of local and national interest. Entry is free, but there is a charge for special exhibitions. For a small annual fee, local residents can become "friends" of the museum; for this they are entitled to reduced entry charges for the exhibitions. Each item in the museum is catalogued with an identity code, name, date of acquisition, where it came from, the room in the museum in which it is currently displayed, and a brief description. Staff of the museum include the chief curator, ten specialist guides and a number of administration staff.
Draw a class diagram to represent this information. Where appropriate, your diagram should include association, aggregation, inheritance and multiplicity.
List sample attributes and operations for the class Item.

5.15   A small dairy company wants to automate orders and payment on their milk rounds. Each milkman sets off on his round with the products that he is going to deliver and his list of customer requirements. As he comes to each house on his list, he checks to see what products are required. Customers have standing orders. If a customer wants to alter the order temporarily, this is classed as an exception (e.g. "1 extra pint today", "6 yoghurts on Thursday"). From time to time the dairy offers certain products at a special rate; orders for these products are known as promotion orders. All orders, Standing, Exception and Promotion, consist of individual order lines for each product ordered. On Fridays the milkman comes round to collect money. Most customers pay cash weekly, although some pay monthly by cheque.
Draw a class diagram to represent this information. Where appropriate, your diagram should include association, aggregation, inheritance and multiplicity.
List sample attributes and operations for the classes Order, Order Line, Standing Order, and Exception Order.
Write a data dictionary definition for the class Product.

5.16   Cute Cards is a small company that sells greetings cards by mail order. Their customers are mostly individuals who place small regular orders, but Cute Cards also sells wholesale to large card shops. The company stock consists of basic cards, which are sold without any message inside, but which may be personalized if the customer wishes. In this case the customer chooses a suitable message from the company's list, plus a typeface and a colour for printing. Payment must be sent with the order in the case of individual customers; wholesale customers are allowed credit.
Draw a class diagram to represent this information. Where appropriate, your diagram should include association, aggregation, inheritance and multiplicity.
List sample attributes and operations for the classes Customer, Individual Customer, Wholesale Customer.

5.17   In the Cute Cards system (Exercise 5.16) an invoice consists of the order number, customer name and address, delivery address (if different from customer's billing address), one or more order lines, any charge for delivery or postage and packing, and the total cost of the order. Write a data dictionary definition for an invoice.

5.18   Cute Cards delivers orders free to customers who live at or within a 20 mile radius, if they order at least £30 worth of cards. For smaller orders, there is a delivery charge of £2.00 and, for orders outside the delivery area, Cute Cards charges postage and packing.

Write a brief description in structured English of the operation to calculate the delivery or postage charge for an order.

References and further reading

Bennett, S., McRobb, S. and Farmer, R. *Object-Oriented Systems Analysis and Design using UML,* London: McGraw-Hill, 1999.

Booch, G., Rumbaugh, J. and Jacobson, I. *The Unified Modeling Language User Guide,* Reading, Massachusetts: Addison-Wesley, 1999.

Fowler, M. with Scott, K. *UML Distilled: Applying the Standard Object Modeling Language,* Reading, Massachusetts: Addison-Wesley, 1997.

Gowers, E. *The Complete Plain Words,* London: Penguin, 1987.

Henderson-Sellers, B. *A Book of Object-Oriented Knowledge,* 2nd edn, Upper Saddle River, N.J.: Prentice-Hall, 1997.

Quatrani, T. *Visual Modeling with Rational Rose and UML,* Reading, Massachusetts: Addison-Wesley, 1998.

Rumbaugh, J., Blaha, M., Premerlani, W., Eddy, F. and Lorensen, W. *Object-Oriented Modeling and Design,* Englewood Cliffs, N.J.: Prentice-Hall, 1991.

Stevens, P. with Pooley, R. *Using UML. Software Engineering with Objects and Components,* Harlow: Addison-Wesley, 1999.

Wirfs-Brock, R., Wilkerson, B. and Wiener, L. *Designing Object-Oriented Software,* Englewood Cliffs, N.J.: Prentice Hall, 1990.

6

Modelling the Behaviour of the System

A system is always developed for a purpose: to provide functionality, or behaviour, that will satisfy the needs and wishes of clients and users. In this chapter we consider how this functionality is modelled in object-oriented system development, from the early stages of requirements engineering through to diagrams that can be used as the basis for writing code. The chapter introduces the techniques of use cases, scenarios, interaction diagrams and state diagrams. At the end of the chapter there is a short section on good practice in modelling.

6.1 Use cases and scenarios

Use cases and scenarios are concerned with the behaviour of the system that is visible externally; they aim to establish what the system does from the user's point of view, in terms that the user can readily understand. Although they have become associated with object-orientation, both use cases and scenarios are functional and can be used in conjunction with any approach to system development.

Use cases specify the functionality that the system will offer from the users' perspective. A use case specifies a set of interactions between a user and the system to achieve a particular goal. If we take a dental surgery as an example, typical use cases would include Make appointment, Invoice patient and Refer patient to GP. The user who drives the use case and whose goal is achieved by it is known as an actor. Figure 6.1 below shows the use case Make appointment and the actor Patient.

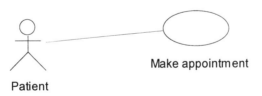

Patient   Make appointment

Figure 6.1 The actor Patient and the use case Make appointment

Actors are people or organizations who interact with the system in some way. An actor inputs and receives information from the system and is associated with at least one use case (major functional activity). Identifying actors in a system is a good starting point for uncovering the principal use cases.

We can think about the use cases in a system at various levels of detail. In the early stages of development, identifying the main use cases with clients is a useful way of establishing the boundary of the system to be developed. Figure 6.2 illustrates the principal use cases in the *Just a Line* car park system. As this is a very simple system, there are only three use cases at this level: entering and leaving the car park and updating the list of cards that the system recognizes as valid.

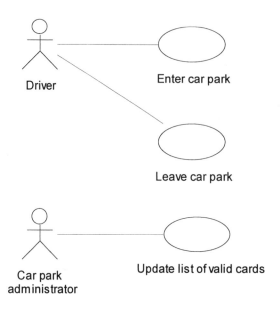

Figure 6.2 Principal use cases in the *Just a Line* car park system

Figure 6.2 shows two different actors in the *Just a Line* system. For the use cases that cover entering and leaving the car park the actor is the driver of the car, since it is the car driver who has the goal of entering or leaving and whose actions will trigger the appropriate use case. When it comes to updating the list of valid cards, this is a goal of the person who looks after that side of the car park system, possibly Jane, the *Just a Line* receptionist.

The behaviour of the system as a whole is described by the set of its use cases, which are uncovered by talking to clients and users. However, users are rarely, if ever, able to come up with a complete set of use cases out of thin air; they need to be prompted to identify exactly what they want the system to do for them. One of the most effective ways of achieving this is to use scenarios.

The relationship between use cases and scenarios is that of the generic to the specific. A scenario represents one instance of a use case, describing a particular sequence of events that may occur in trying to reach the use case goal. Let us go back to our example above of the dental surgery and the use case Make appointment (see Figure 6.1). The receptionist may list what usually happens as follows:

- the patient phones or calls in at the surgery
- he or she asks for an appointment, usually within certain time constraints
- the receptionist asks which of the three dentists usually sees the patient
- the receptionist asks if there is any specific problem (as this may determine the length of the appointment)
- the receptionist offers the patient the next free slot within the patient's time constraints

- the patient accepts the appointment
- the receptionist asks for the patient's name
- the receptionist records the patient's name, and the date and time of the appointment.

This is a normal scenario; it is what generally happens in the dental surgery when a patient makes an appointment. However, there are other sequences of events that may achieve the same goal of making an appointment, such as when the appointment is an emergency. The scenario in this case could be as follows:

- patient phones or comes into surgery
- he or she asks for an appointment as soon as possible
- the receptionist asks what the problem is
- the receptionist identifies the earliest time that one of the dentists is free
- the patient accepts the appointment
- the receptionist asks for the patient's name
- the receptionist records the patient's name, and the date and time of the appointment.

Cases where the goal of the use case is not achieved also need to be considered, so that users and developers can decide how the system is to respond to such situations. The following scenario illustrates the case where the dentist who usually sees the patient is booked up:

- patient phones or comes into surgery
- he or she asks for an appointment with a particular dentist within certain time constraints
- the receptionist is unable to find a free slot with that dentist within the time requested
- the receptionist offers the patient an appointment with the dentist at a time that is outside the patient's time constraints
- the patient refuses the appointment
- the receptionist offers the patient an appointment with one of the other dentists
- the patient refuses
- three months later, the receptionist sends a standard reminder to the patient.

6.1.1 Working with use cases and scenarios

Use cases and scenarios are valuable techniques throughout the development of the system. We have already mentioned in Chapter 4, Section 4.3.1, that scenarios are an effective way of eliciting requirements. Walking through scenarios with users helps to identify the use cases that define the overall behaviour of the system, and clarifies the user requirements that must be satisfied. When talking to users, there are certain questions that are useful in building up scenarios; these include questions such as:

- what do you typically do when you want to ....?
- who else is involved in carrying out this task?
- what information do you need before you start to ....?
- is there any information that has to be saved, modified or deleted during this task?
- how often do you carry out this task?

- what sort of problems do you find when you are carrying out this task?

A scenario consists of a goal (which may or may not be achieved) and a sequence of actions that lead to it. The goal must be well defined, in such a way that it is clear whether or not it has been successfully achieved. Goals such as 'make appointment' and 'leave car park' are well defined, but 'improve patient satisfaction' and 'make car park more secure' are too vague to be useful in a scenario. The sequence of actions leading to the goal must have definite start and end points and be expressed in a way that is as simple and concrete as possible. Vague terms, such as 'quite a few times', 'after a while' or 'rather a lot' should be avoided. One good test for this is whether the scenario could be represented in pictures, as a storyboard; if this is not possible, then the actions need to be described in a more concrete way. Another thing to watch out for when constructing scenarios is that they should be free of implementation details or anything that presupposes that the developed system will have a particular implementation feature.

Use cases should also be described as clearly as possible, in terms that users will understand. A very brief description of the purpose of the use case in jargon-free English should be provided for each one identified. For example, in the dental surgery system, the Make appointment use case could be described as follows:
"When a patient wants to see a dentist, he or she contacts the surgery and is allocated a convenient date and time for an appointment."

A good use case represents some behaviour of the system that delivers something of benefit to an actor and which can be thought about as an independent activity. If you find that two use cases always have to be considered and tested together, then they should probably be merged into one. There are no rules about the size or granularity (level of detail) of a use case, so it is often difficult to know how many use cases to identify. For example, the receptionist in a dental surgery has to add, delete and modify patients' records; is that one use case or three? Use cases at a lower level are useful for project management, since each use case can be seen as satisfying a separate goal, but too many use cases can be overwhelming, both for developers and clients. The problem is exacerbated by the fact that each use case will give rise to a number of different scenarios, creating a huge amount of information that has to be organized and managed. In the example here of adding, deleting and modifying patients' records, we would treat that as one single use case, Maintain patient records.

6.1.2 The advantages of use cases and scenarios

Use cases and scenarios are popular with both users and developers. They are easy to understand for people who are not computer specialists, yet, at the same time, they provide a sound foundation for the design of the system's functionality.

Scenarios are particularly attractive to users, since their narrative form makes them a very effective means of communication. A scenario can be seen as a simple story, a means of recording how things happen currently in the problem domain, and of visualizing how users would like them to happen in the future system. During requirements elicitation, scenarios can help users to explain what they do to carry out particular tasks, what information they need and what the output will be. Walking through the scenarios prompts users to add more detail, and to identify errors and gaps in their original account.

The fact that scenarios are readily accessible to clients and users is also a benefit to the developer, since any technique that promotes a shared understanding of requirements is valuable in system development.   Scenarios are particularly helpful when used in conjunction with CRC (class-responsibility-collaboration) cards (see Chapter 5, Section 5.2.1).   A CRC card documents a class with its responsibilities and the classes that it collaborates with to fulfil these. Walking through scenarios helps to allocate functionality between the various classes and to uncover other classes that may have been missed at an earlier stage.

From a technical point of view, use cases and scenarios bring many benefits to the developer. The purpose of a system is contained in its functionality, the way it behaves in response to input from its environment. Functionality is revealed by studying interactions between the system and the actors in its environment, and the most effective way of studying interactions is by identifying use cases and building up scenarios. Well specified use cases are a prime source of functional requirements for the system, suggesting design features and providing a sound basis for the final code. They are especially useful during testing, when user requirements, as expressed in scenarios, can be compared with performance of the final system. This persistence throughout development of the system means that use cases are also helpful to project managers, since they provide a framework for defining the scope of the project, tracing requirements and monitoring progress.

6.1.3 Use cases and scenarios in the *Just a Line* car park case study

In Figure 6.2 we identified three principal use cases in the *Just a Line* car park system: Enter car park, Leave car park and Update list of valid cards. In this section we give examples of how two of these use cases can be fleshed out by constructing scenarios.

Use case: Enter car park

Let us imagine that Mark Barnes of D&B Systems has asked Sue Preston to describe what she would like to happen when she wishes to use the new, secure car park at *Just a Line*. Sue's first attempt produces the following scenario for the usual sequence of events. This is sometimes referred to as the 'happy day' scenario.

- Sue's car arrives at the entrance to the car park
- Sue inserts her card in the card reader
- the card is recognized as one that is known to the *Just a Line* system
- the entrance barrier is raised
- Sue drives into the car park
- the barrier is lowered.

When Sue reads through this scenario, she realises at once that there are several things that she has forgotten. What if the car park is full when the car arrives? What happens if someone inserts a card when no car is present? How does the driver get his or her card back? And, most important of all, how long does the barrier stay up and how does it avoid crashing down on top of a car that is still under it? Sue's second happy day scenario aims to address these problems.

- Sue approaches the car park and can see that the full sign is off
- Sue's car arrives at the entrance to the car park
- her car's arrival at the barrier is detected
- Sue inserts her card in the card reader
- the card is recognized as one that is known to the *Just a Line* system
- Sue's card is returned
- the entrance barrier is raised
- Sue drives into the car park
- her car's departure is detected
- the barrier is lowered.

Sue also has to consider what is to happen when things do not go as expected. This is her scenario for the situation when the card that is inserted is not known to the *Just a Line* system.

- Sue approaches the car park and can see that the full sign is off
- Sue's car arrives at the entrance to the car park
- her car's arrival is detected
- Sue inserts her card in the card reader
- the card is not recognized as known to *Just a Line*
- the card is returned
- Sue drives away.

Although this covers the basic events, Sue feels that it is not very satisfactory for her as the car driver. The card may have been rejected for a number of reasons: for example, it may be out of date, or the number may have been mistakenly removed from the list. Whatever the reason, the system really ought to indicate why the card has been rejected. This is an example of how scenarios can give rise to new requirements: in this case the need for some way of displaying messages to car drivers.

Use case: Update list of valid cards

It has not yet been decided who is going to be in charge of the day-to-day administration of the car park, so Sue is also asked to think about scenarios for the use case Update list of valid cards. Her happy day scenario for adding a card is as follows. It makes the assumption that the list of cards will be kept in card number order in the developed system.

- the administrator is asked to add card number JL253
- the administrator checks that the new card number is not already in the list
- the administrator finds the place in the list where the new card number is to be inserted
- the new card number is added in the correct slot
- the administrator informs the Personnel Department that card number JL253 has been added.

The main thing that can go wrong here is that the card number is already in the list. This case is covered by the following scenario. Note that this use case merely passes on the information that there is a duplicate number, it does not try to sort out the problem itself.

- the administrator is asked to add card number JL472
- the administrator checks the list and finds card number JL472 already on it
- the administrator informs the Personnel Department of the problem.

At the end of this chapter you will find exercises asking you to construct other scenarios for these use cases.

6.2 Interaction diagrams

During requirements elicitation, use cases and scenarios are usually recorded using informal text but, as development progresses and more details are added, it is a good idea to use interaction diagrams to show what is going on. There are two sorts of interaction diagram that are typically used in object-oriented development: sequence diagrams and collaboration diagrams. Sequence diagrams illustrate interactions that occur between actors and objects in the system in order to carry out the behaviour specified in the scenarios; they are discussed in the following section. Collaboration diagrams also illustrate the behaviour specified in the scenarios, but the interactions are organized around the objects and the links between them, rather than shown in a time sequence.

6.2.1 Sequence diagrams

If we look at the scenarios that we have constructed, we can pick out the objects that are involved and the interactions that take place between them. As an example, let us take the second happy day scenario for the Enter car park use case. This is shown again here.

- Sue approaches the car park and can see that the full sign is off
- Sue's car arrives at the entrance to the car park
- her car's arrival at the barrier is detected
- Sue inserts her card in the card reader
- the card is recognized as one that is known to the *Just a Line* system
- Sue's card is returned
- the entrance barrier is raised
- Sue drives into the car park
- her car's departure is detected
- the barrier is lowered.

The interactions in this scenario are between the actor, Sue (in her role as a car driver) and objects of the following classes: Car Park, Valid Cards, Card Reader, Full Sign, Barrier and Sensor. However, as soon as we begin to draw the sequence diagram, we find that there are more issues that have to be sorted out; for example, what turns the Full Sign on and off? Where does the sensor send the message that a car has been detected? Where do the instructions to raise and lower the barrier come from? Sorting out these types of question is not part of requirements elicitation; these issues involve events that are internal to the system, not part of its interaction with the actors in its environment. We are beginning to move from analysis into design and from a list of events to a sequence of messages. These sorts of question are things that the developer has to decide, not the client.

We mentioned in the section on modelling in Chapter 5 (Section 5.1.2) that one of the purposes of constructing a model is to identify gaps and inconsistencies. We can see here how drawing a sequence diagram reveals new issues in a scenario that we thought was complete. Figure 6.3 shows the sequence diagram for the scenario. At the top of the figure we can see the actor and the objects involved in the interactions when a car enters the car park. The actor is represented by a stick figure (on the left), and the objects (in no particular order) by named rectangles. The fact that the names are underlined shows that it is specific objects that take part in interactions, not the classes themselves. The dotted line underneath each actor and object is called its lifeline; the arrows represent messages and information passing between the actor and objects.

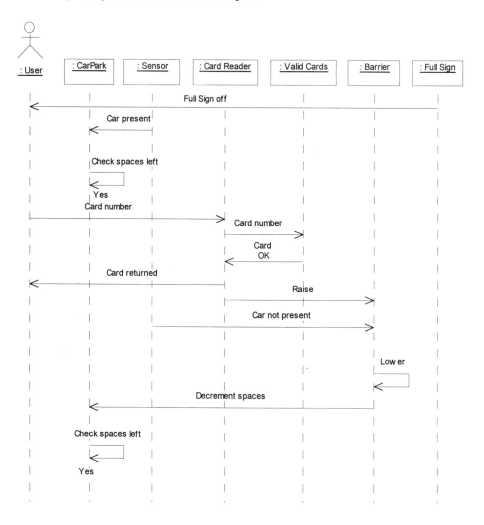

Figure 6.3 Sequence diagram for the happy day Enter car park scenario

If we follow the arrows down the diagram in Figure 6.3, we can see the exactly what happens when a car enters the *Just a Line* car park. The sequence of events is as follows:

- the car driver sees that the Full sign is off
- a car's arrival is detected by the sensor and this information is passed to the car park
- the car park checks to see if there are still spaces[1]
- there is still at least one space available
- a card is inserted into the card reader by the car driver
- the card reader reads the card number and checks that it is in the list of valid cards
- the card is recognized as known to the system
- the card is returned
- the card reader tells the barrier to raise itself
- the sensor sends a message to the barrier that the car is no longer detected
- the barrier lowers itself
- the car park subtracts 1 from the number of available spaces
- the car park checks to see if there are still spaces
- there is still at least one space available.

The events in this sequence are not exactly the same as those in the original scenario, since the sequence diagram illustrates not only interaction between actor and system, but also exchanges of information between the objects inside the system. The sequence diagram is based on the requirements elicited in the scenario, but also illustrates early design decisions on the way that these requirements are going to be implemented and how the functionality is going to be shared out between the classes.

It is possible to show more information on a sequence diagram, by including conditions under which specific interactions take place, and symbols for repeated interactions. However, the extra notation often clutters the diagram, and for beginners it is generally better to produce a separate diagram for each scenario. Many authors also advocate putting comments on the diagram down the left-hand side. This can be very useful in the case of a complicated sequence diagram, but there is always a trade-off between adding extra information and losing the clarity of the diagram (for a discussion of this problem, see Section 6.4).

As a second example of a sequence diagram, Figure 6.4 shows the diagram for the situation when the card that is inserted is not known to the *Just a Line* system. First, the scenario is repeated below. An extra event has been added to make the system more user-friendly by displaying the reason that the card has been rejected.

- Sue approaches the car park and can see that the full sign is off
- Sue's car arrives at the entrance to the car park
- her car's arrival is detected
- Sue inserts her card in the card reader
- the card is not recognized as known to *Just a Line*
- a message is displayed to say that the card has not been recognized
- the card is returned
- Sue drives away.

---

[1] This check is an added precaution in case a driver ignores the illuminated Full sign and attempts to enter the car park.

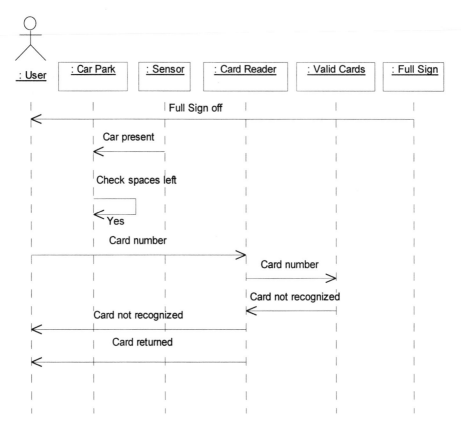

Figure 6.4 Sequence diagram for scenario where the card that is inserted is not recognized

6.2.2 Collaboration diagrams

Collaboration diagrams are an alternative way of illustrating scenarios. They show the same information as sequence diagrams, but represent the interactions organized around the objects and the links between them.

Figure 6.5 shows the collaboration diagram for the scenario where the card that is inserted is not recognized. By comparing it with Figure 6.4, which shows the same information in the form of a sequence diagram, you can see the difference between the two sorts of interaction diagrams.

In Figure 6.5 the named rectangles represent the objects and the lines show the links between them. Numbered arrows indicate the messages and the order in which these occur.

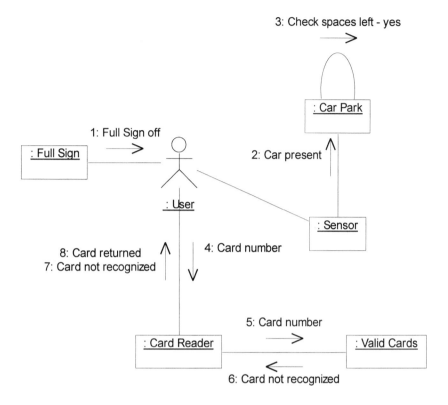

Figure 6.5 Collaboration diagram for scenario where the card that is inserted is not recognized

6.3 State diagrams

Sequence and collaboration diagrams are ways of representing all the interactions that take place between the objects involved in a particular use case. Sometimes, however, we need to focus on a specific class to illustrate how its objects behave during their lifetimes and how they react to all the use cases in which they are involved; in this situation we use a state diagram.

A state diagram only ever describes the behaviour of a single class. In most systems, only a few of the classes are complicated enough to merit one. If a class always responds in exactly the same way to events, then there is no point in drawing a state diagram for it. The interesting classes are those where the response of an object of the class to a particular event varies, depending on the state the object is in at the time. Interaction diagrams, particularly sequence diagrams, are more common than state diagrams; however, when you want to find out what is going on inside a class, you need a state diagram.

A state diagram describes how a class of objects behaves in the system, in other words, how the class responds to all the use cases that affect it. All the objects that are members of the class have the same range of ways in which they can behave, but the actual way an individual object does behave during the running of the system depends on the sequence of events that it experiences.

As an example of this, imagine two objects of the class Balloon, one red and one blue. Both balloons have been blown up, but the blue one has had some of the air let out of it. If someone now tries to blow up the balloons, they will respond in different ways: the blue one will simply become slightly more inflated, but the red one (which is already fully blown up) will burst. We can illustrate these alternative behaviours in a very simple state diagram for the class Balloon, as shown in Figure 6.6.

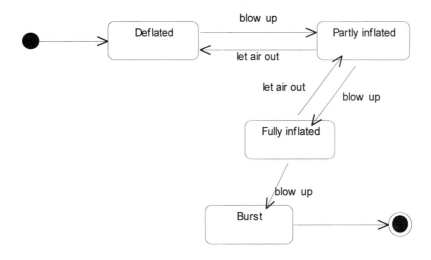

Figure 6.6 Simple state diagram for the class Balloon

In Figure 6.6 we can see the principal components of a state diagram: states (shown by rectangles with rounded corners) and transitions (shown by labelled arrows).

States

The state of an object represents a period of time during which the object satisfies some condition or waits for an event. There are two special states shown in Figure 6.6: the start state (represented by a filled circle) and the stop state (represented by a bull's-eye). Each state diagram must have only one start state, since all objects of the same class must begin life in the same state. However, the diagram can have multiple stop states, since the way in which an object ends its life depends on the sequence of events that it undergoes during its lifetime.

We can tell if an object is in a particular state by looking at the values of its attributes. In the *Just a Line* car park system, for example, objects of the Barrier class have an attribute 'up', which may take the value true or false. If we see that the value of the 'up' attribute for a particular Barrier object is false, then we know that this barrier is currently in the state of being down. This is shown in Figure 6.7, where we can see, for example, that while a barrier is in the Down state, a lower event leaves it in that state, but a lower event acting on a barrier in the Up state shifts it into the Down state.

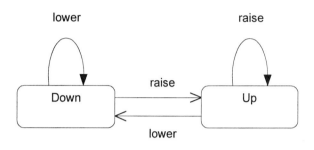

Figure 6.7 Diagram of the Barrier class, showing how the state of an object can be seen from the values of its attributes

Transitions

A state transition represents the response of an object to an event; the response may involve movement of the object from one state to another, or the object remaining in the same state (sometimes referred to as self-transition). A state transition is regarded as instantaneous and cannot be interrupted. It consists of three parts, event, guard, and action; though all of these are optional. An event triggers a state transition; examples are 'blow up' in Figure 6.6 and 'raise' in Figure 6.7. A guard is a condition that allows the transition to take place only if the condition is true; guards are written inside square brackets [ ], examples can be seen in Figure 6.8, below. An action is the behaviour that occurs when a transition takes place, and is preceded by a slash /. An example of an action can be seen in Figure 6.8 which shows the state diagram for a class Petrol Tank; when a Petrol Tank object moves into state Empty, an action occurs to turn on the warning light.   Both guards and actions are generally implemented as operations on the class in the final system code. You can find all the features mentioned here in Figure 6.8, the state diagram for a petrol tank.

There are one or two things to note about Figure 6.8. In order to reduce clutter in the diagram, we have omitted details of guards and actions on some of the state transitions (transitions between Part full and Full, and Part full and Empty). You will also notice that, apart from the start and stop states, all the other states are enclosed in one large superstate. This, again, is to avoid clutter; a tank object may end its life while in any of its three states, but to include separate arrows for each possibility would result in a very messy diagram. Instead of that, we nest the three main states in one large superstate and show the transition to the stop state leading from that. The start state is also shown outside the superstate, but, in this case, it is directly linked to the Empty state, since all Petrol Tank objects begin life empty.

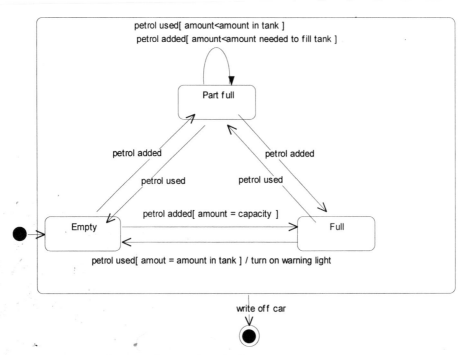

Figure 6.8 State diagram of a Petrol Tank class

As a final example, we return to the *Just a Line* car park case study. We mentioned above that it is only necessary to draw state diagrams for classes with complex or significant behaviour. In the *Just a Line* system, the only diagram that is needed is one for the Car Park class; this is shown on the following page in Figure 6.9. The diagram summarizes the range of behaviours for objects of the Car Park class. These behaviours can also be seen in the lifelines of the Car Park in the various sequence diagrams.

6.4 Good practice in modelling

We have now introduced the principal modelling techniques that are used in object-oriented system development. Many other techniques exist and all of them have advocates who swear that they are essential for object-oriented modelling. However, this book is an introduction, and so we have restricted ourselves to the main techniques covered in Chapters 5 and 6.

Modelling techniques can be taught, and most people will be able to use them proficiently with practice. However, producing a good model requires skill and creative talent. An effective model is accurate, precise, easy to understand, easy to modify, a vehicle for discussion with users and a basis for further development—all in all, a pretty tall order. Good modelling comes with experience, but we mention here one or two points that may be helpful to beginners.

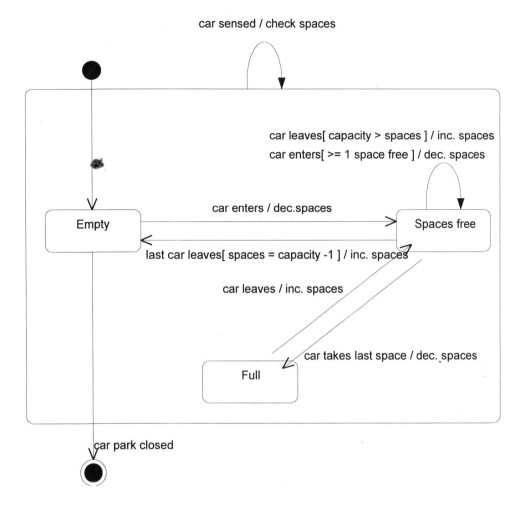

Figure 6.9 State diagram for the Car Park class

Avoiding clutter

In the notes on Figure 6.8, we mentioned that we had left out some of the labelling details because they would have made the diagram too cluttered. Clutter is a common problem in models; there is nearly always a choice to be made between including all appropriate information and producing a clear, easily readable model. Although it is tempting to include anything that may be relevant, we have to remember that a model that is not clear or easy to understand is of very little use. This is particularly the case where the model is used as the basis for discussion with people who may not be familiar with the diagramming techniques used to produce it.

There are various ways in which cluttered, messy diagrams can be avoided. One approach is to use two or more diagrams, instead of trying to crowd all the information into one. We saw this in the section on sequence diagrams in this chapter (Section 6.2.1), where separate diagrams are drawn for each scenario in the use case, rather than putting all the alternative paths on one diagram. Another example can be found in Chapter 5, Figure 5.19, where attributes and operations have been omitted from the class diagram for the *Just a Line* car park system, in order to emphasise the relationships between the classes.

Another way of reducing clutter is to choose names and labels that are short. If more explanation is needed, this can be provided in a key to the diagram or, more fully, in a data dictionary. For example, the Car Park class has two attributes, which are simply labelled capacity and spaces (see Figure 6.10).

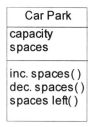

Figure 6.10 The Car Park class from the *Just a Line* system

These attribute names are explained in the data dictionary entry for the Car park:
capacity = *the total number of parking places in the car park*
spaces = *the number of currently free spaces in the car park*

What makes a good class

Choosing classes is one of the most important, yet the most difficult, of the activities in object-oriented system development. An object-oriented software system is built on classes of data objects, so if some significant classes are missed, or if the wrong classes are identified in the early stages of development, this will have a detrimental effect on the whole system. We list here a few informal guidelines that are helpful in choosing good classes, although some of these contradict each other and it will not be possible for all the classes identified in a system to satisfy all the guidelines. Ultimately, you have to rely on common sense, knowledge of the problem domain and, eventually, experience.

- 'God' classes—those that do most of the controlling in a system—should be avoided. The object-oriented approach aims to provide a set of decentralized classes that communicate with each other, not a single class that is in complete control. This is one of the reasons for omitting an Entrance class in the *Just a Line* car park system, since this class would have directed a large part of the functionality of the system.
- A point that is related to the one above is that all classes in the system should have similar amounts of functionality; there should be a roughly even distribution of intelligence between the classes. The Barrier class in the *Just a Line* system could have been implemented as a very passive class, which merely responds to messages from other classes. In fact, it has been designed to take a more active part, including telling the car park to decrement the number of spaces. This can be seen in the sequence diagram, Figure 6.3.

- A class should not simply be one big function, but should include some data attributes. In the car park system, a Display class would have had no purpose other than to display information and so we do not include it.
- A class should have more than basic functionality, such as setting and retrieving data. This guideline would suggest that we omit the Full Sign class from the car park system, but this class is included for another reason (see next guideline).
- Generally, one of the main reasons for choosing a class is that it corresponds to something in the real world and is easy for people to understand; for this reason, we include the Full Sign class in the *Just a Line* car park system.
- A class should be concerned with a single abstraction only, whether it is a physical object, such as a book, a transaction, such as a loan, or an organisation, such as a department. This is important, because it means that the class is more cohesive, easier to understand and simpler to test and maintain.

Unique identifiers for objects

Figure 6.11 shows an example of a class, which we can use to illustrate an important point about modelling attributes.

Staff Card
number name dept.

Figure 6.11 Staff Card class with three attributes

We do not normally include as attributes numbers or codes which are simply there to identify each individual object in the new system; most object-oriented languages automatically generate unique identifiers and it is not appropriate to record them in the early stages of development. However, the card numbers shown in Figure 6.11 are not simply to identify each individual employee in the new system. The numbers are issued by *Just a Line* and make sense in the problem domain, since the car park card reader will need to recognize specific card numbers; therefore we should include them as part of the problem analysis.

A further point is illustrated by Figure 6.12, which shows three objects of the Staff Card class.

<u>:Staff Card</u> number = JL437 name = Sam Parker dept. = Marketing	<u>:Staff Card</u> number = JL722 name = Mira Patel dept. = Marketing	<u>:Staff Card</u> number = JL209 name = Chris Doolan dept. = Design

Figure 6.12 Three objects of class Staff Card, with specific values

Each of the objects in the class has its own identity, but may have the same values as other objects for one or more of its attributes. In Figure 6.12 two of the objects have the value Marketing in the department attribute.

We should also note that different classes might have the same attribute names. If we were developing a complete security system for *Just a Line,* to cover the building as well as the car park, we would include classes such as Employee and Room. Both of these classes would have an attribute recording the department with which the employee or the room is associated; however, since Employee and Room would be separate classes, there would be no confusion between the two department attributes.

Using aggregation

Aggregation is usually described as a part-whole relationship—an aggregation relationship exists between classes if one can be seen as part of the other, or conversely, one consists of, or is made up of, an aggregation of others. A car is said to consist of an engine, wheels, doors, windows etc. The wheels form part-of the car. In this, car is a class, and so are wheel, engine, door. Aggregation is also said to occur when one class is made up of several occurrences of another class; for example, a paragraph is made up of lots of sentences; a sentence is made up of several words, a word is made up of several letters. The concept is quite straightforward, but the point of it is obscure.

Ultimately, one of the main points of creating a model is to use it to produce code. It will be better code if the model can also be used for other useful purposes such as communicating with the client, suggesting a robust code structure, and producing a format that is easier to read, understand and maintain. However, if some feature of the model has no direct counterpart in the code and has nothing useful to say about the way the code should be written, then there does not seem to be a great deal of point in using that feature in the model. This would appear to be the case with aggregation. It is possibly the single feature of O-O about which there is least consensus amongst the community. It has been suggested that if you removed all aggregation from a class diagram and replaced it with association, it would produce the same code as if you left the aggregation in.

There is only any point in modelling aggregation if the development team can find some use for it. It may be the case that it is a useful concept when communicating with the client to increase mutual understanding of the problem domain. It may be that the team can use a more rigorous definition of aggregation (see Chapter 7, Section 7.3.2 for the definition used in this book). The Unified Modelling Language, see Section 3.2.3, offers the notion of composition or containment, which is a more rigorous version of aggregation. The composition relationship dictates that a class can only be part-of a single class, in other words, it can participate in only one 'part-of' relationship. The UML composition also insists that the parts live and die with the whole. Both of these constraints give the concept some concrete meaning, which translates directly into the implementation.

Exercises

6.1   In Section 6.1.3 we described two scenarios for the use case Update list of valid
        cards, successfully adding a new card and trying to add a new card when the card

number is already on the list. Study these, and then write a scenario to describe what happens:
a)   when a card is successfully removed from the list
b)   when the card number to be removed is not on the list.

6.2
a)   Write a simple scenario to describe what happens when someone phones a restaurant to order a large Napolitana pizza to be delivered.
b)   Amend the scenario you wrote in (a) to show what happens when a requested pizza topping is not available.

6.3
a)   Look at the scenario which describes what happens when a car enters the *Just a Line* car park (Section 6.1.3). How would you need to modify this scenario for the situation in which the car entering the car park takes the last available space?
b)   Modify the sequence diagram in Figure 6.3 to match the changes you have made to the scenario.

6.4   Read through the scenario below, describing what happens when someone gets the balance of his or her bank account from an ATM. Draw a sequence diagram to illustrate this information.

- ATM displays Welcome screen with request to insert card
- user inserts card
- ATM reads card number and requests PIN number
- user enters PIN number
- ATM checks card and PIN numbers with bank
- bank verifies card and PIN numbers
- ATM displays services available
- user selects 'Balance of account'
- ATM gets balance of user's account from bank
- ATM displays balance to user
- ATM asks if user requires any further service
- user does not want any other service
- ATM displays request to user to take the card
- user takes the card
- ATM displays Welcome screen.

6.5   Read through the scenario below, which describes what happens when someone is on the second floor of a building and calls the lift to go to the first floor. Draw a sequence diagram to illustrate the information

- user on second floor presses lift button to descend
- lift button lights up
- lift button alerts lift to go to second floor
- lift goes to second floor
- lift button light goes out
- the lift doors open

- user enters and presses button for first floor
- the lift doors close.

6.6   The sequence diagram below illustrates what happens when someone buys a book over the Internet. Write a scenario using natural language to describe the sequence of events from the user's point of view.

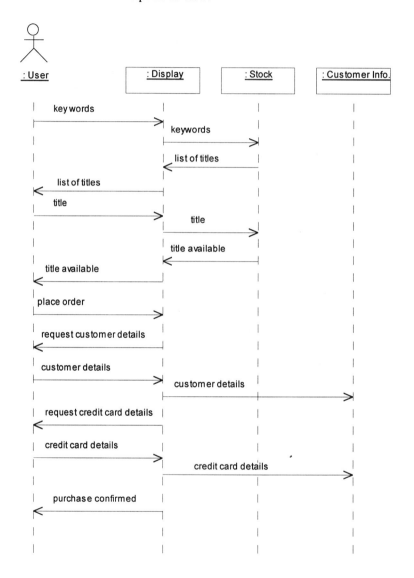

6.7
a)   Write a short, simple scenario, to describe what happens when a caller obtains a phone number by calling Directory Enquiries.
b)   Draw a sequence diagram to illustrate the scenario in (a).
c)   Modify the scenario to cope with the situation where the operator can't find the number and has to ask the caller to spell the name.
d)   Draw a sequence diagram to illustrate the situation in (c).

6.8   Look at Figure 6.7 and then draw a very simple state diagram for the Full Sign class in the car park system.

6.9   Modify the state diagram for the class Balloon, shown in Figure 6.6, to include guards on some of the transitions, a self-transition on the state, Partly inflated, and a new state, Tied up.

6.10   Draw a state diagram to illustrate the behaviour of a child's bank account, where no overdraft is allowed. The account is empty to start with. Money can then be deposited, to put the account in credit, and taken out as long as the account does not become overdrawn. The account can only be closed when the balance is zero.

6.11   Study the state diagram below, which illustrates a kitchen timer.
       Write a brief description of the behaviour of the timer.

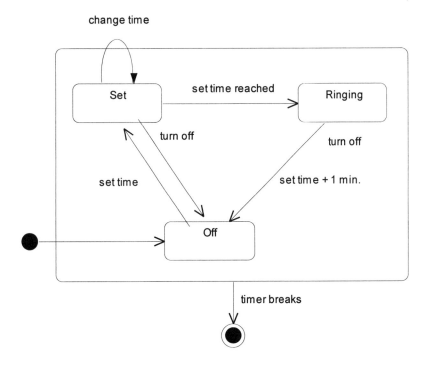

6.12   Draw a state diagram to illustrate a machine for selling crisps, as described in the following paragraph. You do not have to include a stop state on the diagram.

To begin with, the machine is idle. When the user selects the type of crisps he or she wants, the machine requests payment. The user inserts coins until the correct amount, or more, has been entered (the machine does not give change). The packet of crisps is then dispensed. The transaction is now complete and the machine returns to the idle state.

References and further reading

Bennett, S., McRobb, S. and Farmer, R. *Object-Oriented Systems Analysis and Design using UML,* London: McGraw-Hill, 1999.

Booch, G., Rumbaugh, J. and Jacobson, I. *The Unified Modeling Language User Guide,* Reading, Massachusetts: Addison-Wesley, 1999..

Fowler, M. with Scott, K. *UML Distilled: Applying the Standard Object Modeling Language,* Reading, Massachusetts: Addison-Wesley, 1997.

Henderson-Sellers, B. *A Book of Object-Oriented Knowledge,* 2nd edn, Upper Saddle River, N.J.: Prentice-Hall, 1997.

Jacobson, I., Christerson, M., Jonsson, P. and Overgaard, G. *Object-Oriented Software Engineering: A Use Case Driven Approach,* Wokingham: Addison-Wesley, 1992.

Quatrani, T. *Visual Modeling with Rational Rose and UML,* Reading, Massachusetts: Addison-Wesley, 1998.

Rumbaugh, J., Blaha, M., Premerlani, W., Eddy, F. and Lorensen, W. *Object-Oriented Modeling and Design,* Englewood Cliffs, N.J.: Prentice-Hall, 1991.

Stevens, P. with Pooley, R. *Using UML. Software Engineering with Objects and Components,* Harlow: Addison-Wesley, 1999.

7

Moving Towards Implementation

The purpose of all modelling, ultimately, is to produce a working system. Once the system developers and clients are happy that the models they have devised represent the system as they want it, it is time to think about implementation. The models discussed in Chapters 5 and 6 are of the style used at the analysis stage of system development—they deliberately minimize references to implementation details. This simplifies the models and makes them suitable vehicles for discussions with the client. All features of these early models are drawn from the problem domain. Separating the analysis models from the implementation models also avoids premature assumptions about the implementation technology for the system.

In this chapter we focus on the models from the implementation perspective. We discuss the difference this makes in the way the models are interpreted and explore additional features that may be added at this stage. We refer to this as the design stage.

To allow us to concentrate on software issues we implement a car park simulation rather than a full scale car park system with real card readers, sensors and barriers. The issues involved in a full scale implementation are beyond the scope of this book.

7.1 The design view

At the design stage, we look at the system from the implementation perspective. Changes need to be made to the models created during the analysis stage. New classes need to be added to cope with implementation considerations; we must also think in more detail about what the implementation will require in terms of relationships or links between classes and we will need to add links and re-interpret those we have already identified. All of the changes made at this stage add detail which is not visible to the user of the system. We add classes and relationships that enable the system to produce the required functionality, but are not part of the problem domain.

Before discussing the details of the design model, we need to consider how the car park simulation will work. The software will simulate the arrival and departure of cars by using a random number generator. The input of the cards, by car drivers arriving at the entrance barrier, will be simulated in the same way. Once the program has started it will run without input from the user, simulating car arrivals and departures which can be detected by the sensors at the entrance and exit. Card numbers will be generated for each arriving car and sent to the card reader. In this way we simulate the action of a car driver putting a card into the card reader and of the card reader reading the card. We explain below how this affects our models.

Some parts of the system have not been implemented. These include the use case 'Update list of valid cards'—our implementation simply has a hard-coded list of cards. Messages to the user have been kept to a minimum—no use has been made of computer graphics.

7.1.1 Notation for the design model

As we move towards implementation, documentation of the models becomes more precise: closer to the code that will eventually be produced from them. Class and object names take the form they will have in the code. Operation names, also, include the detail required by the code: the operation signature (operation name, names and types of any parameters and the operation return type).

In the design model and in the code, we use a standard notational convention. All names are written without spaces, i.e. separate words are run together. Class names are written in lower case with a capital letter at the start of each word. To distinguish names at the design level and implementatation stages we use a different font as in, for example, `CarPark`, `FullSign`, and `CardReader`. The analysis stage name Visitor's Card becomes `VisitorCard`. Names of objects, attributes and operations are written in lower case with a capital letter at the start of every word except the first one. Examples are: the object `entranceBarrier`, the attribute `maxCardNo` and the operations `decSpaces()`, and `cardReadOK():Boolean`.

For aesthetic reason, large sections of code are presented in the same font as the main text.

7.1.2 Detail in the design model

All of the diagrams allow for detail to be shown or suppressed. For example on class diagrams we can choose to show or suppress attributes and operations. Figure 7.1 shows a class diagram displaying class names and relationships only; whereas Figures 7.5 and 7.6 show attribute and operation names. The models inevitably acquire more detail as the development proceeds, but not all of the detail needs to be shown all of the time. What we decide to display on a particular diagram will depend on the purpose of drawing the diagram. If we simply want to identify the classes in a system and how they relate to one another, then we do not need to know details about attributes and operations. On the other hand, by the time we hand the models over to the programmer, he or she needs to know the exact operation signatures, the name and type of all data attributes, and the exact nature and multiplicity of relationships between classes.

Similarly with the interaction diagrams, the amount of detail shown on a model will be dictated by the purpose of the model. Full operation signatures, for example, are often not shown because the diagrams become impossibly cluttered. CASE tools (computer aided software engineering tools for the automated generation of diagrams) allow full details to be stored, then displayed or suppressed as desired.

7.2 The class diagram at the design stage

Figure 7.1 shows the class diagram for the *Just a Line* car park system at the analysis stage. This is the same diagram that is shown in Chapter 5, Figure 5.19. We must now add to it classes and relationships that represent features required for implementation purposes; these are features not known about or discussable with the user and therefore not part of requirements engineering.

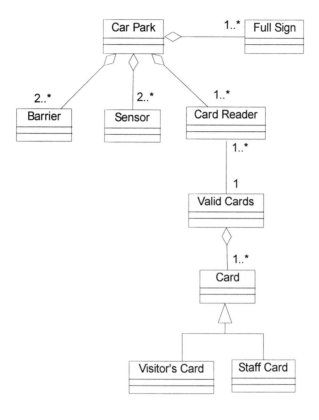

Figure 7.1 Class diagram for the *Just a Line* car park system at the analysis stage

7.2.1 The Barrier class

Figure 7.2 shows a diagram of the car park as envisaged at this stage. To clarify the discussion, we have given names to some of the objects. The entrance and exit are two objects of the Barrier class. We have also named objects of the Sensor class—in and out are two objects of the Sensor class. The in object (of the Sensor class) detects cars coming into the car park and is associated with the entrance barrier, the out object detects cars at the exit barrier.

Figures 7.3 and 7.4 show the 'happy day' behaviour of the Barrier objects as they would be modelled at the analysis stage. When the objects appear on a sequence diagram (for example, in Figure 7.3) the object name is shown in the object box at the top of the object lifeline. The object name comes first, then a colon, then the class name, e.g. `entrance:Barrier` and `in:Sensor`.

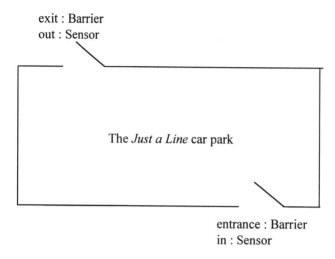

exit : Barrier
out : Sensor

The *Just a Line* car park

entrance : Barrier
in : Sensor

Figure 7.2 Diagram of the car park showing the `Barrier` and `Sensor` objects

Examination of these diagrams tells us that a `Barrier` object behaves significantly differently depending on whether it is an entrance barrier or an exit barrier.

The `entrance` barrier is responsible for:

- raising the barrier when sent an appropriate message
- keeping the barrier up while a car is present and sensed by the `in:Sensor`
- lowering the barrier when the car has passed through and is no longer detected by the `in:Sensor`
- ensuring that the `CarPark` object, which keeps count of the number of spaces left in the car park, knows that a car has just entered.

The `exit` barrier is responsible for:

- raising the barrier when sent an appropriate message
- keeping the barrier up while a car is present and sensed by the `out : Sensor`
- lowering the barrier when the car has passed through and is no longer detected by the `out : Sensor`
- ensuring the `CarPark` object, which keeps count of the number of spaces left in the car park, knows that a car has just left.

The important difference is the message sent to the `CarPark` object. The entrance barrier tells it to decrement the count; the exit barrier tells it to increment the count. This means that entrance and exit barrier cannot simply be two objects of the `Barrier` class with different names, we must create two separate classes: `EntranceBarrier` and `ExitBarrier`.

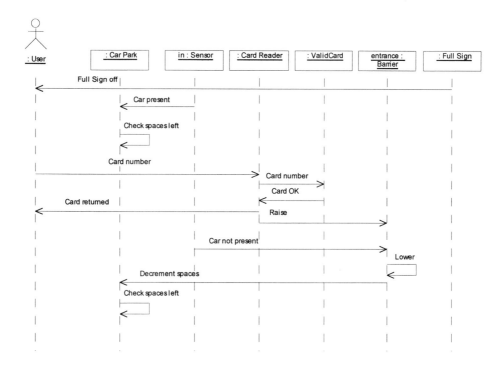

Figure 7.3 Sequence diagram showing entrance barrier behaviour

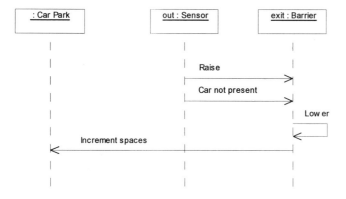

Figure 7.4 Sequence diagram showing exit barrier behaviour

Figure 7.5 illustrates how we create two separate classes, `EntranceBarrier` and `ExitBarrier`, by specializing the `Barrier` class. Although the two sub-classes look identical in this diagram, their operations will be implemented differently.

There is one other difference in the behaviour of the two types of barrier: they communicate with different sensors. However, this on its own would not require us to create separate classes for `entrance` and `exit` barriers. All objects of the `Sensor` class have the same range of ways in which they can behave, but the actual way an individual `sensor` object does behave during the running of the system depends on the sequence of events that it experiences. The two sensors (`in :Sensor` and `out :Sensor`) are simply two objects of the Sensor class and have different names.

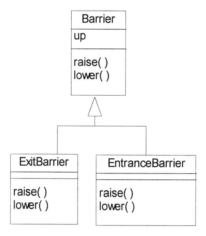

Figure 7.5 Class diagram showing specializations of the `Barrier` class

7.2.2 The Simulator class

As we mention above, our software simulates car arrivals and departures and the input of cards. This could have been done by user input from the keyboard—we could have, for example, asked the user to input a 1 to simulate a car arriving and a 0 to simulate a car leaving. We could then have asked the user to input a number to simulate the reading of the card number by the card reader. However, this would make the running of the simulation a slow and tedious process. Instead we use a new class, the `Simulator` class, to simulate car arrivals and departures. The `Simulator` class (see Figure 7.6) has one attribute: `maxCardNo` (see explanation below) and four operations of interest to us: `arrivalGenerated()`, `departureGenerated()`, `getCardNo()` and `stillThereGenerated()`.

In order not to overcomplicate the code, a very simple simulator is used. The simulation of car arrivals and departures is handled by using a random number generator which produces a number between 0 and 1.. If this number is less than or equal to 0.7, it counts as a car arrival; if it is greater than 0.7, it counts as a car departure. The value of 0.7 is chosen to ensure that there are sufficient arrivals to allow the car park to become full (assuming some cards are invalid). A second random number is used to simulate the detection, by the

Simulator
maxCardNo
arrivalGenerated( )   departureGenerated( )   getCardNo( )   stillThereGenerated( )

Figure 7.6 The Simulator class

sensor, of the presence of a car. If the number is less than 0.5 it means that a car is present at the barrier, i.e. sensed by the sensor; if the number is greater than or equal to 0.5 no car is sensed.

Simulation of the process of putting a card into the card reader is also done by the simulator class. The attribute maxCardNo stores the highest card number issued to date by the *Just a Line* system. The getCardNo() function returns a card number, derived from the random number generator, which is less than or equal to maxCardNo.

Figures 7.7 – 7.9 are fragments of sequence diagrams which show how the Simulator class is used by other classes in the system. In common with all design diagrams, these sequence diagrams use a slightly different notation from the analysis diagrams, as explained in 7.1.1.

Figure 7.7 models the simulation of a car arrival. The CarPark object sends a message to a Sensor object (in:Sensor) asking if a car is present—in the software, in:Sensor will be continually polled by CarPark asking for this information. In turn in:Sensor asks the Simulator if a car is arriving. The Simulator replies that a car is arriving (the arrivalGenerated() function returns true) and this information is passed back to the CarPark.

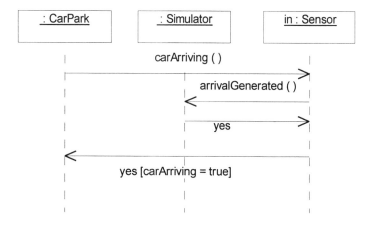

Figure 7.7 Sequence diagram showing how the Simulator is used to simulate car arrivals

The simulation of a car departure, modelled in Figure 7.8, is handled in a similar way, the only differences being that the CarPark is communicating with the out:Sensor object which sends a carLeaving() message to the Simulator.

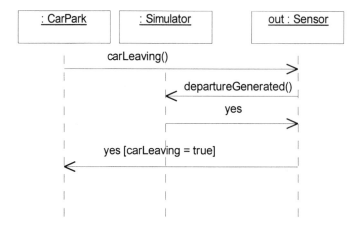

Figure 7.8 Sequence diagram showing how the Simulator is used to simulate car departures

Figure 7.9 shows how the Simulator is used to generate card numbers to be read by the CardReader. The CarPark, knowing at this stage that a car is present at the entrance barrier, needs to know if the car driver has a valid card. The CarPark object sends a message to the CardReader asking if it has read (and checked) the card—cardReadOK(). In the simulation, the CardReader object asks the Simulator for a card number, which is then passed on to ValidCards (the set of valid cards) for checking.

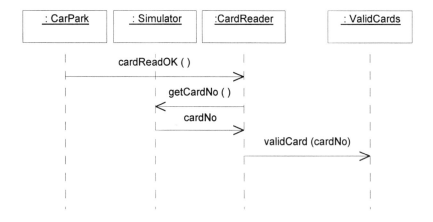

Figure 7.9 Sequence diagram showing how the Simulator is used to generate card numbers

7.2.3 The CarParkSystem class

We add a `CarParkSystem` class to our class diagram simply to serve as a boot strap for the whole system. Our implementation language, Java, insists that every function, even `main()` which sets the whole software system into action, is part of a class. The `CarParkSystem` class therefore serves as a home for the `main()` function. The only job of `main()` in this system is to create an instance of the `CarPark` class—once this has been done the simulation runs itself.

The implementation classes that we need to add to the Figure 7.1 class diagram are: `CarParkSystem`, `Simulator`, `ExitBarrier` and `EntranceBarrier`. The revised class diagram is shown in Figure 7.10 (to avoid clutter we have omitted some of the association relationships).

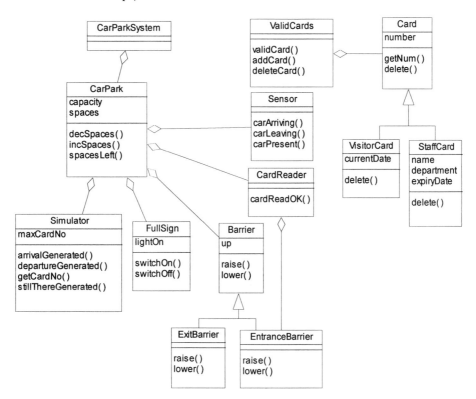

Figure 7.10 Revised class diagram showing implementation classes

7.3 Relationships at the design stage

Relationships modelled in the class diagram at the analysis stage are loosely defined and can be interpreted in a fairly informal way. At the design stage the lines representing relationships between classes must be defined precisely enough to enable the programmer to interpret the diagram without ambiguity.

7.3.1   The analysis model relationships

The relationships modelled on a class diagram (see Chapter 5) are association, aggregation and inheritance.   The interpretation of the inheritance relationship does not vary significantly between the different stages of system design and will not be discussed here. However, how we interpret association and aggregation relationships depends very much on the stage at which we view the model.

Association at the analysis stage models a conceptual relationship between classes; it means only that there is some sort of relationship between instances of classes, which probably mirrors a real-life relationship. The multiplicity of the relationship modelled at this stage also tends to reflect the real-life situation. For example, the one to many association between a company and its employees, see Figure 7.11, represents the fact that in a problem domain a particular company may have many employees, but an employee only works for one company.

Figure 7.11 Association relationship between Company and Employee

Aggregation at the analysis stage is used in a vague and even controversial way. An aggregation represents a whole-part relationship between instances of classes; it is generally agreed to be a tighter form of association, although in what way it is tighter is rarely defined. There is certainly no generally agreed translation of aggregation into code. For a discussion of aggregation, see Chapter 5 Section 5.2.1. For our definitions of association and aggregation, as used throughout the rest of the book, see below.

7.3.2 The design model relationships

As a software system progresses through the stages of its development, association and aggregation relationships acquire more precise meaning. Relationships other than real-life ones are identified and added to the model. When the system developer is at the stage of creating CRC cards (see Chapter 5) it is often discovered that one class needs to use the services (i.e. the operations) of another to fulfil its own responsibilities. In this case, an association relationship exists between the two classes. Further associations of this type may be identified when the sequence diagrams are drawn during the dynamic modelling stage (see Chapter 6). On a design model, therefore, specifying that an association exists is telling us about relationships between software objects, not about real-life relationships. Of course the software objects and their relationships may well mirror a real-life situation, but by this stage there will be objects in our model that are not part of the problem domain (see section 7.1).

Navigability Specifying that a relationship exists between classes has implications at the coding level—the nature of the relationship must be accurately defined for the benefit of the programmer. The programmer needs to know exactly what an association or an aggregation relationship modelled on a class diagram means in terms of the programming language, being used for implementation. For the benefit of the programmer we need to record on the class diagram not only the nature of the relationships, but also decisions about the direction of navigation paths between classes. A navigable path must exist between classes related by either association or aggregation. If one class uses the services of another class, it needs to be able to see that class. To ensure that two classes can see each other, we must build into the model navigable paths between them. For example, re-examination of the dynamic behaviour of the car park system (see Figure 7.12) reveals that the CardReader needs to be able to use the services of the Simulator class, the ValidCards class and the EntranceBarrier class to fulfil its own responsibilities. The CardReader's responsibilities are to read and report back to the CarPark class that a card has been read and checked, and a car allowed through the barrier. All of this responsibility is incorporated in the cardReadOK() operation.

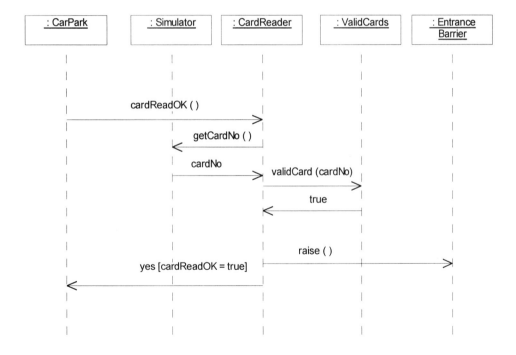

Figure 7.12 Fragment of the sequence diagram for car enters car park

If the CardReader is to use the services of these classes, it has to have a navigable path to them. For reasons which are explained below, it is appropriate to use an association relationship between the `CardReader` and the `Simulator`, and between the `CardReader` and `ValidCards`, and an aggregation relationship between the `CardReader` and the `EntranceBarrier`—see Figure 7.13(a). The `CardReader` can now use the services of `ValidCards`, the `EntranceBarrier` and the `Simulator`, navigable paths exist between them.

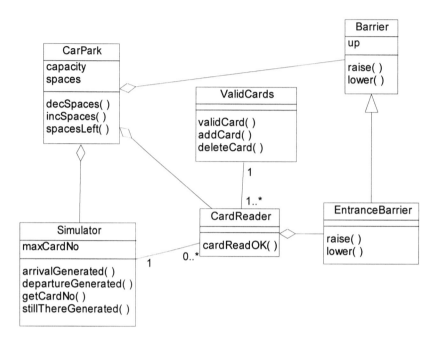

Figure 7.13(a) Partial class diagram showing association and aggregation relationships

Association relationships can be implemented so that they are navigable in one direction or both. We can tell from the sequence diagrams whether a relationship needs to be navigable in one or both directions. For example we can see from the sequence diagram in Figure 7.12, that the `CardReader` needs to able to use the services of the `Simulator`, but not vice-versa. The `Simulator` does pass a value (CardNo) to the `CardReader`, but this is in response to the message `getCardNo()`, it is not a request for a service. The navigability between the `CardReader` and the `Simulator` therefore should be implemented so that it is unidirectional. In the same way, the `CardReader` needs to use the services of the `ValidCards` class but not vice-versa—another unidirectional navigation path. This information is required by the programmer and can be added to the class diagram as shown in Figure 7.13(b)—a relationship that is navigable in one direction only is denoted by an arrowhead indicating the direction of the navigability. If a relationship is navigable in both directions, it has no arrowsheads on it.

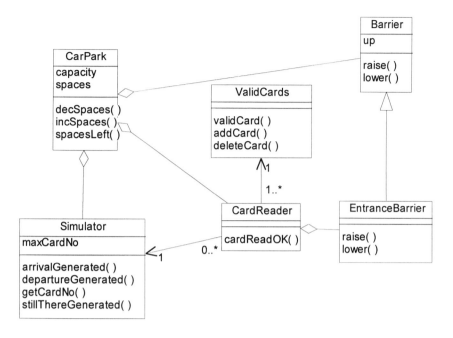

Figure 7.13(b) Associations navigability information added

If a relationship needs to be navigable in one direction only, this means, in terms of the code, that only one class will have a reference (pointer in C++ terms) to the other. For example, the association between CardReader and the ValidCards class only requires unidirectional navigability. This means that CardReader will have a reference to ValidCards, but ValidCards will not have a reference to CardReader.

Association and aggregation   Unless the difference between association and aggregation can be given some semantics that can be meaningfully translated into code, it is not worth modelling them as separate relationships in the design model. In this book we use a precise definition of each, although readers should be warned that not everyone uses the same definitions. We define an association relationship to be one that describes a relationship with an object that already exists. Aggregation is used to describe a relationship between a whole object and one of its parts. The part object is one that has no independent existence from the whole; it will be created when the whole object is created, usually by its constructor (a function that is automatically executed when a new instance of a class is created) and will be destroyed when the whole object is destroyed. The part object can therefore only participate in one aggregation. Association describes a link between two objects of equal standing or importance. Aggregation implies that one object is superior to another—it is a whole-part relationship in which the inferior object is just a part of a more important whole. The inferior object can only belong to one object and it lives and dies with the whole. This definition of aggregation is variously referred to as composition or aggregation by containment.

Specifying that the relationship between two classes is an aggregation relationship, as defined above, gives the programmer information about where to create an instance of a class. For example, the programmer can tell from Figure 7.13(b) that the `CarPark` constructor must create instances of the `Barrier`, `CardReader` and `Simulator` classes, and that the `CardReader` constructor must create an instance of the `EntranceBarrier` class. However, the programmer has no information about where to create an instance of the `ValidCards` class. As we only want one instance of this class (one definitive list of valid cards) it is sensible to create this instance in the `CarPark` class (see Figure 7.14).

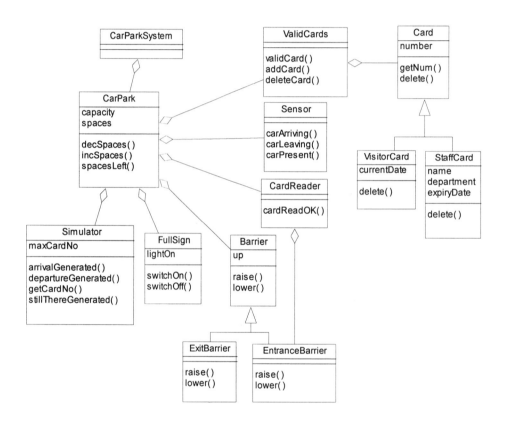

Figure 7.14 Class diagram for the car park simulation, with added aggregation between `CarPark` and `ValidCards`

Implementing association and aggregation relationships   Given our definitions of association and aggregation, the way we enable objects of one class to see objects of another class (in terms of the code) will depend on whether the classes are related by association or aggregation. For an association this means that we must find some way of letting an object see the object it needs to communicate with—it needs to know the appropriate address. For an aggregation relationship we do not need to do any extra work unless the part object needs to use the services of the whole. The whole object knows about its parts. When we create an instance of the whole object, we will also create instances of its parts. In Java, this usually means that the constructor function of the whole class will contain code to create instances of the parts.

To illustrate this, let us look at the code for the section of the CardReader class that implements most of the relationships modelled in the class diagram in Figure 7.13(b). Program line numbers are shown on the left; the two forward slashes, //, indicate comments in the code.

CardReader has an association relationship with ValidCards and an aggregation relationship with EntranceBarrier.

```
01 public class CardReader              // define CardReader class
02 {
03   private ValidCards okCards;        // list of valid cards
04   EntranceBarrier  inBarrier;        // barrier controlled by reader
05   public CardReader(CarPark aCarPark, ValidCards centralList) //constructor
06   {
07    okCards = centralList;            // create association
08    inBarrier = new EntranceBarrier(aCarPark);      // create aggregation
09   }

10   public boolean cardReadOK()        // is card valid?
11   {
12    int cardNo;                       // number of card in machine

13    cardNo = Simulator.getCardNo();   // simulate reading

14    if (okCards.validCard(cardNo))    // validate card
15    {
16      inBarrier.raise();
17      return true;                    // let car in if ok
18    }
19    else
20    {                                 // deny entry
21      System.out.print("Entry refused, invalid card number");
22      return false;
23    }
24   }
25 }
```

Line 01 is the initial definition of the CardReader class.

Line 03 defines a reference okCards to an object of class ValidCards.

Line 04 defines a reference inBarrier to an object of class EntranceBarrier.

So far, there is no difference in the setting up of the links to the two objects—lines 03 and 04 are structurally identical. Both effectively initiate the setting up of references to objects of the required classes. The references are declared but not given any value—not yet given an address to point to.

Line 05 defines the constructor function for the CardReader class—this function is automatically executed when an object of class CardReader is created. An object centralList of class ValidCards is passed in as a parameter to this function. What is actually passed in is the address of the object centralList. The significance of this is that the object centralList already exists, it was created in the CarPark constructor. If you refer to the diagram in Figure 7.14, you can see that the CarPark class creates the instance of ValidCards.

Line 07 connects the reference okCards to the address passed in as a parameter. If we assume that the address in memory of the object centralList is 1000 then Figures 7.15 (a), (b) and (c) illustrate what happens.

Figure 7.15(a) Line 03 defines a reference okCards to an object of class ValidCards

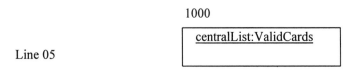

Figure 7.15(b) Line 05 passes in (the address of) the object centralList of class ValidCards

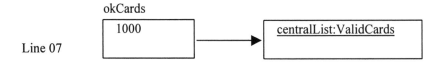

Figure 7.15(c) Line 07 connects the reference okCards to the object centralList

Lines 03, 05 and 07, therefore, implement a unidirectional association link between the CardReader and okCards, an object of the ValidCards class.

The aggregation link between CardReader and EntranceBarrier is created in lines 04 and 08.

Line 08 creates a new instance of the EntranceBarrier class (assumed to be at memory address 2000); the reference, inBarrier, created in line 04 now points to this new EntanceBarrier object as illustrated in Figure 7.16 (a) and (b). However, inBarrier has no separate existence from the CardReader object of which it is part: it will be destroyed when the CardReader object is destroyed.

Line 04

Figure 7.16(a) Line 04 defines a reference inBarrier to an object of class EntranceBarrier

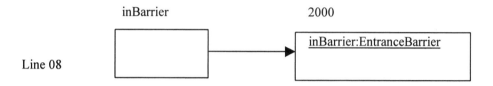

Line 08

Figure 7.16(b) Line 08 connects the reference inBarrier to an object of class EntranceBarrier

Different interpretations at different stages The meaning of a relationship modelled on a class diagram, therefore, is quite different depending on the development stage at which it is viewed. In very early analysis models, when classes are first identified, an association represents a conceptual relationship that exists in the problem domain. During dynamic modelling, as class responsibilities are firmly established, relationships will be added to the model to indicate that classes use each other's services. Finally we need to make decisions about the extent to which classes are to be allowed existences independent of each other—this will decide whether a relationship is an aggregation or an association. It means that the relationships on the class model are interpreted at this stage in terms of references to other classes.

7.4 Sequence diagrams at the design stage

The main difference between sequence diagrams drawn at the analysis stage and those drawn at the design stage is that the design model will also include design objects (implementation-oriented objects of the type mentioned above in Section 7.1) and the messages passed between objects will contain detail of operation signatures. The diagrams can also specify object and class names more accurately, show conditional behaviour, control and iteration. Interaction diagrams can also be used to show the sequence in which objects are created and deleted. In fact the notation supporting sequence diagrams is so rich and diverse that it is easy to include so much detail that the diagrams become confusing. We find it best to keep the diagrams simple and clear, even if this is at the cost of some detail. However, some of the supporting notation can be useful.

Conditional behaviour One of the most frequently asked questions concerning sequence diagrams, is how to show conditional behaviour: what to do about recording both outcomes of an *if* statement, or all possible outcomes of an *if .. then .. else* statement. There are two main ways of doing this. One is to draw a different sequence diagram for each conditional outcome or scenario; the other is to annotate the diagrams with details of the conditions. Figure 7.17 shows the sequence diagram for the scenario for the 'Enter car park' use case where the car arriving takes the last available space and the Full sign has to be switched on. In this scenario all the conditions are right for a car to enter the car park. We simulate a car approaching the entrance; it is sensed by the sensor, the car park is not full, the car driver's card is valid, the entrance barrier is raised, the count of the number of spaces left is decremented and, as this car uses up the last space in the car park, the Full sign goes on.

We have used something of both techniques in this sequence diagram. There is some annotation of conditions, but also the diagram only attempts to show one possible path through this part of the system: one scenario. We have annotated conditions where we felt there was some danger of confusion. The annotation is made in square brackets and indicates the condition and the outcome. The condition controls whether the message it annotates is sent. For example, in Figure 7.17, there is an annotated condition on the fourth horizontal line—yes[carArriving = true], and another near the bottom of the diagram—yes [cardReadOK = true]. This sort of annotation is useful, and often makes it unnecessary to draw separate sequence diagrams for all possible outcomes of simple conditions.

We can, for example, draw a separate sequence diagram to show what happens if the Sensor does not detect a car arriving, as in Figure 7.18, but this adds little to our understanding of the system's behaviour—we could have worked this out from Figure 7.17. How much annotation is used and how many different scenarios are illustrated with a sequence diagram, is very much a subjective decision.

Use of returns One of the things that causes the most problems to newcomers to O-O programming, is following the flow of control from object to object. A well designed O-O system (see Chapter 6, Section 6.4, What makes a good class) will have a collection of decentralised objects democratically sharing the work between them. As each object shoulders its share of the work burden, it takes over control. When its share of the work is complete, it passes control back to the object that messaged it. Sequence diagrams are useful for documenting flow of control. Where it gets complicated, i.e. control does not immediately return to the original object but is passed to another object and so on, it can be useful to document *returns*. A *return* is represented by a horizontal arrow that does not have a message label. In Figure 7.17, the first two horizontal arrows represent messages, the next two represent *returns*.

On the whole, *returns* tend to be omitted as they can be assumed—control always returns to the object that sent the message. Overuse of *returns* can clutter the diagram unnecessarily. The diagram in Figure 7.17 can be simplified by omitting the *returns*. In this case it means that the comments about conditions must be attached to the next message, which will only fire given the condition specified in the comment. Figure 7.19 shows the initial sequence of messages from Figure 7.17, without *returns*.

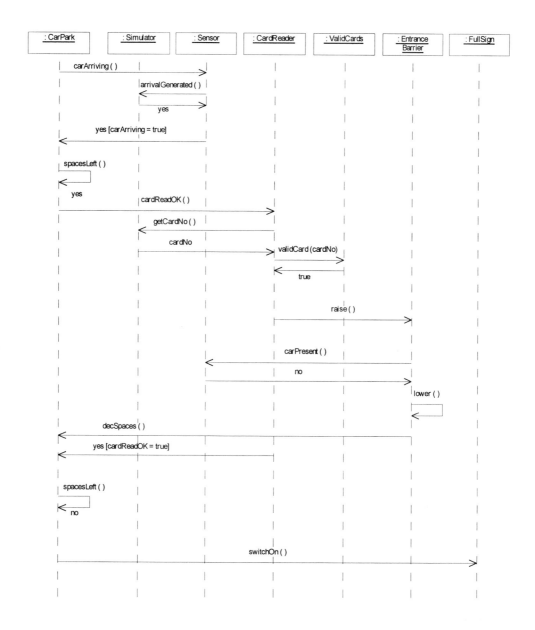

Figure 7.17 Sequence diagram for 'Enter car park', where the car arriving takes the last available space

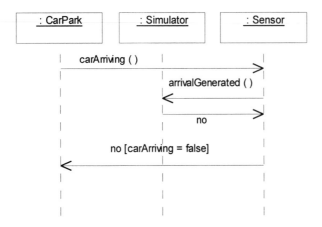

Figure 7.18 Sequence diagram showing car not detected by the `sensor` object

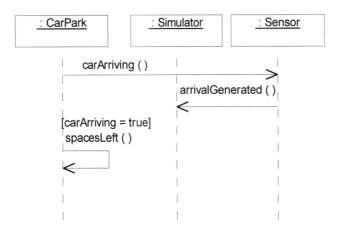

Figure 7.19 Sequence diagram without *returns*

If you are keen to avoid showing *returns*, but the operation invoked returns a value, there is a notation to allow you to do this. Figure 7.20 shows a fragment of the complete sequence diagram shown in Figure 7.17. When `CardReader`'s `cardReadOK()` operation is invoked, the `CardReader` sends a `getCardNo()` message to the `Simulator`, which reurns a `cardNo`. The `cardNo` is then passed to the `ValidCards` object for checking. The label `cardNo:= getCardNo()` indicates that the variable `cardNo` is set to the value returned by the operation `getCardNo()`.

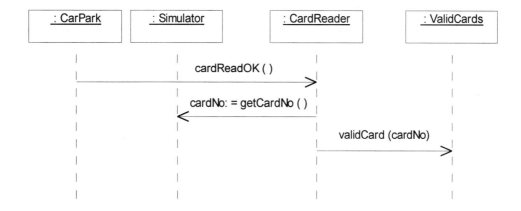

Figure 7.20 Fragment of sequence diagram avoiding use of return

Activation When a message is sent to an object, the corresponding operation is invoked and starts to execute. The duration of that execution can be shown on the sequence diagram by drawing a narrow vertical rectangle over the object's lifeline; this is known as activation. If, before the end of the operation's execution, a message is sent to another object, the original object remains active and an activation of the new object begins. The activation end represents the end of the execution of the operation and can be marked by a return to the calling object.

For example in Figure 7.21 the CarPark object sends a cardReadOK() message to the CardReader object and the CardReader's lifeline becomes activated. The lifeline remains activated while it invokes the Simulator's getCardNo() operation and waits for a response. The getCardNo() message in turn starts a period of activation on the lifeline of the Simulator object, which ends when the Simulator returns a cardNo to the CardReader.

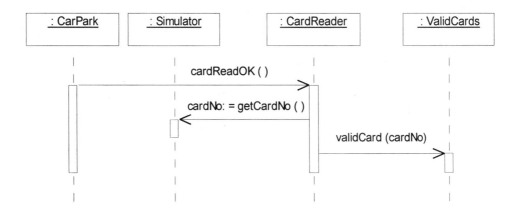

Figure 7.21 Sequence diagram showing activation

Iteration Sequence diagrams can show iteration; for example they can indicate that a particular message is sent repeatedly to many different objects of the same class. We can find an example in the implementation of operation of the `ValidCard` class. Up to this point we talked about validating card numbers without saying precisely how this is to be carried out. What actually happens is that an object of the `ValidCards` class, during its validation operation, `validCard(cardNo)`, sends a `getNum()` message to each `Card` object in turn. In response each `Card` object sends its number which is compared to the number being validated. As soon as a match is found, the number is deemed to be valid. On a sequence diagram, we can show this repetition by placing an * before the repeated message. This is illustrated in Figure 7.22.

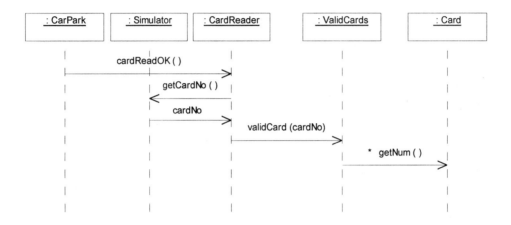

Figure 7.22 Sequence diagram showing iteration

Creation and deletion Sequence diagrams can show the creation and removal of objects. The creation of a new object is indicated by a message arrow, which meets the object symbol. Dotted, directed lines indicate return of control.

This notation is useful for emphasising the relative timing of the creation of objects. Figure 7.23 shows part of the object creation process at the beginning of the car park simulation. This diagram is helpful in that it clarifies which objects are the creators of other objects and the order in which they create them[1].

Object deletion is indicated by adding a large cross on the object's lifeline at the end of its activation. See Figure 7.24.

---

[1] In the Figure 7.23 CarParkSystem is a class, not an object. This is because of the way Java handles the main() function which starts the system running

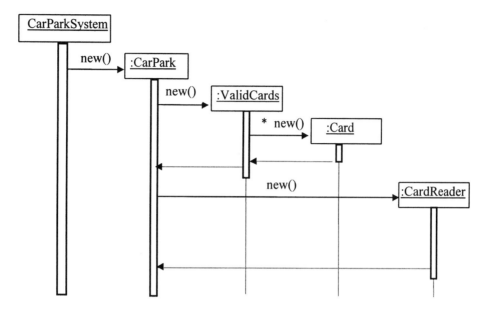

Figure 7.23 Notation for object creation

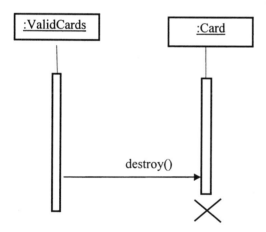

Figure 7.24 Notation for object deletion

The notation for sequence diagrams is based on Buschmann's work (Buschmann et al., 1996) and allows for many features not mentioned here. If you find your diagrams need a richer syntax, read this text.

Exercises

7.1   Draw design stage sequence diagrams for the car park simulation scenarios:
a)   a car attempts to enter the car park but there are no spaces left;
b)   a car attempts to enter the car park but its driver's card is not valid.

7.2   Draw a design stage sequence diagram for the use case 'Leave car park'.

7.3   Redraw the whole of the sequence diagram shown in Figure 7.17, without using returns. Use annotation of conditional behaviour as appropriate.

7.4   Redraw, showing activation, the sequence diagram in Figure 7.17.

7.5   Draw the collaboration diagram that corresponds to the sequence diagrams in:
a)   Figure 7.8
b)   Figure 7.9
c)   Figure 7.20.
        You can find an example of a collaboration diagram in Chapter 6, Section 6.2.2.

References and further reading

Bennett, S., McRobb, S. and Farmer, R. *Object-Oriented Systems Analysis and Design using UML,* London: McGraw-Hill, 1999..

Buschmann, F., Meunier, R., Rohnert, H., Sommerlad, P. and Stal, M. *Pattern-Oriented Software Architecture: A System of Patterns,* Chichester: John Wiley & Sons, 1996.

Fowler, M. with Scott, K. *UML Distilled: Applying the Standard Object Modeling Language,* Reading, Massachusetts: Addison-Wesley, 1997.

Oestereich, B. *Developing Software with UML: Object-oriented Analysis and Design in Practice,* Harlow: Addison-Wesley, 1999.

Quatrani, T. *Visual Modeling with Rational Rose and UML,* Reading, Massachusetts: Addison-Wesley, 1998.

Stevens, P. with Pooley, R. *Using UML. Software Engineering with Objects and Components,* Harlow: Addison-Wesley, 1999.

8

Implementation

This is not a book about programming; however it is about developing an object-oriented system from requirements analysis through to code. This chapter is concerned with issues relating to converting the final models into code and demonstrates the mapping between the models and the code. It covers:

- how classes and relationships specified in the class diagram translate into code;
- how objects are created from these classes;
- how the message passing and flow of control modelled in the sequence diagrams are implemented in the code.

We have chosen to do the implementation in Java, simply because we had to choose one object-oriented programming language and Java, as well as being currently very popular, has the following advantages:

- it is relatively small;
- it is supported by a large number of standard libraries;
- it will run on a variety of platforms;
- it has extensive network capabilities;
- it is strongly typed and therefore robust.

This chapter assumes a working knowledge of Java—for information about how to use the language, readers are referred to the Java programming books in the References and further reading section of this chapter.

8.1 Implementing the class diagram

Even for a small system like the car park simulation, it is impossible to squeeze into one class diagram all of the known facts. The class diagram, in Figure 8.1 shows all of the classes we implement and most of the relationships—but omits details about attribute types, parameter types and return types. Most CASE (automatic modelling) tools allow the user to selectively suppress or view detail in this way. Full details about the class diagram are given in Chapter 7. In this chapter, we show full details where the mapping between models and code is demonstrated. The full code listing is presented in Appendix C.

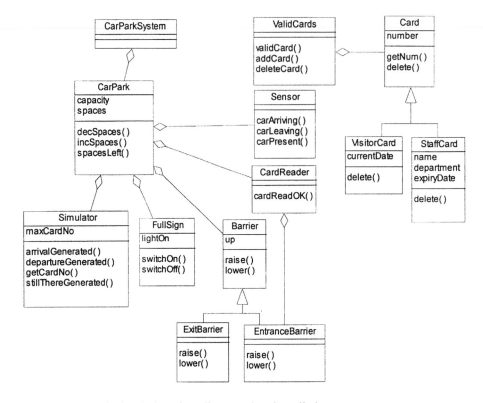

Figure 8.1 Car park simulation class diagram showing all classes

To give readers an idea of how to convert a class diagram into code, we demonstrate the technique with just a few classes—the three classes shown in Figure 8.2: `Card`, `StaffCard` and `VisitorCard`. In order to simplify the Java code, the date for `StaffCard` and `VisitorCard` has been implemented as expiry date.

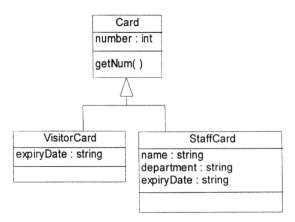

Figure 8.2 The classes `Card`, `StaffCard` and `VisitorCard`

8.1.1 The Card class

We start with the Card class modelled in Figure 8.3 and implemented in the fragment of code shown. The class name, attribute and operations translate into code, almost without alteration.

The main difference between model and code is the introduction of the constructor operation. A constructor is an operation that is automatically executed when a new object or instance of a class is created. The new object is created by the keyword new, the constructor operation does any initialization specified by the programmer. Constructors are not normally shown in analysis or design models.

When examining the code bear in mind the following points:

- When a new Card object is created, the constructor sets the attribute number to the value of the parameter num.
- Everything between /* ... and ...*/ is treated as a comment.
- Everything between // and the end of a line of code is treated as a comment.

In Figures 8.3, 8.4 and 8.5 arrows are used to indicate where features of the class diagram are implemented in the code.

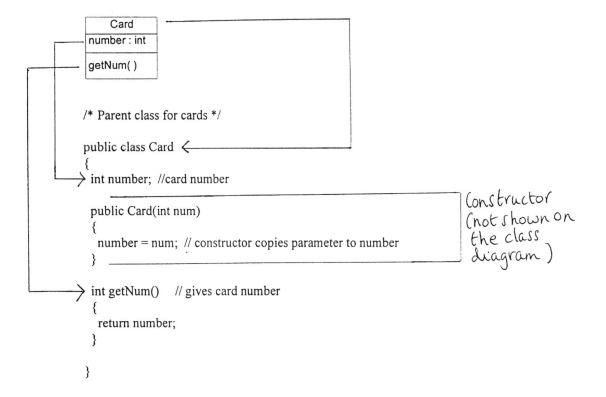

Figure 8.3 The Card class diagram and its implementation code

8.1.2 The StaffCard class

Figure 8.4 models the inheritance relationship between Card and StaffCard—a StaffCard is a specialisation (child) of Card. The code below implements the StaffCard class and the inheritance relationship. The three attributes—name, department and expiryDate—are declared as part of the class definition. When the constructor of this class is called (as part of the object creation process), the attributes are populated with the values passed in as parameters to the constructor. The inherited attribute, number, gets its value by calling the constructor of the parent class (i.e. Card) with the required number as a parameter. It is the responsibility of Card's constructor to assign card numbers.

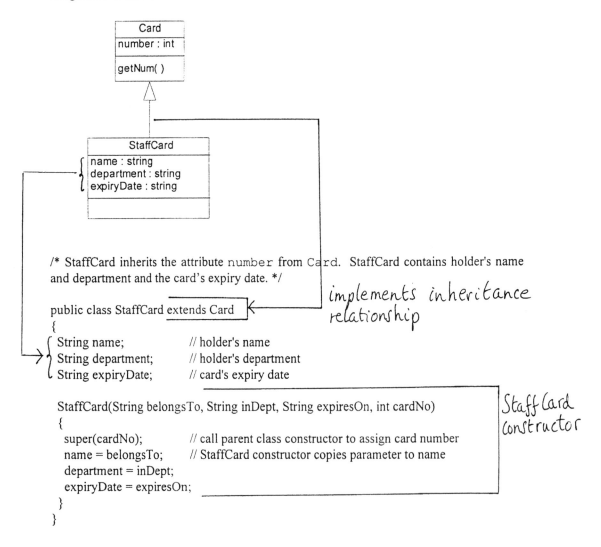

```
/* StaffCard inherits the attribute number from Card. StaffCard contains holder's name
and department and the card's expiry date. */

public class StaffCard extends Card        implements inheritance
{                                          relationship

  String name;          // holder's name
  String department;    // holder's department
  String expiryDate;    // card's expiry date

  StaffCard(String belongsTo, String inDept, String expiresOn, int cardNo)
  {                                                              Staff Card
    super(cardNo);      // call parent class constructor to assign card number   Constructor
    name = belongsTo;   // StaffCard constructor copies parameter to name
    department = inDept;
    expiryDate = expiresOn;
  }
}
```

Figure 8.4 The StaffCard class diagram and its implementation code

8.1.3 The VisitorCard class

VisitorCard works very much as StaffCard, except that no parameters are passed into its constructor (see Figure 8.5). A VisitorCard has only two attributes, expiryDate and the inherited attribute number. A visitor's card is valid for only one day, so the expiryDate is set to whatever the current date is—in this case it is arbitrarily set to 01-01-2000. The system (arbitrarily) sets all VisitorCard numbers to 9. As with StaffCard, the number is set by calling the constructor of the parent class (i.e. Card) with the required number (in this case 9) as a parameter.

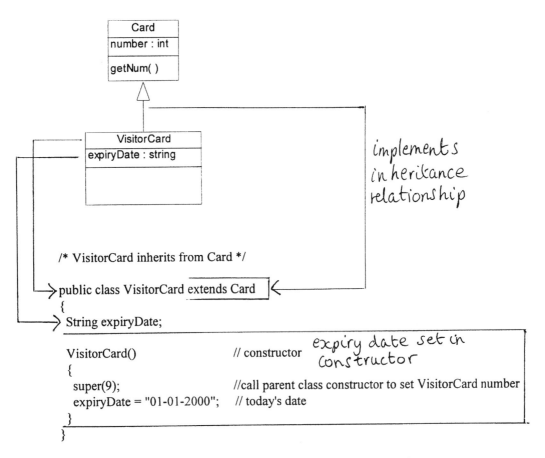

```
/* VisitorCard inherits from Card */

public class VisitorCard extends Card
{
  String expiryDate;

  VisitorCard()                              // constructor
  {
    super(9);                                //call parent class constructor to set VisitorCard number
    expiryDate = "01-01-2000";               // today's date
  }
}
```

implements inheritance relationship

expiry date set in constructor

Figure 8.5 The VisitorCard class diagram and its implementation code

8.2 Implementing the dynamic model

We have found that for students new to the topic, one of the hardest things about implementing an O-O system is coping with distribution of system functionality amongst classes. If we focus on one class, the functionality achieved by its operations is (or should be) cohesive and logically grouped; a class will have a set of responsibilities appropriate to its role in the system. However, if we focus on the overall system functionality, we see a different picture. In order to execute a single (sizeable) bit of functionality, i.e. one major task or use case, we will certainly find that bits of that functionality are distributed amongst different classes. To achieve one use case we will find that we are jumping about between classes. This is especially disconcerting to students used to top-down functional decomposition, where the system is divided into its major functions, then each function is divided into smaller functions, which in turn are divided. With functional decomposition the structure of the code mirrors (or is dictated by) the structure of the functional decomposition. The sequence of execution is often straightforward—it goes straight down the page.

In this section we try to show how the sequence of execution in the code for our O-O design maps to the events (or messages) shown on the sequence diagram.

We have included in this chapter relevant parts of the code—these can be found in Section 8.3.

8.2.1 Creation of the objects

In this section we demonstrate how and where objects are created in the code, following the order specified in the sequence diagram in Figure 8.6. The sequence diagram does not attempt to model the creation of all of the objects in the system, but it shows the creation of the first few and indicates how the model and code fit together.

We have related the diagram to the code by annotating both with matching handwritten letters. For example, on the diagram the creation of a new CarPark object is labelled 'A'; the corresponding line of code in the CarParkSystem class (see Section 8.3), is highlighted, by being boxed, and also labelled 'A'. Objects in the diagram (Figure 8.6) are related to the code as specified in Table 8.1.

Table 8.1

Ref.	Creating class/object	New object	Page
A	CarParkSystem	:CarPark	152
B	:CarPark	:ValidCards	153
C	:ValidCards	:Card	155
D	:CarPark	:CardReader	153
E	:CardReader	:EntranceBarrier	156

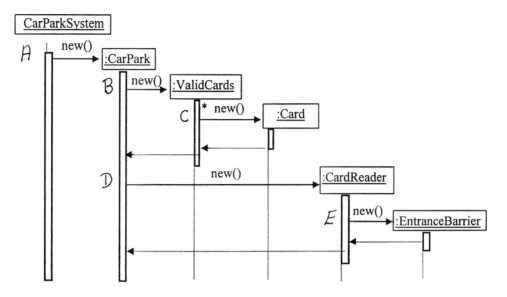

Figure 8.6 Sequence diagram showing creation of objects[1]

8.2.2 Following the sequence of messages

In this section we demonstrate how messages on a sequence diagram relate to the code. We will use the sequence diagram in Figure 8.7 and relate it to the fragments of code in Section 8.3.

The way the demonstration works, is that for each message, or return on the diagram (Figure 8.7) we have marked the line of code that actually sends the message, or return. The demonstration works like a treasure hunt. To find the next message readers must find the class to which the message is sent—the receiving class. On the diagram (Figure 8.7) this class is named in the rectangle at the top of the life-line on which the message arrow terminates. For example the first message is carArriving(), sent from an object of the CarPark class to an object of the Sensor class. The message arrow terminates on the lifeline of the Sensor class; this makes Sensor the receiving class. Once the receiving class has been identified, the reader must find the code for that class (in Section 8.3), then look for the operation that corresponds to the message. When an object receives a message, the appropriate method is fired, i.e. it executes. The reader should follow the execution of the method by tracing through the lines of code in the method. The next step will be taken either when the end of the method is reached (in which case control returns to the object that sent the message) or when we come across a line of code that sends a message to another class object. In this case we proceed to the next stage of the treasure hunt.

The simulation starts in the constructor method of the CarPark class. The CarPark constructor is fired when a new CarPark object (aCarPark) is created by Main() in the

---

[1] In the Figure 8.6 the CarParkSystem is a class, not an object. This is because of the way Java handles the main() function which starts the system running

`CarParkSystem` class. The treasure hunt described here starts inside the constructor method of the `CarPark` class, when the first message is sent..

To assist the reader, we have set out, in Table 8.2, the steps in the treasure hunt. Table 8.2 relates the sequence of messages and returns in the sequence diagram (Figure 8.7) to the relevant parts of the code in Section 8.3. Each message and return has a reference number which matches a corresponding (handwritten) reference number in Figure 8.7 and in the code.

Headings in Table 8.2 are as folows:

- Ref. No.: the reference number as shown in Figure 8.7 and in the code;
- Sending Class: the class from which the message is sent or a return statement occurs;
- Pg.: the page in the code where the message or return is marked with the reference number;
- Message/Return: the text of the message or Boolean value returned;
- Receiving Class: the class to which control is passed via the message or return. Where a specific object is named in the message, receiving class is shown as `objectName : className`.

Table 8.2

Ref. No.	Sending Class	Pg.	Message/Return	Receiving Class
1	CarPark	153	carArriving()	inSensor : Sensor
2	Sensor	157	arrivalGenerated()	Simulator
3	Simulator	158	returns true	Sensor
4	Sensor	157	returns true	CarPark
5	CarPark	153	spacesLeft()	CarPark
6	CarPark	154	returns true	CarPark
7	CarPark	153	cardReadOK()	MainCardReader : CardReader
8	CardReader	156	getCardNo()	Simulator
9	Simulator	158	returns cardNo	CardReader
10	CardReader	156	validCard(cardNo)	okCards : ValidCards
11	ValidCards	155	* getNum()	knownCards[i] : Card
12	Card	156	returns number	ValidCards
13	ValidCards	155	returns true	CardReader
14	CardReader	156	raise()	inBarrier : EntranceBarrier
15	EntranceBarrier	157	carPresent()	inSensor : Sensor
16	Sensor	158	stillThereGenerated()	Simulator
17	Simulator	158	returns false	Sensor
18	Sensor	158	returns false	EntranceBarrier
19	EntranceBarrier	157	lower()	EntranceBarrier
20	EntranceBarrier	157	decSpaces()	ownerCarPark : CarPark
21	CarPark	153	spacesLeft()	CarPark
22	CarPark	154	returns true	CarPark

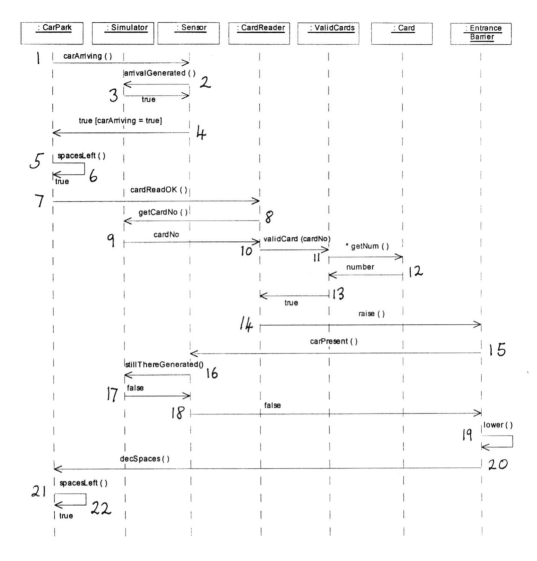

Figure 8.7 Sequence diagram showing message sequence for the 'Enter car park' use case

8.3 Code fragments

The classes listed here are to support the points made in Section 8.2. Not all of the classes are listed. The full set of classes can be found in Appendix C. Readers should note that not all aspects of the simulation have been implemented. Our main concern, when writing the simulation was to produce an uncomplicated body of code with which to illustrate the move from design to implementation. We have, therefore, concentrated on the central features of the car park simulation. We have not, for example, modelled or implemented that part of the system which deals with the addition or deletion of cards. In the interests of simplicity, the car park we model has only one entrance and one exit. This simplifies the required relationship network (for example, we do not need to build in an association between the EntranceBarrier and its Sensor).

Classes are listed in the following order:

Class	Page
CarParkSystem.java	152
CarPark.java	152
ValidCards.java	154
Card.java	155
CardReader.java	156
EntranceBarrier.java	157
Sensor.java	157
Simulator.java.	158

CarParkSystem.java

```
/* Main driver class for Car Park simulation */

public class CarParkSystem
{
  public static CarPark aCarPark;

  public static void main(String[] args)
  {
    // set up car park with 1 entrance, 1 exit,
    // 5 spaces, 3 of which are full initially
    aCarPark =  new CarPark(1,1,5,3);
  }
}
```

A

CarPark.java

```
/* Class representing Car Park */

public class CarPark
{
  private int capacity;        // max number of spaces
  private int spaces;          // actual spaces
  Sensor inSensor;             // sensors for entry/exit
  Sensor outSensor;
  ExitBarrier outBarrier;      // barrier for exit
  ValidCards currentCards;     // list of valid cards
```

```
      CardReader mainCardReader;        // card reader at entry
      FullSign fullLight;

      public CarPark(int noExits, int noEnts, int inCapacity, int noSpaces)
      {
        Simulator.setMaxCardNo(10);       // set max number for attempted cards
        capacity = inCapacity;            // give value to capacity
        spaces = noSpaces;                // and to spaces
B       currentCards = new ValidCards();   // create list of valid cards
D       mainCardReader = new CardReader(this, currentCards); // create card reader

        // 'this' is the standard Java term used to refer to the class currently being defined

        inSensor = new Sensor();          // create sensors
        outSensor =  new Sensor();
        fullLight = new FullSign();
        outBarrier = new ExitBarrier(this);  // create exit barrier
        for(int carNo = 0; carNo<50; carNo++) // simulate for 50 cars
        {
1         if (inSensor.carArriving())     // if next event is car arrival
          {
            System.out.print("\nCar Arriving ");
5           if (spacesLeft())             // if room in park
            {
7             if (mainCardReader.cardReadOK())  // if valid card entered
              { // the card reader will handle car's entry
21              if (!spacesLeft())        // switch on full light if full
                  fullLight.switchOn();
                fullLight.display();      // displays full sign status
              }
            }
            else
              System.out.print("No entry - Car Park Full ");
          };

          if (spaces != capacity && outSensor.carLeaving())//if car park not empty
                                          //and exit simulated
          {
            System.out.print("\nCar Leaving  ");
            outBarrier.raise();
            if (spaces == 1)         // if only space is one just vacated
              fullLight.switchOff(); // switch off full sign
            fullLight.display();     // display full sign status
          }
        }
      }
```

```
public void decSpaces()
{
  spaces = spaces -1;
  System.out.print(" Spaces left = " + spaces + " ");
}

public void incSpaces()
{
  // add 1 to spaces available
  spaces = spaces + 1;
  System.out.print(" Spaces left = " + spaces + " ");
}

public boolean spacesLeft()
{
  // indicates if space available
  if (spaces > 0 )
  {
    return true;
  }
  else
  {
    System.out.print("No spaces left ");
    return false;
  }
}
}
```

6 and 22

ValidCards.java

```
/* Class representing list of valid cards */

public class ValidCards
{
Card knownCards[];  // list of valid cards
 int i;

 ValidCards()
 {
  // set up list of known cards. Better system would store in
  // e.g. linked list or file
  knownCards = new Card[8];  // assign memory for 8 valid cards
  // add 6 staff cards
```

```
        knownCards[0] = new StaffCard("Fred","Sales","17-11-1999",1);
        knownCards[1] = new StaffCard("Sue","Sales","21-03-2001",2);
        knownCards[2] = new StaffCard("Frank","Research","03-06-2000",3);
        knownCards[3] = new StaffCard("Mary","Testing","29-02-2000",4);
        knownCards[4] = new StaffCard("Bill","Research","05-12-2000",5);
        knownCards[5] = new StaffCard("Jill","Testing","13-01-2000",6);

        // add 2 visitors' cards
        knownCards[6] = new VisitorCard();
        knownCards[7] = new VisitorCard();
    }

    public boolean validCard(int cardNo)
    {
      boolean valid = false;   // initial value

      // search known cards to see if number corresponds
      for (i = 0; i < 8; i++)
      {
        if (knownCards[i].getNum() == cardNo)
        {
          valid = true;       // change to true when one is found
        }
      }

      if (valid)
      {
        System.out.print(" Valid card " + cardNo + ". ");
        return true;
      }
      else
      {
        System.out.print(" Invalid card " + cardNo + ". ");
        return false;
      }
    }
}
```

Card.java

```
/* Parent class for cards */

public class Card
{
  int number;  //card number
```

```
    public Card(int num)
      {
        number = num;  // constructor copies parameter to number
      }

    int getNum()    // gives card number
      {
        return number;
      }

    }
```

12 (handwritten, pointing to `return number;`)

CardReader.java

```
    /* Class representing Card reader */

    public class CardReader
      {
        private ValidCards okCards;       // list of valid cards
        EntranceBarrier  inBarrier;       // barrier controlled by reader

        public CardReader(CarPark aCarPark, ValidCards centralList) //constructor
          {
            okCards = centralList;         // create association
            inBarrier = new EntranceBarrier(aCarPark);   // create aggregation
          }

        public boolean cardReadOK()    // is card valid?
          {
            int cardNo;             // number of card in machine

            cardNo = Simulator.getCardNo(); // simulate reading

            if (okCards.validCard(cardNo)) // validate card
              {
                inBarrier.raise();
                return true;           // let car in if ok
              }
            else
              {                         // deny entry
                System.out.print("Entry refused, invalid card number ");
                return false;
              }
          }
      }
```

E (handwritten, pointing to `inBarrier = new EntranceBarrier(aCarPark);`)

8 (handwritten, pointing to `cardNo = Simulator.getCardNo();`)

10 (handwritten, pointing to `if (okCards.validCard(cardNo))`)

14 (handwritten, pointing to `inBarrier.raise();`)

EntranceBarrier.java

/* Entrance Barrier class which specialises Barrier */

```java
public class EntranceBarrier extends Barrier
{
  public EntranceBarrier(CarPark aCarPark)
  {
    super(aCarPark);   // pass parameter to parent Barrier class
  }

  public void raise() // let a car in
  {
    super.raise();     // use parent's method to raise barrier
    while (ownerCarPark.inSensor.carPresent())
    {
      // do nothing - just wait
    }
    lower();

  }

  void lower()        // car is now in. 1 space fewer
  {
    super.lower();
    ownerCarPark.decSpaces();
  }
}
```

15 (while (ownerCarPark.inSensor.carPresent()))

19 (lower();)

20 (ownerCarPark.decSpaces();)

Sensor.java

/* Class to indicate presence of a car at entrance or exit sensor */

```java
public class Sensor
{
  public boolean carArriving() // simulated arrival of car
  {
    return (Simulator.arrivalGenerated());
  }

  public boolean carLeaving()  // simulated departure of car
  {
    return (Simulator.departureGenerated());
  }

  public boolean carPresent()  // simulates sensor detecting car
  {
```

2 and 4 (return (Simulator.arrivalGenerated());)

```
          System.out.print(" Car present. ");
16 and 18  return (Simulator.stillThereGenerated());
          }
        }
```

Simulator.java

```
/* Class to produce random arrivals, departures and card numbers */

public class Simulator
{

  static int maxCardNo;      // highest card number that could be issued

  public static void setMaxCardNo(int maxNo)
  {
    maxCardNo = maxNo;
  }

  public static boolean arrivalGenerated()
  {
    //This method returns true if an arrival has occurred
3   return (Math.random() <= 0.7);   // returns true or false depending on no. generated
                                      // 0.7 is empirical value
  }                                   // to give full range of car park states

  public static boolean departureGenerated()
  {
    //This method returns true if a departure has occurred
    return (Math.random() > 0.7);   // returns true or false depending on no. generated
  }                                  // as above

  public static boolean stillThereGenerated()
  {
    //This method returns true if car is still detected by sensor
17  return (Math.random() < 0.5); // returns true or false depending on no. generated
  }

  public static int getCardNo()
  // generates a card number at random
  {
9   return (int)(maxCardNo*Math.random()); //returns number generated
  }
}
```

Exercises

8.1   Figure 8.6 models the creation of the first few objects in the car park system, assuming the sequence of events modelled in Figure 8.7. Draw a similar diagram that shows the order of creation of the rest of the objects that would be required to complete the scenario: 'Car enters car park, no spaces are left and the full sign is switched on'.

8.2   Using the sequence diagram you drew as the answer to Exercise 7.2, trace the sequence of messages through the code. Use the code in Appendix C as the listing in Section 8.3 is incomplete.

8.3   Figure 8.8 shows the class diagram and the Java code for the CarPark class.
a)   From the class diagram, identify the CarPark attributes.
b)   Identify the lines of code where these attributes are defined.
c)   Identify the lines of code where the attributes are initialized.
d)   Using the complete program listing in Appendix C, identify the code where the values for the CarPark attributes are specified and then passed to the CarPark constructor as parameters.

8.4   Using the class diagram and the Java code in Figure 8.8 (below):
a)   Identify the CarPark operations.
b)   Identity these operations in the code.

```
┌─────────────────────┐
│      CarPark        │
├─────────────────────┤
│ capacity            │
│ spaces              │
├─────────────────────┤
│ decSpaces( )        │
│ incSpaces( )        │
│ spacesLeft( )       │
│                     │
└─────────────────────┘
```

CarPark.java

```java
/* Class representing Car Park  */

public class CarPark
{
    private int capacity;        // max number of spaces
    private int spaces;          // actual spaces
    Sensor inSensor;             // sensors for entry/exit
    Sensor outSensor;
    ExitBarrier outBarrier;      // barrier for exit
    ValidCards currentCards;     // list of valid cards
    CardReader mainCardReader;   // card reader at entry
    FullSign fullLight;
```

```java
public CarPark(int noExits, int noEnts, int inCapacity, int noSpaces)
{
  Simulator.setMaxCardNo(10);      // set max number for attempted cards
  capacity = inCapacity;           // give value to capacity
  spaces = noSpaces;               // and to spaces
  currentCards = new ValidCards();  // create list of valid cards
  mainCardReader = new CardReader(this, currentCards); // create card reader

  // 'this' is the standard Java term used to refer to the class currently being defined

  inSensor = new Sensor();         // create sensors
  outSensor = new Sensor();
  fullLight = new FullSign();
  outBarrier = new ExitBarrier(this);  // create exit barrier
  for(int carNo = 0; carNo<50; carNo++) // simulate for 50 cars
  {
   if (inSensor.carArriving()) // if next event is car arrival
   {
    System.out.print("\nCar Arriving ");
    if (spacesLeft())          // if room in park
     {
      if (mainCardReader.cardReadOK()) // if valid card entered
      { // the card reader will handle car's entry
       if (!spacesLeft())    // switch on full light if full
         fullLight.switchOn();
       fullLight.display();   // displays full sign status
      }
     }
     else
       System.out.print("No entry - Car Park Full ");
    };

    if (spaces != capacity && outSensor.carLeaving())//if car park not empty
                              //and exit simulated
    {
      System.out.print("\nCar Leaving ");
      outBarrier.raise();
      if (spaces == 1)       // if only space is one just vacated
        fullLight.switchOff(); // switch off full sign
      fullLight.display();    // display full sign status
    }
   }
  }
}


public void decSpaces()
{
```

```
      spaces = spaces -1;
      System.out.print(" Spaces left = " + spaces + " ");


   }

   public void incSpaces()
   {

      // add 1 to spaces available
      spaces = spaces + 1;
      System.out.print(" Spaces left = " + spaces + " ");


   }

   public boolean spacesLeft()
   {

      // indicates if space available
      if (spaces > 0 )

      {
         return true;
      }

      else

      {
         System.out.print("No spaces left ");
         return false;
      }
   }
```

Figure 8.8 CarPark class diagram and Java code

8.5   Figure 8.9 (below) shows the class diagram and the Java code for the ValidCards
       class.
a)   Identify, in the ValidCards class code, a operation that is used polymorphically.
b)   In which class is this polymorphic operation defined?
c)   Which classes are involved in the polymorphic execution of the operation?

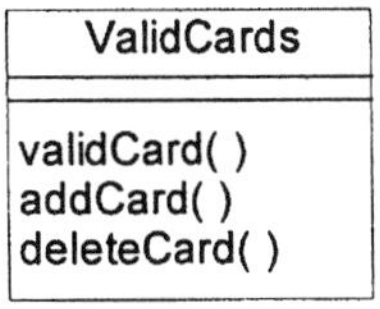

```
┌─────────────────────┐
│     ValidCards      │
╞═════════════════════╡
│ validCard( )        │
│ addCard( )          │
│ deleteCard( )       │
└─────────────────────┘
```

ValidCards.java

```
/* Class representing list of valid cards */

public class ValidCards
{
 Card knownCards[];   // list of valid cards
 int i;

  ValidCards()
  {
   // set up list of known cards. Better system would store in
   // e.g. linked list or file
   knownCards = new Card[8];   // assign memory for 8 valid cards
   // add 6 staff cards
   knownCards[0] = new StaffCard("Fred","Sales","17-11-1999",1);
   knownCards[1] = new StaffCard("Sue","Sales","21-03-2001",2);
   knownCards[2] = new StaffCard("Frank","Research","03-06-2000",3);
   knownCards[3] = new StaffCard("Mary","Testing","29-02-2000",4);
   knownCards[4] = new StaffCard("Bill","Research","05-12-2000",5);
   knownCards[5] = new StaffCard("Jill","Testing","13-01-2000",6);

   // add 2 visitors' cards
   knownCards[6] = new VisitorCard();
   knownCards[7] = new VisitorCard();
  }

  public boolean validCard(int cardNo)
  {
   boolean valid = false;   // initial value

   // search known cards to see if number corresponds
   for (i = 0;i < 8;i++)
   {
    if (knownCards[i].getNum() == cardNo)
    {
     valid = true;      // change to true when one is found
    }
   }

   if (valid)
   {
    System.out.print(" Valid card " + cardNo + ". ");
    return true;
   }
   else
   {
    System.out.print(" Invalid card " + cardNo + ". ");
```

```
      return false;
    }
  }
}
```

Figure 8.9 ValidCards class diagram and Java code

8.6   Figure 8.10 (below) shows the (undocumented) Java code for the Family Hierarchy
      example from Chapter 2.
a)   Identify the class constructors in this code.
b)   What initialization is done by the Toddler class constructor?
c)   What are the attributes of the Grandad class, and how are they initialized?
d)   Which operation is used polymorphically, and to which classes is it applied?

Family Hierarchy

```java
import java.lang.String;

class Person
{
  Person()
  {

  }

  void talk()
  {
    System.out.println("A Person says: I'm not saying anything");
  }
}

class Baby extends Person
{
  Baby()
  {

  }

  void talk()
  {
    System.out.println("A Baby cries: Wah, Wah" );
  }
}

class Toddler extends Person
```

```
{
  String vocabulary;

  Toddler()
  {
    vocabulary = "Mama, NO";
  }

  void talk()
  {
    System.out.println("A Toddler shouts: " + vocabulary );
  }
}

class Teenager extends Person
{
  char gender;

  Teenager(char sex )
  {
    gender=sex;
  }

  void talk()
  {
    if (gender=='M' || gender =='m')
      System.out.println("A male teenager says: Grunt, Grunt");
    else
      System.out.println("A female teenager says: Where's my mascara");
  }
}

class Mother extends Person
{
  Mother()
  {
  }

  void talk()
  {
    System.out.println("A Mother says: Have you tidied your room?");
  }
}

class Father extends Person
{
  Father()
  {
  }
```

```java
  void talk()
  {
   System.out.println("A Father says: I'm going to football");
  }
}

class Grandad extends Person
{
 String currentYear;
 String yearOfBirth;

 Grandad(String thisYear, String birthYear)
 {
   currentYear = thisYear;
   yearOfBirth = birthYear;
 }

 void talk()
 {
    int age;

    age = new Integer(currentYear).intValue()-
        new Integer(yearOfBirth).intValue();
    System.out.println("A Grandad says: I'm " + age + " years old");

 }
}




class Granny extends Person
{
 Granny()
 {
 }

 void talk()
 {
   System.out.println("A Granny says: When's the boxing on?" );
 }

}




public class FamilyTalking
{

  public static void main(String[] args)
```

```
{
  Person familyMember[];
  int i;
  familyMember = new Person[8];
  familyMember[0] = new Baby();
  familyMember[1] = new Toddler();
  familyMember[2] = new Teenager('F');
  familyMember[3] = new Teenager('M');
  familyMember[4] = new Mother();
  familyMember[5] = new Father();
  familyMember[6] = new Granny();
  familyMember[7] = new Grandad("99", "01");

  for  (i=0;i<8;i++)
  {
  familyMember[i].talk();
  }

 }
}
```

Figure 8.10 Java code for Family Hierarchy example

References and further reading

Bennett, S., McRobb, S. and Farmer, R. *Object-Oriented Systems Analysis and Design using UML,* London: McGraw-Hill, 1999.

Bishop, J.M. *Java Gently,* Harlow: Addison-Wesley, 1998.

Buchanan, W. *Mastering Java,* Basingstoke: Macmillan, 1998.

Fowler, M. with Scott, K. *UML Distilled: Applying the Standard Object Modeling Language,* Reading, Massachusetts: Addison-Wesley, 1997.

Parsons, D. *Introductory Java,* London: Letts, 1998.

Quatrani, T. *Visual Modeling with Rational Rose and UML,* Reading, Massachusetts: Addison-Wesley, 1998.

9

Dealing with Persistent Data

9.1 The problem of persistent data

Persistent data refers to objects that continue to exist after the program that creates and uses them has stopped executing. We need to think about persistent data in the *Just a Line* car park problem, since an important feature of the system is the validation of cards that are inserted into the card reader. The validation is performed by the ValidCards class, which checks the card number entered. The programming language Java has no facilities for easy storage and retrieval of persistent data, but we can address this problem in various ways:

- input the data each time we run the program (by typing it in or reading it from a file);
- hard-code the data as part of the program;
- link the program to a database.

For the sake of simplicity in the code shown in Appendix C, we have chosen the second of these options, as shown in the code extract below.

```
{
    // set up list of known cards.

    // assign memory for 8 valid cards
    knownCards = new Card[8];

    // add 6 staff cards
    knownCards[0]=new StaffCard("Fred","Sales","17-11-1999",1);
    knownCards[1]=new StaffCard("Sue","Sales","21-03-2001",2);
    knownCards[2]=new StaffCard("Frank","Research","03-06-2000",3);
    knownCards[3]=new StaffCard("Mary","Testing","29-02-2000",4);
    knownCards[4]=new StaffCard("Bill","Research","05-12-2000",5);
    knownCards[5]=new StaffCard("Jill","Testing","13-01-2000",6);

    // add 2 visitors' cards
    knownCards[6]=new VisitorCard();
    knownCards[7]=new VisitorCard();
}
```

Although this is a relatively uncomplicated approach, there are serious disadvantages when the list of cards needs to be updated, since users of the system would have to be knowledgeable enough to be able to access and modify the program code.

In this chapter we discuss briefly the third of the options mentioned above. This involves linking the Java program to a database that stores the data and allows it to be accessed and queried in a straightforward way by users who are not trained software engineers.

9.2 Different types of database

One of the main advantages of the object-oriented approach to software development is the potential for a seamless transition from analysis through design to implementation. The best way to achieve this when dealing with persistent data is to use an object database.

Object databases are designed specifically to implement the complex data structures found in object-oriented analysis and design models, while providing the same storage, access and query facilities found in more traditional databases. For certain types of software system, those that are built from complicated data objects, an object database is the usual means of storing, manipulating and retrieving data. Such systems include multimedia, computer aided design, and geographical information systems.

Although, in theory, an object database is the best way of storing data in an object-oriented system, in practice this is not always feasible. For many years, the database market has been dominated by relational database technology. Relational databases have a sound mathematical foundation; they are mature, flexible and extremely efficient for the sort of data that they were designed to handle. Object databases, on the other hand, are relatively new and the technology on which they are based is still subject to change. Many organizations have invested money, time and effort into creating and maintaining their relational database systems; for the majority of these organizations, changing to an object database is not yet worth the risk. It is a safer option to find some way of allowing new object-oriented applications to share the existing relational database.

In the case where part of a system is to be implemented in an object-oriented programming language and part in a relational database, two questions must be considered:

- how are the object-oriented models from the analysis and design stages of development to be implemented within the constraints of a relational database?
- how is the object-oriented part of the system going to access the data in the database?

These issues are discussed in Sections 9.4 and 9.5 of this chapter.

9.3 Microsoft Access: a typical relational database

We briefly describe below three of the features of Microsoft Access, a popular relational database.

Tables A database in Microsoft Access is built around tables; all other parts of the database, such as queries, forms and reports, depend on the data in the tables. Tables store data in a row-column format; each column stores a field, or attribute of the data, and each row stores a record, typically the complete set of values for a single data object. Figure 9.1 below shows a small example table that contains data about customers. Every table should have a primary key (an attribute, or combination of attributes, that uniquely identifies each record). In Figure 9.1, the primary key is CustNo.

Queries The tables in the database contain all the data that the users need, but not in a very accessible form. Users frequently want to view data structured in a particular way, or they want to retrieve only those records that satisfy a certain condition. In order to allow this, Access provides the query mechanism, which enables users to retrieve and analyse the data in an appropriate and convenient way. Figure 9.2 below illustrates the result of a query on the data in Figure 9.1, requesting details of customers who live in Hansford.

Customer

CustNo	Name	FirstName	Street	Town	PostCode	PhoneNo
1	Leary	John	14 High St.	Hansford	SG7 4DG	01483 876594
2	Trip	Chris	2 Long Ave.	Boxeth	SG8 5TR	01485 324906
3	Jones	Ellen	67 Bow Rd.	Hansford	SG7 4RF	01483 897885
4	Brown	Lisa	124 High St.	Hansford	SG7 4DF	01483 874553
5	James	Bob	21 Park Rd.	Boxeth	SG8 7YH	01485 347236

Figure 9.1 Example of a small table of customers in an Access database

HansfordCustomer

CustNo	Name	FirstName	Street	Town	PostCode	PhoneNo
1	Leary	John	14 High St.	Hansford	SG7 4DG	01483 876594
3	Jones	Ellen	67 Bow Rd.	Hansford	SG7 4RF	01483 897885
4	Brown	Lisa	124 High St.	Hansford	SG7 4DF	01483 874553

Figure 9.2 Result of a query requesting details of customers who live in Hansford

Forms Tables are the core of the database, but they are not very user-friendly when it comes to viewing and manipulating data. A form in Access allows the user to display, enter and modify data on screen. Forms are based on tables, but may include labels, boxes, lines and even pictures to make the user's task easier. Figure 9.3 shows a form based on the table in Figure 9.1 and displaying the first record in the table.

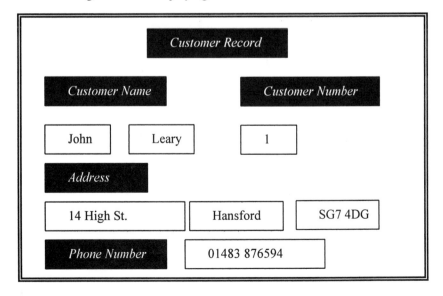

Figure 9.3 Form displaying the first record from the table in Figure 9.1

9.4 Implementing object-oriented models in a relational database, such as Microsoft Access

If part of a system is to be implemented in an object-oriented programming language and part in a relational database, one of the issues that needs to be considered is how the object-oriented models from the analysis and design stages of development are to be implemented within the constraints of a relational database. This is still a relatively new area of research and there is currently no generally accepted way of dealing with the problem. Authors who are expert in databases tend to advocate a method based on the principles of normalization; we do not cover this here, as normalization is beyond the scope of this book. Several authors of books on object-orientation who have addressed the problem suggest guidelines to follow in converting classes in the class diagram into tables in the database. This approach is discussed briefly in this section.

9.4.1 Converting a class diagram into tables

In order to explain the guidelines for converting a class diagram into tables, we will illustrate them with a small example. Figure 9.4 shows a very simple analysis class diagram illustrating how *Just a Line* deals with customer orders for greetings cards.

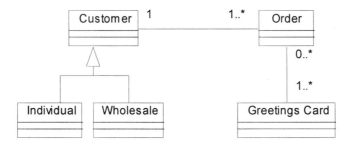

Figure 9.4 Simple class diagram for the *Just a Line* greetings card ordering system

We can see from the diagram that a greetings card can be included in zero or more orders, an order must be for at least one card; an order can be for only one customer, but a customer may have more than one order. In addition, the system caters for two types of customer: individual and wholesale.

Individual classes

The basic guideline when converting a class diagram into a set of tables is that one class maps to one or more tables. Certain other details will also need to be supplied, such as the primary key (to uniquely identify each separate record in the table) and whether a field in the table must be filled in or can be null. Figure 9.5 shows the design class GreetingsCard with its attributes. We do not include the class operations here, because all but the most basic operations will be implemented in the object-oriented programming language, not in the code associated with the database; we are concerned here with data, not the functionality of the system. Figure 9.6 shows the `GreetingsCard` class as a table in Microsoft Access and Figure 9.7 shows a form displaying details of the first record in the table.

```
GreetingsCard
name
size
unit price
message
picture
```

Figure 9.5 The class `GreetingsCard`

GreetingsCard

CardID	CardName	CardSize	UnitPrice	Message	Picture
1	Forgot again	6 x 4	1.00	Forgot again! HAPPY BIRTHDAY	Query.bmp
2	The Champ	6 x 4	1.00	Have a great day, Champ!	Champ.bmp
3	Waves	6 x 6	2.00	With best wishes	Waves.bmp
4	Mona Lisa 1	6 x 6	1.50		ML1.bmp
5	Mona Lisa 2	6 x 6	1.50		ML2.bmp
6	Shells	6 x 6	2.00	Thinking of you	Shells.bmp

Figure 9.6 The `GreetingsCard` class as a table in Microsoft Access

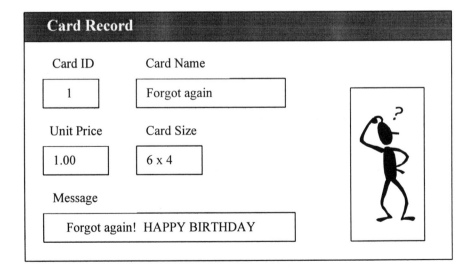

Figure 9.7 Form displaying the first record of the table in Figure 9.6

Many to many associations

A many to many association in a class diagram is always represented with one table each for the related classes and a separate table to represent the association. Primary keys from the two related classes become fields in the association table.   The many to many association from the analysis class diagram in Figure 9.4 is shown again at the design stage in Figure 9.8.

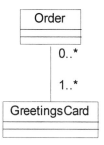

Figure 9.8 A many to many association in a class diagram

This part of the class diagram will be converted into three tables: GreetingsCard, Order and Card/Order, which can all be seen below in Figure 9.9.

GreetingsCard

CardID	CardName	CardSize	UnitPrice	Message	Picture
1	Forgot again	6 x 4	1.00	Forgot again! HAPPY BIRTHDAY	Query.bmp
2	The Champ	6 x 4	1.00	Have a great day, Champ!	Champ.bmp
3	Waves	6 x 6	2.00	With best wishes	Waves.bmp
4	Mona Lisa 1	6 x 6	1.50		ML1.bmp
5	Mona Lisa 2	6 x 6	1.50		ML2.bmp
6	Shells	6 x 6	2.00	Thinking of you	Shells.bmp

Order

OrderID	Date	OrderCost	DeliveryCharge	TotalCost
99-8743	08/12/99	10.00	1.00	11.00
99-9438	12/12/99	15.00	1.00	16.00
00-0774	13/01/00	25.00	0.00	25.00
00-1065	22/02/00	10.00	1.00	11.00
00-1174	25/02/00	30.00	0.00	30.00

CardOrder

CardID	OrderID
1	00-0774
2	99-8743
3	00-1065
5	00-1174
6	99-9438

Figure 9.9 Separate tables representing the class diagram extract in Figure 9.8

The fields in the CardOrder table are the primary keys that uniquely identify each instance of a card and of an order. Each row of the table represents an actual link between a card and an order; so, for example, we can see from the first row of the table that card number 1 is part of order number 00-0774.

One to many associations

In the case of one to many associations implementers have two options:

- create a separate table, as for a many to many association
- include a foreign key[1] in the table for the many class.

Figure 9.10 shows the one to many association between the Customer and Order classes, Figure 9.11 shows the first option of three separate tables and Figure 9.12 illustrates the second option of using a foreign key.

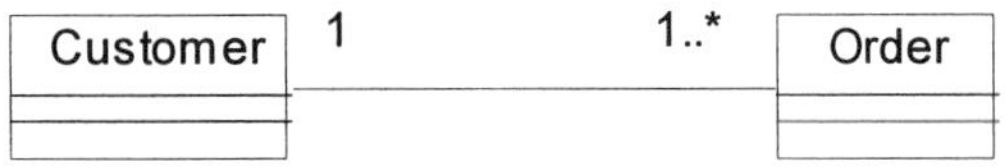

Figure 9.10 One to many association from the class diagram

Customer

CustNo	Name	FirstName	Street	Town	PostCode	PhoneNo
1	Leary	John	14 High St.	Hansford	SG7 4DG	01483 876594
2	Trip	Chris	2 Long Ave.	Boxeth	SG8 5TR	01485 324906
3	Jones	Ellen	67 Bow Rd.	Hansford	SG7 4RF	01483 897885
4	Brown	Lisa	124 High St.	Hansford	SG 7 4DF	01483 874553
5	James	Bob	21 Park Rd.	Boxeth	SG8 7YH	01485 347236

---

[1] If one table contains the primary key of another, this is called a foreign key. A foreign key permits a link between the two tables. This can be seen in Figure 9.12, where CustNo, the primary key of the Customer table, also appears in the Order table.

Order

OrderID	Date	OrderCost	DeliveryCharge	TotalCost
99-8743	08/12/99	10.00	1.00	11.00
99-9438	12/12/99	15.00	1.00	16.00
00-0774	13/01/00	25.00	0.00	25.00
00-1065	22/02/00	10.00	1.00	11.00
00-1174	25/02/00	30.00	0.00	30.00

CustomerOrder

CustNo	OrderID
1	99-9438
2	00-1065
3	00-0774
4	99-8743
5	00-1174

Figure 9.11 First option: separate tables for the one to many association and classes

Customer

CustNo	Name	FirstName	Street	Town	PostCode	PhoneNo
1	Leary	John	14 High St.	Hansford	SG7 4DG	01483 876594
2	Trip	Chris	2 Long Ave.	Boxeth	SG8 5TR	01485 324906
3	Jones	Ellen	67 Bow Rd.	Hansford	SG7 4RF	01483 897885
4	Brown	Lisa	124 High St.	Hansford	SG7 4DF	01483 874553
5	James	Bob	21 Park Rd.	Boxeth	SG8 7YH	01485 347236

Order

OrderID	CustNo	Date	OrderCost	DeliveryCharge	TotalCost
99-8743	4	08/12/99	10.00	1.00	11.00
99-9438	1	12/12/99	15.00	1.00	16.00
00-0774	3	13/01/00	25.00	0.00	25.00
00-1065	2	22/02/00	10.00	1.00	11.00
00-1174	5	25/02/00	30.00	0.00	30.00

Figure 9.12 Second option: implement tables for Customer and Order only, but include foreign key (CustNo) in the table for the Order class

The choice of which of these options to implement depends on the particular application. The second alternative (including a foreign key in the table for the class at the many end of the association) has the advantages that there are fewer tables, which results in simpler navigation around the database. However, from another point of view, the first option may be considered preferable, since the tables, such as Order, are a more direct representation of the original classes.

Aggregation For the purposes of converting a class diagram to tables, aggregation is treated as a one to many association (see above).

Inheritance

Figure 9.13 shows an example of an inheritance relationship identified in the analysis class diagram in Figure 9.4. This diagram shows the relationship at the design stage, with the super-class, Customer, which has the attributes, name and address, common to all customers. There are also two sub-classes, representing individual and wholesale customers. The Individual class inherits the name and address attributes from Customer, and also has an attribute recording the number of previous cards bought (*Just a Line* offers a free gift to individual customers who have bought 500 cards). The sub-class Wholesale also inherits name and address from Customer and has the extra attributes to record the contact name and the discount allowed on orders.

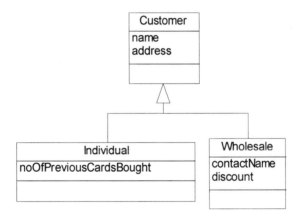

Figure 9.13 Inheritance relationship from the class diagram

There are three possible ways of implementing this relationship in a relational database:

- map each of the three classes to a separate table, using a shared number or code to link the tables
- implement tables for the sub-classes only (in this case, Individual and Wholesale)
- combine all three classes in one table.

The first option, implementing the relationship as three separate tables, is a simple, clean design. However, if used throughout the database, it will result in a large number of tables.

and slow navigation. It can also cause maintenance problems if the super-class (in this case, Customer) is modified.

The second option, implementing sub-classes only, is suitable in the case where the super-class is abstract, in other words, there are no actual instances of it. This is the case here, since all the customers in the *Just a Line* system are either individual or wholesale. This option is also appropriate when the super-class has very few attributes and the different sub-classes each have many. Implementing only two tables results in faster performance than when the first option is chosen, but all the attributes of the super-class have to be replicated in each sub-class table.

In the third option the attributes of all three classes are included in a single table. This works well if the sub-classes differ from the super-class more in their behaviour than in their attributes. However, if the sub-classes do have many attributes of their own, putting all the classes together in a single table will result in lots of null values.

Each case of inheritance has to be considered individually. In the example in Figure 9.13 Customer is an abstract class; all the customers in the system are either individual or wholesale. The attributes seem to be fairly evenly divided between the three classes but in analysing the data, we may have found that the name attribute will probably be quite different for the two types of customer. Individual customers will have a first name, possibly an initial, and a last name; wholesale customers, on the other hand, will probably have an organization name and possibly a department. The data that we wish to store about the two types of customer is not particularly similar, and would suggest that the best way to implement this inheritance relationship is in a table for each of the sub-classes, the second option on the list above. In this way we can design the separate tables so that each represents the data as accurately as possible. The two tables are shown in Figure 9.14.

Individual Customer

CustNo	Name	FirstName	Street	Town	PostCode	PreviousCards
1	Leary	John	14 High St.	Hansford	SG7 4DG	50
2	Trip	Chris	2 Long Ave.	Boxeth	SG8 5TR	150
3	Jones	Ellen	67 Bow Rd.	Hansford	SG7 4RF	400
4	Brown	Lisa	124 High St.	Hansford	SG7 4DF	0
5	James	Bob	21 Park Rd.	Boxeth	SG8 7YH	80

Wholesale Customer

CustNo	Name	Street	Town	PostCode	Contact	Discount
21	Cards 4 All	1–2 High St.	Hansford	SG7 0HY	Ray	20%
27	Westons	42 Mays Rd.	Boxeth	SG8 9TR	Janet	25%
34	Mac & Son	29a Pine Rd.	Hansford	SG7 4ES	Joe	20%
49	The Card	9–12 King St.	Hansford	SG7 6JK	Tim	30%
52	Haines	68 Lime Rd.	Boxeth	SG8 8LG	Les	15%

Figure 9.14 Tables representing the two sub-classes from the inheritance relationship in Figure 9.13

9.5 Linking Java code to a relational database

JDBC (sometimes referred to as Java Database Connectivity) is a set of classes and interfaces written in the Java programming language that allow Java applications to access data stored in virtually any relational database. JDBC makes it possible to set up a connection between the Java program and the database, access and manipulate the data in the database, and process the results. It is beyond the scope of this book to describe in detail how JDBC works; in this section we simply give some idea of how data held in a relational database can be accessed by a Java program.

As an example, we return to the *Just a Line* car park case study and, in particular, the validation of cards that are inserted into the card reader. Figure 9.15 shows an extract from the analysis class diagram for the *Just a Line* car park system, showing the classes Visitor's Card, Staff Card and the Card super-class. The full class diagram can be seen in Chapter 5, Figure 5.19.

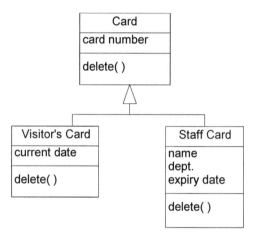

Figure 9.15 Visitor's and staff cards in the *Just a Line* car park system

For the sake of simplicity, we have chosen to model the three classes, Card, Visitor's Card and Staff Card, as a single table in the Access database. Figure 9.16 shows the Access table with details of six staff cards and three visitors' cards. In line with the Java code (see Chapter 8 and Appendix C), the date attribute for both classes of card is implemented as expiry date and all visitors' cards have the number 9^2.

In order to provide a link between the Java code and the data it needs, the programmer has to use Java's JDBC facility. This involves creating a data source and entering the data source name into the Java program. The JDBC driver manager locates a driver that can connect to the database and establishes a link through which data can be accessed. The actual code to establish the link between the object-oriented Java code and the Access

---

[2] We should point out here that the use of number 9 as a visitor's card number would have a limit of one card if the table was set up with CardNo as the primary key.

database is too complex to include here. It can be found on the web site for this book at http://www.mcgraw-hill.co.uk/textbooks/britton, together with more detailed instructions on how to set up the link.

Card

CardNo	Name	Department	ExpiryDate
1	Sam Parker	Marketing	31/01/00
2	Mira Patel	Marketing	31/03/00
3	Chris Doolan	Design	29/02/00
4	Annie Raines	Accounts	30/04/00
5	Sue Preston	Management	30/04/00
6	Harry Preston	Management	30/04/00
9			02/12/99
9			02/12/99
9			03/12/99

Figure 9.16 Table in Access showing details of the staff and visitor's cards in the *Just a Line* car park system

The problem of how to deal with persistent data in an object-oriented system has not yet been resolved, particularly where objects are built from more complex data structures than we have considered in this chapter. Although object-oriented databases are clearly the way forward, their use throughout the industry is so far neither practical nor feasible. JDBC is an example of an approach that allows companies to retain their existing relational databases, but it has not yet been tried and tested enough to win widespread support. For beginners to object-oriented system development, it is important to be aware that there is a problem with persistent data and to wait and see how successful the different approaches are at solving it.

Exercises

9.1   You can see below three objects of class Employee. Design a table to store information about employees in a relational database, such as Microsoft Access. Insert the employee details given here as the first three records in the table.

: Staff Card	: Staff Card	: Staff Card
number = JL437	number = JL722	number = JL209
name = Sam Parker	name = Mira Patel	name = Chris Doolan
dept. = Marketing	dept. = Marketing	dept. = Design

9.2   The following diagram illustrates an association relationship between employees and rooms in a security system. An employee can enter one or more rooms, and each room can be entered by one or more employees.
Design tables to show how you would implement this relationship in a relational database.

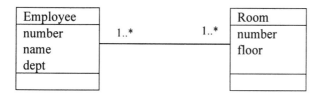

9.3   The diagram below shows an association relationship between employees and their cars. The association indicates that an employee can own 0, 1 or 2 cars, but a car can be owned by only one employee.
Use two different ways to implement this relationship in a relational database.

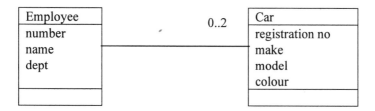

9.4   The diagram below illustrates an inheritance between the super-class Employee and sub-classes Full-timer and Part-timer. Show how you would implement this relationship in a relational database.

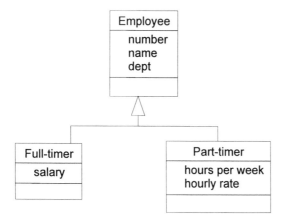

References and further reading

Bennett, S., McRobb, S. and Farmer, R. *Object-Oriented Systems Analysis and Design using UML,* London: McGraw-Hill, 1999. Pages 388–390

Rumbaugh, J., Blaha, M., Premerlani, W., Eddy, F. and Lorensen, W. *Object-Oriented Modeling and Design,* Englewood Cliffs, N.J.: Prentice Hall, 1991. Pages 373–386.

Ullman, J.D. and Ullman, J. *A First Course in Database Systems,* Upper Saddle River, N.J.: Prentice Hall, 1997.

Java web site http://java.sun.com/docs/books/jdbc/intro.html

10
Testing

Software testing must be done in essentially the same way whatever development method is used. To know what is involved in testing O-O software and what special advantages and problems it presents, we must first understand conventional testing techniques and procedures. This chapter discusses the development stages at which testing activities take place, standard testing activities and who does the testing. We also discuss problems with testing that are peculiar to O-O software and the extent to which an O-O design benefits the tester.

For clarity and ease of understanding, examples are written in pseudo-code rather than any particular programming language.

10.1 Stages of testing

Testing software should involve essentially the same procedures and techniques whatever design paradigm has been used. A software product developed using an O-O approach will be subjected to unit, integration and system testing in much the same way as software developed using a traditional approach. However, O-O designed software will give the tester some advantages over conventionally designed software; at the same time it brings problems not present in conventional software testing.

In the process of software development, testing has historically been left until the code has been written. However, testing or quality assurance activities can take place throughout the entire development process. Events in the testing process can be categorized as either validation activities or verification activities. Validation addresses the question: are we building the correct system, i.e. the one that satisfies the agreed requirements? Verification addresses the question: are we building the system correctly? Verification activities test the code and therefore cannot take place until the implementation stage. We discuss the activities involved in validation and verification under the headings pre-implementation testing and post-implementation testing.

10.1.1 Pre-implementation testing

Testing the software product can, and should, be done throughout the software development process. In the early stages of development, i.e. at the analysis and design stages, the type of testing that can be done is of a different nature from the testing that is done during and after implementation. Before implementation, ideas are being tested; during and after implementation, code is being tested. Pre-implementation testing is not done by programmers or even, normally, by members of a testing team but by a team of reviewers who may be project managers, customers or system developers—anyone actively involved in the development process. Early testing is more often thought of as a review of work done so far; a walkthrough of ideas or concepts. In the traditional life cycle approach this work will be done at the end of each of the development stages and will take the form of a review of the deliverable for the stage just completed. It corresponds to the backward pointing arrows in Figure 10.1 labelled 'validation'.

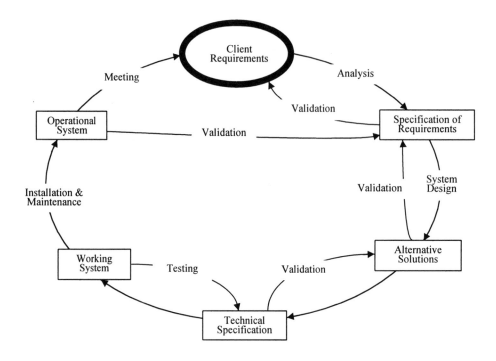

Figure 10.1 Simplified life cycle

Reviewers check that the specification document produced at the end of the analysis stage accurately captures the client requirements and that the requirements specified are consistent and feasible. The set of alternative solutions produced at the system design stage will be reviewed to check that they can meet the specified requirements, that they are feasible technically, operationally and financially, that they would fit in with client or company policies and resources. In the technical specification produced at the end of the detailed design stage it is still ideas not code that are being checked, although these ideas are now more formally expressed in the design documents. One of the proposed solutions will have been selected and designed in detail. Reviewers will check that the design meets the requirements outlined in previous stages, that the design is complete and that it is compatible with logical and physical performance requirements.

The next stage is to test the code; testing moves into the post-implementation phase and initially will be done by the programmer or a dedicated testing team.

10.1.2 Post-implementation or code testing

Whatever software development method has been used, the tester can apply two main testing techniques:

- white box testing
- black box testing.

White box testing

White box testing, variously known as white box, structural, program-based or glass box testing, is done by someone who has access to the source code—usually the programmer. Test cases are selected to exercise those parts of the code likely to cause trouble; for example, branches, loops, boundaries, case statements and complicated algorithms.

Black box testing

Black box testing is also known as specification or functional testing. A program or unit is tested without knowledge of the internal structure of the code. Therefore it can (and should) be done by someone other than the programmer. The tester treats the code as a black box into which he or she cannot see. Test cases are selected on the basis of the externally visible behaviour of the code, as specified in the program documentation. The tester is only interested in what the code does, not how it works. The code is tested by inputting data to the black box and checking that the output is as expected.

Test phases

Traditionally code testing falls into three distinct phases:

- unit testing
- integration testing
- system testing.

Unit testing There is not total agreement over the definition of a unit. It has been variously defined as:

- a single cohesive function or procedure
- the smallest segment of code that can be separately compiled
- a function that fits on to a single page
- code that one person can write in a given amount of time.

The most commonly used definition is the first one: that a unit comprises a single procedure or function. During unit testing a unit is tested by itself; any units which are called by it (server units) are replaced by stubs—short sections of code which substitute for missing units. A stub is required, for example, when the unit being tested calls (or messages) another unit which has not yet been written. A dummy unit (the stub) is written which, typically, does nothing except output a message such as 'Unit x has been reached'. This allows the unit undergoing testing to execute without the compiler or linker protesting about the missing units. The normal procedure is that a driver program will be written to act as a test harness for the unit being tested.

At unit testing level both black box and white box testing are appropriate. For O-O systems a unit is usually assumed to be a single class.

Integration testing Integration testing checks that units tested in isolation work properly when put together. When units have successfully completed the unit testing stage, they are combined into logically coherent groups for testing. For example, units forming a sub-system might be tested together. When testers are happy that a sub-system works, it will be combined with another sub-system for testing; when that combination works, another will be added and so on until the whole system is tested. The emphasis in integration testing is on checking that units work together; the testers concentrate on unit interaction rather than functionality. The code being tested gets progressively bigger—first a group of co-operating units will be tested together, then a sub-system, then several sub-systems; finally the whole system is tested.

System testing During system testing, testers check that the system behaves correctly when used as the client might typically use it. At this stage, testing assesses whether the system can cope with mainstream data and conditions—the type of data users will expect the system to handle on a routine basis, under normal conditions. The tester will also check the system's performance behaviour—how long it takes to execute given tasks. The system will undergo volume, stress and storage tests to check its performance under extreme conditions, for example huge volumes of input, high speed input, large numbers of users, peak bursts of activity. All computations are checked for correctness with expected and unexpected data and conditions. The system's error handling and recovery will be tested to establish that the correct error messages are issued and that the system recovers gracefully from fatal errors. The tester will also be expected to check that the system has an appropriate degree of security—that unauthorised users cannot gain access to the system.

Other types of test

Other types of testing may be appropriate, depending on how essential it is to minimize software failure, and how much time and effort the customer is prepared to put into testing. The options include:

- regression testing
- acceptance testing by user or a testing team
- beta testing
- release testing.

Regression testing It is a well-recognized phenomenon that correcting software faults very often leads to the introduction of new faults. The wise programmer therefore, when he or she has corrected a fault, should rerun all applicable tests and check that the program still produces the same results. This rerunning of tests and checking of results is known as regression testing. As regression testing is often a very tedious and expensive business, programmers are encouraged to organize their testing activities so that regression testing can be as automated as possible.

Acceptance testing Acceptance tests are done by the customer when the software is delivered. Normally, acceptance tests are a formal set of tests run to determine whether or not a system meets the customer's acceptance criteria. This, in turn, will determine whether or not the customer is prepared to accept and pay for the software. The main functionality of the system is tested, using the type of data a user might be expected to input.

Acceptance tests are often circulated in advance so that the programmer or development team can run them before formally handing over the software. This can save everyone time and embarrassment.

Beta testing If a software product such as a word processor, a web browser or a stock control system is being developed for general release, the software developers may decide to have it tested by outsiders before it is finally shipped. Beta testing is done by teams of 'friendly' outsiders who represent the type of users likely to purchase the software being developed. Their role is to give feedback on their experience of using the product in a working environment.

Release testing Release tests check that the product about to be sent out is complete: that all the disks or CDs are there with the right files on them; that the correct versions of the files are being used; that the disks or CDs are virus-free and that the correct set of documentation is included. The tester will do a high level check that the software does what it claims to do by comparing the software, the requirements documentation, the marketing material and the user documentation.

Who does the testing?

The testing of the code may be done by different people at different times. Who does the testing will depend both on the stage at which testing is being done and the resources allocated to testing a particular software product. Testing may be done by:

- the programmer
- a team of testers
- beta testers—people who represent the market for the software
- the customer
- the maintainer (often a programmer other than the one who wrote the code).

Unit testing is normally done by the programmer who wrote the unit. The programmer is not necessarily the best person to do this job as no-one wants to find errors in their own code. Studies indicate a reluctance on the part of the developers to put much effort into trying to prove that their own work is flawed. Also, programmers are rarely trained testers—it is estimated that only 10% of programmers are given adequate training. Nevertheless, resource limitations usually dictate that it is the programmer who does the unit testing.

Integration and system and testing are often done by a testing team. The customer will subject bespoke software to acceptance tests. Beta testing is done by potential users on non-bespoke software.

Path coverage criteria

In an ideal world, the programmer would test all paths through the code he or she is testing. However, this is usually an impossible goal given normal limitations on time and effort. Myers (1976) famously wrote a 20-line program, which he demonstrated to have 100 trillion paths through it. He estimated it would take approximately a billion years for a very fast tester to test all of those paths.

A path can either mean a route through an entire program (end-to-end path) or through part of a program (sub-path). An end-to-end path traces the sequence of statements executed from the start to the exit point in an execution of a program. A sub-path traces the statements executed from one logical point in the program to another. Paths are considered to differ if, on any pass through the code, the program executes a different set of statements or the same statements in a different order.

As it is impossible, except in the case of very small programs, to test all paths through a program, the tester usually adopts agreed coverage criteria to define achievable path testing. Three commonly used criteria are:

- statement coverage
- branch coverage
- condition coverage.

To achieve complete *statement coverage* the tester must find test cases that ensure that every statement of the program is executed at least once. For example consider the program fragment:

```
if ((A > 1) AND (B=0))
{
// Sub-statement 1
}
else
{
// Sub-statement 2
}
```

and the test cases:

1. $(A > 1)$ AND $(B = 0)$
2. $(A <= 1)$ AND (B NOT= 0)
3. $(A <= 1)$ AND $(B = 0)$
4. $(A > 1)$ AND (B NOT= 0)

Statement coverage requires that every decision is executed once. In the above example statement coverage requires only that the if..else statement be executed once. Therefore, if either sub-statement 1 or sub-statement 2 is executed, statement coverage is achieved— test case 1 (for example) is enough.

To achieve *branch coverage* the programmer must find test cases that will ensure that wherever there is a branch in the code, test data values exercise both routes through the branch; both sub-statement 1 and sub-statement 2 must be exercised. To achieve branch coverage requires test case 1 and any one of the other three test cases. Branch coverage does not insist that both parts of the predicate ((A>1) and (B=0)) be exercised in each condition (true and false).

Condition coverage requires that both parts of the predicate be tested in both conditions. To achieve condition coverage all four test cases would be required. This will achieve the combination of conditions:

A>1		**B=0**
True	and	True
False	and	False
False	and	True
True	and	False

Coverage analysis measures the thoroughness with which code has been tested. Typically code will be considered to be adequately tested if testing achieves 100% statement coverage and 85% branch coverage.

10.2 Special requirements for testing O-O software

In testing O-O systems the three traditional code testing phases—unit testing, integration testing and system testing—map on to class testing, object integration testing and system testing. System testing is done from the users' point of view using a black box approach; the software design paradigm is therefore immaterial. The differences between traditional and O-O system testing are in the class and object integration phases.

10.2.1 Class/object testing

Unit testing of O-O systems normally means class testing, which in practice means testing instantiations of the class concerned. With any unit testing, the larger the unit the more complicated its testing will be. In traditional systems the unit being tested is most often a single function or procedure. Unit testing in O-O systems is inevitably a more complex and involved process as the basic unit is larger: a class will normally comprise several methods, attribute values, an inheritance burden and relationships with other classes.

Unit testing of O-O software, therefore, needs to take into account certain features not normally part of traditional unit testing:

- encapsulated state
- method interaction
- inheritance and polymorphism.

Encapsulated state Operations cannot be tested in isolation as their behaviour may be affected by the object's current attribute value—its state. For example a method `withdrawCash` on a bank account object may produce different results depending on the current value of the `amountInAccount` attribute; certain types of bank account do not permit the customer to overdraw. We need to check that methods interact correctly with the object's data—that a deposit method does actually update the amount by the required figure and that its value persists between method calls.

Method interaction An object's methods need to be tested in relation to one another to check that they interact correctly. We need to know for example what happens if we try to withdraw money from an account before that account has had a deposit, or before it has been opened.

Inheritance There seems to be general agreement in O-O literature that if inheritance is used properly then unchanged features inherited from a parent class do not need to be re-tested in a child class. Inheritance is used correctly only if a proper IS-A relationship exists between parent and child classes (see Chapter 2).

However, the tester will have to consider the following points even with unchanged inherited features:

- Abstract classes can only be tested indirectly—we can only test an abstract class by testing instances of its descendant specialized classes. In Figure 10.2 we revisit the family hierarchy we first met in Chapter 2. Let us assume that Person is an abstract class—it cannot be instantiated because (in our system) everyone in the family has to be an instantiation of one of the specialized classes. We can only test the Person class indirectly, therefore, by testing instantiations of the specialized classes and checking that inherited features work as we expect them to.
- Special test cases should be written just to test that the inheritance mechanism is working, e.g. that a child class can inherit from the parent and that we can create instances of the child class.

Even if the parent class is concrete, fully tested and partakes in a proper IS-A relationship with its specialized classes, there are circumstances under which we need to test inherited operations. If a class modifies an inherited instance variable which has an effect on how an inherited operation works, that operation needs to be retested. For instance, let us revisit the family hierarchy we first met in Chapter 2 (see Figure 10.2).

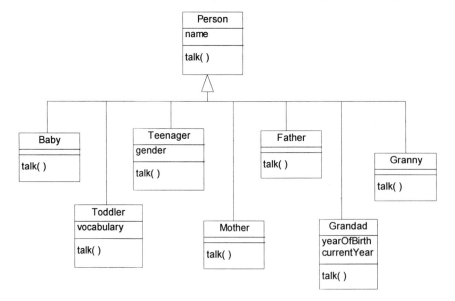

Figure 10.2 Family hierarchy

We invent a new class `PoliteToddler`, a specialization of `Toddler` (see Figure 10.3). `PoliteToddler` inherits unaltered the `Toddler` method for the `talk()`
operation.   However, the value of the attribute `vocabulary` is changed in the `PoliteToddler` class. The `PoliteToddler` class inherits from the `Toddler` class the attribute `vocabulary` and its value "Mama, NO". The `PoliteToddler` class adds to the value of `vocabulary` the words 'Please' and 'Thank you', so that the value of `vocabulary` becomes: 'Mama, NO, Please, Thank you'. The `talk()` method outputs the value of the attribute `vocabulary`.   As `vocabulary` is altered in the `PoliteToddler` class, the `PoliteToddler` version of the `talk()` method should be retested.

```
class Toddler extends Person
{
 String vocabulary;
 Toddler()
 {
  vocabulary = "Mama, NO";
 }
 void talk()
 {
  System.out.println("A Toddler shouts:" + vocabulary );
 }
}

class PoliteToddler extends Toddler
{
  PoliteToddler()
  {
  vocabulary = vocabulary + ", Please, Thank you";
  }
}
```

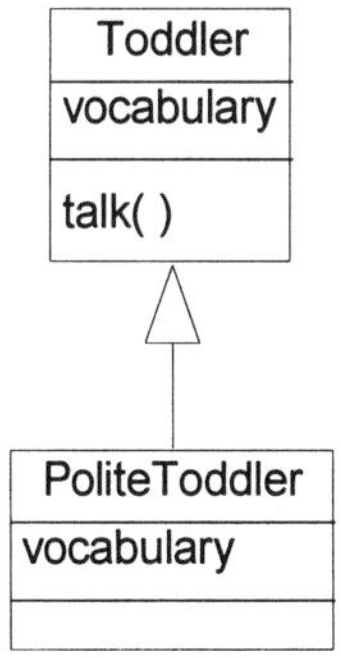

Figure 10.3 The PoliteToddler class diagram and Java code

If operations are changed or over-ridden they need to be re-tested. For example in Figure 10.2, we can see that the `talk()` method of the class `Person` is over-ridden in each of the specialized classes; the method will have to be tested in each class. Still assuming that the Person class is abstract, as none of its specialized classes inherit its method unchanged, we would have to write a special test case to test it. We could, for example, invent a class GreatAunt which inherits the Person talk() method unaltered. An instantiation of this class, GreatAunt Madeleine, when invited to talk, should respond "I'm not saying anything". A complete implementation of the family hierarchy can be found in Appendix E.

Polymorphism The use of polymorphism can produce beautifully elegant and compact code but it can also make testing more complicated. The identification of all of the paths through a section of code that uses polymorphism is harder because the criteria which indicate different paths are not specifically mentioned in the code as they are in procedural code.

For example let us look at the problems we could have in identifying all the test cases in a section of code which sends the message talk to an array of family members.

```
2001    for (i =0; i <8; i++)
2002    {
2003      familyMember[i].talk;
2004    }
```

This section of code, on its own, gives the tester no information about which classes are involved. The tester will have to do some detective work before he or she can identify all the test cases required to test these lines of code adequately. In this case, the population of the array familyMember[] would have to be examined.

```
0101    Person familyMember[];        //declare array of Person objects
0102
0103    familyMember = new Person[8];    //assign memory for 8 person objects

0104    // populate the array

0105    familyMember[0]=new  Mother();
0106    familyMember[1]=new  Granny();
0107    familyMember[2]=new  Teenager('F');
0108    familyMember[3]=new  Teenager('M');
0109    familyMember[4]=new  Baby();
0110    familyMember[5]=new  Father();
0111    familyMember[6]=new  Grandad("2000", "1902");
0112    familyMember[7]=new  Toddler();
```

This code sets up and populates an array of family members. Provided the tester locates this array, he or she can see which test cases to use. However, these lines might easily be separated from the code which uses the array.

To do the same thing in a conventional programming language (which does not use polymorphism), we would have to name the classes involved. The code would look something like:

```
for  (i =0;  i <8; i++)
{
switch (familyMember[i])
{
case Mother: Mother.talk();  break;
case Granny: Granny.talk();  break;
case Teenager('F'): FemaleTeenager.talk();  break;
case Teenager('M'): MaleTeenager.talk();  break;
case Baby: baby.talk();  break;
case Father:father.talk();  break;
case Grandad: Grandad.talk();  break;
case Toddler: Toddler.talk();  break;
}
}
```

This makes clumsier code than the elegant polymorphic version, but it does clearly identify the different test cases.

In the O-O version, if we substitute `PoliteToddler` for `Toddler` in the familyMember array the code that exercises the array (lines 2001–2004) does not need to changed. However, as a new path has been introduced, it should be re-tested.

Although there are not yet agreed standards for testing O-O systems, it is generally accepted that the class testing phase should test each method, method to method interaction, encapsulated state and the inheritance structure of the class.

10.2.2 Object integration testing

Object integration testing has the same purpose as traditional unit integration testing: to check that units (objects) which worked when tested in isolation still work when combined with other units. A logical group or cluster of objects is identified and tested; this cluster is then combined with others until the whole system is combined and tested. A cluster may be a group of objects that work together to fulfil a function or form a sub-system, or it may be a group of objects that are used in the execution of a use case. Object integration has been identified as one of the greatest causes of faults in O-O systems, therefore thorough testing at this level is very important.

Use cases and scenarios (see Chapter 6) are a useful source of test cases; the complete set of scenarios identified during requirements elicitation will provide all of the test cases required for black box testing of the system. During the integration phase we can begin to test some of the functionality specified in the use cases and identify the different paths through a group of objects. The number of different paths through the objects increases exponentially when they are combined and tested as a cluster. Failures will appear that were impossible to detect at class testing level. Integration testing can be a daunting experience for the tester of a system with several thousand classes.

The bonus for the tester of O-O systems is that incremental integration is easy to achieve—small clusters of objects can be thoroughly tested and certified before being combined with other certified clusters. Another benefit is that in O-O systems the interfaces between objects are clearly defined, which avoids undocumented and problematic links between objects.

10.2.3 Coverage criteria

Testing of O-O systems is still too immature for industry to make confident rulings about coverage criteria: how much testing is required for a system to be considered safe. Researchers and O-O theorists have proposed bases for calculating minimal requirements in class testing. For example, the McCabe complexity metric has been used to define the number of test cases that should be applied to each method (McCabe, 1994). However, there are unresolved problems with such metrics and their use in the calculation of the amount of testing required. Only accumulated experience combined with the rigorous analysis of faults found in working systems will bring the required confidence.

Exercises

10.1   To test the boundary conditions of the program fragment:

```
i = 1;
while (i <= 10)
{
//      sub-statement 1;
i = i + 1;
}
```

a)   What values of i would you test to convince yourself that the loop was working under normal conditions?

b)   What abnormal values of i would you test to be sure that the upper and lower loop boundaries were functioning properly?

10.2   Consider the program fragment:

```
if (A==TRUE)
{
// sub-statement 1
}
else
{
// sub-statement 2
}
```

and the two test cases:

i)   A==TRUE

ii)   A==FALSE.

Which of the test cases must be used to give statement coverage? Which of the test cases must be used to give branch coverage?

10.3   Consider the program fragment:

```
if (A OR B)
{
// sub-statement 1
}
else
{
// sub-statement 2
}
```

and the test cases:

i)   A==FALSE   B==FALSE
ii)   A==FALSE   B==TRUE
iii)   A==TRUE   B==FALSE
iv)   A==TRUE   B==TRUE.

Which of the test cases must be used to give:

a)   statement coverage
b)   branch coverage
c)   condition coverage?

10.4   Consider the program fragment:

```
if ((A > 1) AND (B > 0))
{
// sub-statement 1
}
else
{
// sub-statement 2
}
```

Devise test cases to ensure:

a)   statement coverage
b)   branch coverage
c)   condition coverage.

References and further reading

Firesmith, D. *Testing Object-Oriented Software,* Proceedings of TOOLS, March 1993.

Harrold, M.J., McGregor, J. and Fitzpatrick, K. *Incremental Testing of Object-Oriented Class Structure,* 14th Conference on Software Engineering, 1992.

Huffman Hayes, J., *Testing of Object-Oriented Programming Systems: A Fault Based Approach,* Proceedings. of the International Symposium on O-O Methodologies and Systems, ed. Bertino and Urb, 1994.

Jacobson, I., Christerson, M., Jonsson, P. and Overgaard, G. *Object-Oriented Software Engineering: A Use Case Driven Approach,* Wokingham: Addison-Wesley, 1992.

Kaner, K., Falk, J. and Nguyen, H.Q. *Testing Computer Software,* 2nd edn., Boston: International Thomson Computer Press, 1993.

McCabe, T., Dreyer, A., Dunn, A. and Watson, A. 'Testing an Object-Oriented Application', *The Quality Journal,* October 1994.

Myers, G.J. *Software Reliability: Principles & Practices,* New York: John Wiley and Sons, 1976.

Myers, G.J. *The Art of Software Testing,* New York: John Wiley and Sons, 1979.

Wirfs-Brock, R., Wilkerson, B. and Wiener, L. *Designing Object-Oriented Software,* Englewood Cliffs, N.J.: Prentice Hall, 1990

Appendix A: Background material for the case study

Background to the case study: the _Just a Line_ security problem

Just a Line is a company that designs and sells greeting cards for all occasions. The company was founded in the early 1990's by Harry and Sue Preston to sell their own card designs by mail order, but has grown so rapidly that _Just a Line_ products have now taken over a large share of the market, both at home and abroad. Much of this success is due to Harry's flair for innovative ideas and understanding the market; his edible cards and non-crease wrapping paper have been especially popular, while the 'Juvenile Jokes' and 'Tasteless Titters' card ranges are regular best sellers. Sue, meanwhile, has been in charge of managing the company, making sure that profits are healthy, staff happy and that everything runs smoothly.

On the whole, things are going well and recently _Just a Line_ has moved into large new premises on the edge of town. Sue's only problem at present concerns security at the new company site. A few months ago _Just a Line's_ new line of 'touchy-feely' card sculptures was scooped by _Global Greetings,_ a rival company. Harry is devastated that his ideas have been stolen, and is convinced that there must have been a leak from someone inside _Just a Line_. He wants to tighten security, so that management can see which employees are in the _Just a Line_ building at any time and casual visitors are discouraged from wandering around the site.

Sue is sympathetic to Harry's point of view and agrees that stricter security is needed, but she is worried that new security measures may be unpopular with the staff, many of whom have been with them since the early days of _Just a Line_. She decides to talk to D&B Systems, the company who developed the original computer system for _Just a Line_, to discuss the situation and see what solutions might be available. During the past few years, D&B have expanded from business application software, such as the system they developed for _Just a Line,_ into computer security products and integrated security systems providing computerized control of buildings and site access.

Plan for the first interview with Sue and Harry from *Just a Line*

D&B Systems – Interview Plan			
System: *Just a Line*		**Project reference:** JaL/MB/00	
Participants:	Sue Preston (*Just a Line*) Harry Preston (*Just a Line*) Mark Barnes (D&B)		
Date: 10/4/00	**Time:** 14.30	**Duration:** 45 minutes	**Place:** Sue's office

Purpose of interview:
Preliminary meeting to identify problems and requirements regarding security at the *Just a Line* site.

Agenda:
- problems with security and any other concerns
- current security procedures
- initial ideas
- follow-up actions

Documents to be brought to interview:
- rough plan of building and site
- any documents relating to current security procedures

Initial interview between Sue and Harry Preston of *Just a Line* and Mark Barnes of D&B Software.

Sue: Hello, Mark, good to see you. Come and sit down.

Harry: Hello again. It must be quite a while since we last met; I expect you'll notice a few changes.

Mark: Hello there. Yes this is certainly different from your other place; you've come a long way. Mind you, I'm not surprised, I see your cards all over the place nowadays.

Harry: Excellent—we've been trying really hard to increase our market share and I think we're doing OK at the moment. Of course, the hard thing is to keep one step ahead all the time. You get a winning idea—like those edible cards for example, they've been brilliant – but then you have to think up something else that's just as good, if not better. You can't relax for a minute.

Sue: Yes, you can see why it was such a blow when *Global Greetings* produced their card sculptures just weeks before ours were due to come out. And they are so similar; it's absolutely sickening. Harry and his group worked incredibly hard for months on that line and we were counting on them being something really different when they hit the market.

Harry: Well, I can't believe it's a coincidence. I mean, just look at this site; anyone can wander in and out at any time more or less as they please. Of course, we know our own employees, and we do get a lot of bona fide visitors, but you are always seeing people around that you don't recognize, and really, it could be anyone. We even get locals using our car park, just because it's free and convenient for the new shopping centre opposite.

Mark: I think that's what you wanted to talk to me about, isn't it—security on the site, I mean?

Sue: Well, basically yes, we do need to tighten up on security, but at the same time I really think it's very important that we don't antagonize the staff, or make them think that we don't trust them. We don't know how *Global Greetings* got wind of our card sculptures, but I honestly can't believe any of our staff would have told them.

Harry: Most people here have been with us for quite a while, we have a friendly, informal, hard-working atmosphere and we don't want to spoil that, by bringing in draconian measures that will just get up people's noses.

Mark: Yes, I can see that; it's a bit of a problem, but I'm sure we can work round it. Can you just give me a brief idea of what security procedures you have at the moment?

Sue: Well, not a lot really. There's Jane on reception—that's on the left as you come in. But the site's a funny sort of shape, with the building on a corner, then the delivery area next to it and the car park off to the side opposite the shopping precinct. Look I've drawn it for you.

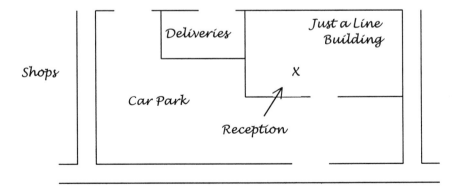

Mark: OK, I see. Can you give me some idea of how many of your employees use their cars to get to work?

Harry: Well most of them I should think, but I'm afraid I couldn't give you an exact number at the moment. We've got ninety-six people on the staff here if that's any help to you.

Mark: Right, and can people drive in and out of both the car park entrances, or is it one way?

Sue: No, you can come in and out of either entrance and park wherever you can find a space. It's all pretty casual.

Harry: That's another problem we've got. Staff come and go quite a bit during an average day, going to see customers, meetings off site etc. Then, when they get back here, they often can't find a space because the car park's full of shoppers. It's extra irritating because the car park is an odd sort of L-shape, so you have to drive right round it just in case there's a space you've missed. It's a terrible waste of time.

Mark: Does anyone check the cars that are parked on site during the day?

Sue: Jane on reception has a list of employees' cars. Here's a copy for you. She's supposed to go out two or three times during the day to make sure that only our staff cars are in the car park and slap a notice on any that are nothing to do with *Just a Line*. Trouble is, that doesn't really have much effect and we haven't thought about what to do when we find cars that aren't part of the company, but that keep using our car park. And that's when Jane actually goes out and checks—I'm sure she spends most of the day on the phone to that dopey boyfriend in marketing.

Harry: Now, that's not really fair, Sue. Jane's quite an asset. A lot of our customers like the image she projects.

Sue: A lot of our customers like . . . . sorry, Mark, we seem to be wandering from the point rather.

Mark: What about Jane's other duties? You said she's on reception, so does that mean that she checks people coming in and out of the building?

Sue: Well she knows our staff, and visitors are supposed to report to her when they arrive. You can see from the diagram, though, where she sits is a bit out of the way and she is on the main switchboard as well, so really it would be dead easy for someone to walk in and she wouldn't notice. Actually, it would be dead easy for someone to be standing right in front of her and she wouldn't notice!

Mark: So, let's see. It looks as if you've got two problems: you've got to tighten up a bit on security, though you have to be careful that you don't offend your staff, and you want to keep outsiders from using your car park.

Sue: Yes, that's pretty much it, except that, of course, it would be nice to have something in place as soon as possible. I expect you're used to clients saying that, aren't you, but I am a bit worried about things. It's not just the security side. What about our legal liability if someone gets injured in our car park, even if they're not supposed to be there?

Mark: Well, I think there are a couple of things that you can do straight away. First of all, why don't you move Jane's desk out into the foyer, facing the main entrance? It would look more welcoming and give her a much better view of who is coming and going. Then, look at the car park; at the moment people can drive in and out of either entrance, which isn't a good idea. There's no reason why you can't make one of the car park entrances for coming in only and the other for exits. The entrance would be the one near the front of the building and the exit the one in the far corner. That would make it impossible for shoppers to pop in and out the back way. Look I'll show you what I mean on the drawing you did for me.

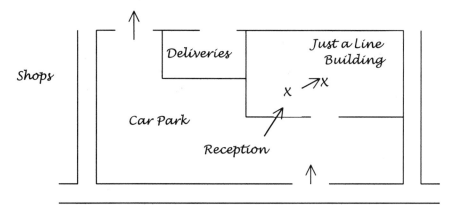

Sue: Yes, I see. I think that would help. It would take a lot more brass neck to drive into the car park through the main entrance than to slip in and out at the back where nobody can see you.

Harry: And I like the idea of putting Jane in a more central position. I think she'd enjoy it and it would certainly be harder for casual visitors to wander around the building.

Sue: And it would be easier for us to see what she gets up to all day. Those ideas are both fine for now, they'll be an improvement, but, on the other hand, I don't think they'll solve our problems in the long term.

Mark: No, you will have to do more than move Jane's desk and put up a few notices in the car park, but I'd like a bit of time to think about the best way to approach this. Obviously you could go for a sophisticated system with swipe cards for employees that allow entry into different parts of the building, but my gut feeling is that that would be overkill in your case. I think the answer is to start by seeing what we can do with the car park. Keeping your staff happy is a very important issue, so I'd like to arrange to talk to one or two of your employees, you know, chat to them about how they would feel about added security on site and also whether they have problems with car parking.

Sue: Yes, of course, that's no problem. I should think Annie Raines would be a good person to start with. She's been doing the accounts for us since shortly after we started *Just a Line* and she's definitely someone that I want to keep on side. I'll have a word with her and tell her you'll be contacting in the next few days.

Mark: Thanks, and there's another thing. I need to get a much more accurate idea of how many of your employees use their cars for work and how the car park is actually used during the day. Would it be OK with you if I circulate a simple questionnaire to all staff? It wouldn't take them any time to fill it in and it would give them the feeling that they are being consulted.

Sue: Of course, we can get Jane to give them out and collect in the replies if you like. I think she can just about manage that.

Mark: So finally, could we fix up another meeting to talk about the next stage when I've had a chat to Annie and got the questionnaire information—say in about 10 days time?

Harry: Yes, good idea. Sue'll fix that up for you and in the meantime come along and I'll introduce you to Jane.

Questionnaire to investigate use of the car park at *Just a Line*.

D&B Systems – Car park survey for *Just a Line*

We have commissioned D&B Systems to investigate use of the company car park and current problems, so that the present system can be improved. This is your car park and we would like your opinion on how it should be organized. Please spare a few minutes to answer the questions below and return the form to Jane in reception by Friday 14th April.

Please circle your answers to the following questions:

1. How many times a week do you use your car to get to and from work?
    never / once or twice / two or three times / every day / no regular pattern

2. Which car park entrance do you normally use to come into the car park?
    main entrance / back entrance / either

3. Which car park entrance do you normally use to leave the car park?
    main entrance / back entrance / either

4. How often do you need to use your car for work during the day?
    never / rarely / about once a day / two or three times a day / no regular pattern

5. Do you have problems finding a space in the car park?
    never / sometimes / frequently / always

6. If you have problems finding a space, when does this usually happen?
    at the start of work / during the morning / lunchtime / during the afternoon /
    at the end of the day / no regular pattern

7. Would you like to see more security in the car park?
    yes / no / don't mind

8. Please note below any comments you have on the current car parking system.
    _____
    _____
    _____

9. Please note below any suggestions for improving the car parking at *Just a Line*.
    _____
    _____
    _____

Your name: _____

Your department: _____

Thank you for completing this questionnaire.

Summary of the initial interview with Sue and Harry Preston of *Just a Line*

D&B Systems – Interview Summary			
System: *Just a Line*		**Project reference:** JaL/MB/00	
Participants:	Sue Preston (*Just a Line*) Harry Preston (*Just a Line*) Mark Barnes (D&B)		
Date: 10/4/00	**Time:** 14.30	**Duration:** 45 minutes	**Place:** Sue's office
Purpose of interview: Preliminary meeting to identify problems and requirements regarding security at the *Just a Line* site.			

No.	Item	Action
1	Very little security at present, both in building and on site.	
2	Lack of security on site appears to have allowed leaks about designs.	
3	Any new security measures must not offend staff.	Interview some staff members (start with Annie Raines).
4	Receptionist not in central position in entrance to building.	Move receptionist's desk to foyer, facing main entrance.
5	Staff often need to use cars during the day; problem finding a space when they get back.	
6	Not clear exactly how staff use car park.	Ask staff to fill in questionnaire on car park usage.
7	Car park frequently used by people not connected to company (close to shopping centre and no charge).	
8	Two entrances to car park (one opposite shopping centre). No route system in car park.	Introduce one-way system; entrance to car park via front only.
9	No penalty for unauthorized parking.	
10	Impossible to tell if car park is full without driving round it.	
11	Further discussions needed when more info. available.	Arrange follow-up meeting with Sue and Harry (in about 10 days' time).

Part of the *Just a Line* car park list for April 2000

Just a Line Car Park List						April 2000
Name	**Dept.**	**Ext.**	**Car make**	**Model**	**Number**	**Colour**
Sue Preston		361	Renault	Clio	P409 JPG	red
Harry Preston		360	Porsche	Carrera	JAL 1	silver
Annie Raines	Accounts	579	Volvo	340	H53 KJN	white
Chris Doolan	Design	488	VW	Golf	R401 CDV	grey
Chris Doolan	Design	488	Renault	Espace	L43 JKB	green
Sam Parker	Marketing	640	Peugeot	406	R339 BJS	blue
Mira Patel	Marketing	636	Ford	Mondeo	T324 TSS	red
....	....	....	....	....	....	....
....	....	....	....	....	....	....

Prototype identity card for *Just a Line* staff

Just a Line **Staff Identity Card**

Name: _____   Photo

Department: _____

Employee Number: _____

A requirement from the *Just a Line* system in tabular form

No.	Source	Date	Description	Priority	Related Reqs.	Alter-native Reqs.	Related Docs.	Change Details
4.4	Meeting with Sue & Harry Preston	10/4/00	Ensure that only staff and visitors are able to use the car park.	E	2.9 4.6		List of staff car nos.	

A brief description of the *Just a Line* car park problem

Just a Line management wishes to increase security, both in their building and on site, without antagonizing their employees. They would also like to prevent people who are not part of the company from using the *Just a Line* car park.

It has been decided to issue identity cards to all employees, which they are expected to wear while on the *Just a Line* site. The cards record the name, department and number of the member of staff, and permit access to the *Just a Line* car park.

A barrier and a card reader are placed at the entrance to the car park. The driver of an approaching car inserts his or her numbered card in the card reader, which then checks that the card number is known to the *Just a Line* system. If the card is recognized, the reader sends a signal to raise the barrier and the car is able to enter the car park.

At the exit, there is also a barrier, which is raised when a car wishes to leave the car park.

When there are no spaces in the car park a sign at the entrance displays "Full" and is only switched off when a car leaves.

Special visitors' cards, which record a number and the current date, also permit access to the car park. Visitors' cards may be sent out in advance, or collected from reception. All visitors' cards must be returned to reception when the visitor leaves *Just a Line.*

Exercises

A.1   List some of the questions that Mark Barnes could ask Annie Raines during his interview with her about parking problems and added security on the *Just a Line* site.

A.2   Design a questionnaire to be given to the employees at *Just a Line* to gather information on how they would feel about extra security measures in the building and around the site.

A.3   Organize a future workshop with a small group of people to identify initialrequirements for a full security system for *Just a Line.* The workshop should cover the three stages of critique, fantasy and implementation. Details about future workshops can be found in Chapter 4, Section 4.3.1.

Appendix B: Models for the car park system

This appendix contains the collected set of analysis and design diagrams from which the Java code was derived. They are reproduced here for ease of reference.

Analysis model

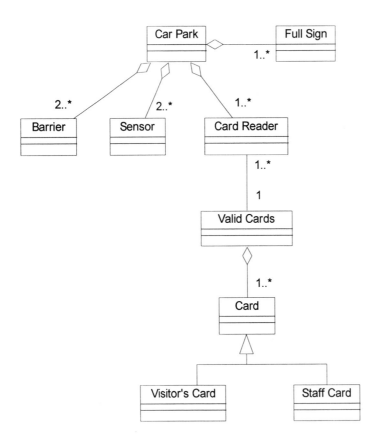

Class diagram for the *Just a Line* car park system at the analysis stage

Initial data dictionary

Car Park: represents the physical car park and keeps count of the number of spaces available.

Staff Card: a card, issued to a member of the *Just a Line* staff, that records the staff member's number, name and department. The number uniquely identifies the member of staff within *Just a Line*. The card also permits access to the *Just a Line* car park.

Visitor's Card: a card, which permits access to the *Just a Line* car park, given to someone visiting the company. The card records a number and the current date. Visitors' cards may be sent out in advance or collected from reception, and all cards must be returned to reception when the visitor leaves *Just a Line*.

Card Reader: a machine that reads a card that is input and checks the card number against a list of valid numbers. If the card is valid, the reader sends a signal to raise the barrier.

Barrier: a bar, which raises or lowers itself according to signals received from either one of its associated sensors, or from the card reader.

Sensor: a device for detecting the presence of a car

Informal descriptions of some of the classes in the *Just a Line* car park problem

Data dictionary

Barrier = Barrier type + up
    Barrier type = ["Entrance " | "Exit "]
    up = ["True " | "False "]
    raise: If the barrier is not already raised, this operation takes as argument an object of the Barrier class and returns an object of the same class, with the up attribute set to "True ". If the barrier is already up, the operation returns the error message "Barrier already raised ".
    lower: If the barrier is not already lowered, this operation takes as argument an object of the Barrier class and returns an object of the same class, with the up attribute set to "False ". If the barrier is already down, the operation returns the error message "Barrier already lowered".

Card = number + [Staff Card | Visitor's Card]
delete: This operation removes the card from the set of cards known to *Just a Line*.

Card Reader = location
read card: This operation takes a card number as input and checks it against the set of numbers of known cards in the Valid Cards class.

Car Park = capacity + spaces
capacity = *the total number of parking places in the car park*
spaces = *the number of currently free spaces in the car park*
inc. spaces: This operation checks that the car park is not empty (the number of spaces left is not equal to the capacity of the car park). If this is the case, the value of 'spaces' is incremented by 1.

dec. spaces: This operation checks that the value of the attribute 'spaces' in the car park is greater than 0. If this is the case, the value of 'spaces' is decremented by 1. If this results in there being no spaces left, the Full Sign is turned on.

Full Sign = location + on
on = ["True " | "False "]
switch on:
switch off:

Sensor = car sensed
car sensed = ["True " | "False "]
sense car: If a car is detected by the sensor, this operation sets the car sensed attribute to "True ".

Staff Card = name + dept. + expiry date
name = first name + last name
dept. = ["Accounts " | "Design " | "Marketing " | "Administration "]
expiry date = *date after which card is no longer valid*
delete: If the expiry date on the card has passed, this operation removes the card number from the list of cards known to *Just a Line*.

Valid Cards = known cards *the set of cards whose numbers are recognized by *Just a Line*.*

Visitor's Card = current date *date that the card is issued*
delete: If the date on the card has passed, this operation removes the card number from the list of cards known to *Just a Line*.

Part of a data dictionary for the *Just a Line* car park

Analysis model (continued)

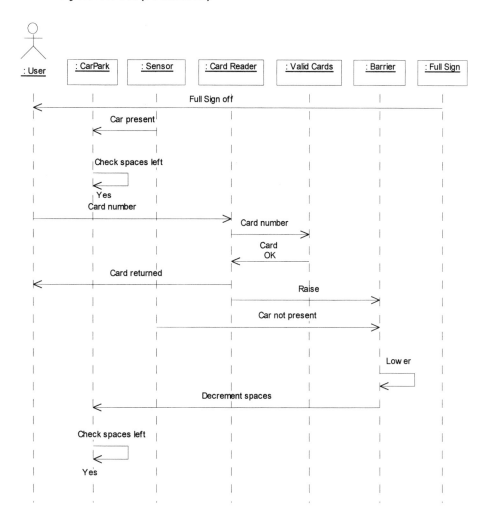

Sequence diagram for the happy day Enter car park scenario

Analysis model (continued)

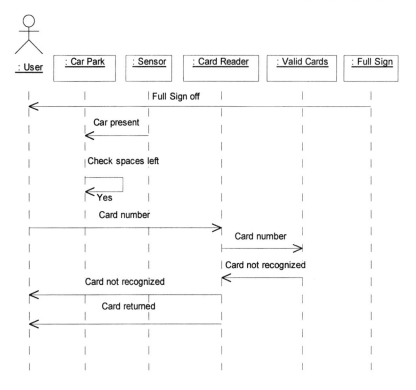

Sequence diagram for scenario where the card that is inserted is not recognized

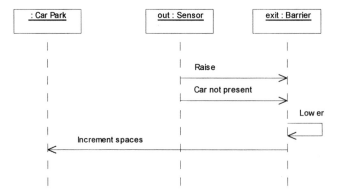

Fragment of sequence diagram showing behaviour of exit barrier

Design model

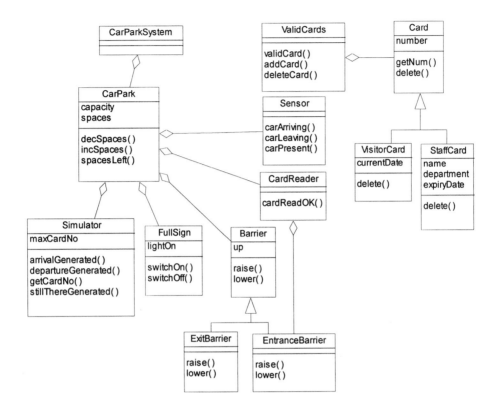

Car park simulation class diagram showing all classes

Design Model (continued)

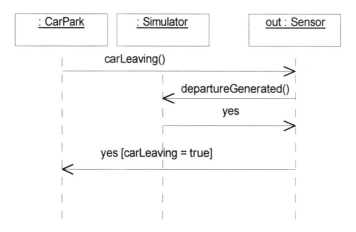

Sequence diagram showing how the Simulator is used to simulate car departures

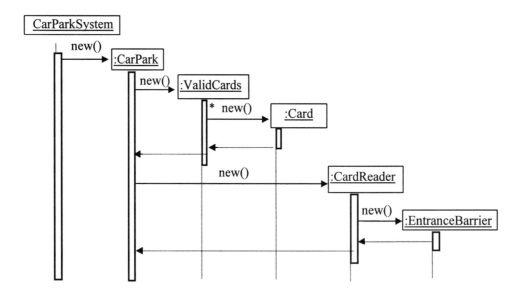

Notation for object creation

Design Model (continued)

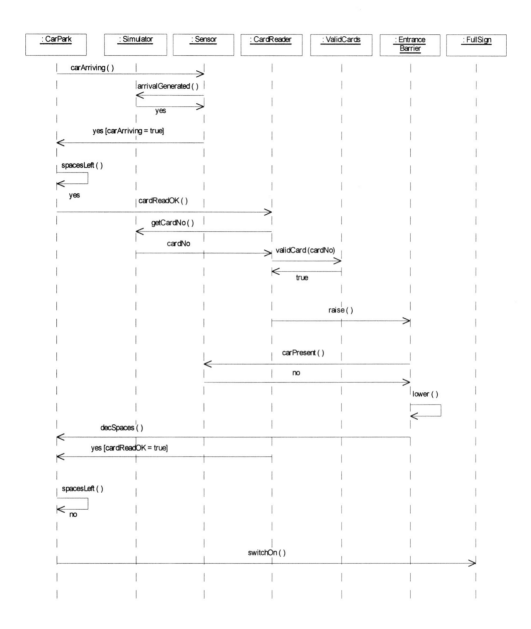

Sequence diagram for 'Enter car park', with Full sign turned on after car arrives.

Exercises

B.1   In a full security system for *Just a Line,* there would be a class Employee. List sample attributes and operations for this class.

B.2   Write a scenario to describe what happens when a car leaves the *Just a Line* car park and there are no unusual circumstances.

B.3   Draw a sequence diagram to illustrate the scenario you wrote for Exercise B.2.

B.4   Write a scenario to describe what happens when a car leaves the full *Just a Line* car park and the Full sign turns off.

B.5   Draw a sequence diagram to illustrate the scenario you wrote for Exercise B.4.

B.6   Draw a collaboration diagram for the scenario you wrote in Exercise B.4.

B.7   To standardize a future housekeeping routine for deletion of out-of-date cards, the dates on StaffCard and VisitorCard have both been implemented as expiryDate. Redraw the relevant part of the design model car park simulation class diagram to show how it can be improved by efficient use of inheritance.

B.8   Draw a state diagram to illustrate the behaviour of the `EntranceBarier` class.

Appendix C: Java code for the *Just a Line* car park simulation

List of file names

The Java files are listed in the following order:

CarParkSystem.java
CarPark.java
ValidCards.java
Card.java
StaffCard.java
VisitorCard.java
CardReader.java
Barrier.java
EntranceBarrier.java
ExitBarrier.java
Sensor.java
FullSign.java
Simulator.java

CarParkSystem.java

```java
/* Main driver class for Car Park simulation */

public class CarParkSystem
{
  public static CarPark aCarPark;

  public static void main(String[] args)

  {
    // set up car park with 1 entrance, 1 exit,
    // 5 spaces, 3 of which are full initially
    aCarPark = new CarPark(1,1,5,3);
  }
}
```

CarPark.java

```
/* Class representing Car Park */

public class CarPark
{
  private int capacity;           // max number of spaces
  private int spaces;             // actual spaces
  Sensor inSensor;                // sensors for entry/exit
  Sensor outSensor;
  ExitBarrier outBarrier;         // barrier for exit
  ValidCards currentCards;        // list of valid cards
  CardReader mainCardReader;      // card reader at entry
  FullSign fullLight;

  public CarPark(int noExits, int noEnts, int inCapacity, int noSpaces)
  {
    Simulator.setMaxCardNo(10);   // set max number for attempted cards
    capacity = inCapacity;        // give value to capacity
    spaces = noSpaces;            // and to spaces
    currentCards = new ValidCards();   // create list of valid cards
    mainCardReader = new CardReader(this, currentCards); // create card reader

    // 'this' is the standard Java term used to refer to the class currently being defined

    inSensor = new Sensor();      // create sensors
    outSensor = new Sensor();
    fullLight = new FullSign();
    outBarrier = new ExitBarrier(this);   // create exit barrier
    for(int carNo = 0; carNo<50; carNo++) // simulate for 50 cars
    {
      if (inSensor.carArriving()) // if next event is car arrival
      {
        System.out.print("\nCar Arriving ");
        if (spacesLeft())         // if room in park
        {
          if (mainCardReader.cardReadOK()) // if valid card entered
          { // the card reader will handle car's entry
            if (!spacesLeft())    // switch on full light if full
              fullLight.switchOn();
            fullLight.display();  // displays full sign status
          }
        }
        else
          System.out.print("No entry - Car Park Full ");
      };
```

```java
        if (spaces != capacity && outSensor.carLeaving())//if car park not empty
                                //and exit simulated


    {
      System.out.print("\nCar Leaving ");
      outBarrier.raise();
      if (spaces == 1)        // if only space is one just vacated
        fullLight.switchOff(); // switch off full sign
      fullLight.display();    // display full sign status
    }
  }
}


public void decSpaces()
{
  spaces = spaces -1;
  System.out.print("Spaces left = " + spaces + " ");
}

public void incSpaces()
{
  // add 1 to spaces available
  spaces = spaces + 1;
  System.out.print("Spaces left = " + spaces + " ");
}

public boolean spacesLeft()
{
  // indicates if space available
  if (spaces > 0)
  {
    return true;
  }
  else
  {
    System.out.print("No spaces left ");
    return false;
  }
 }
}
```

ValidCards.java

```java
/* Class representing list of valid cards */
public class ValidCards
{
Card knownCards[];  // list of valid cards
 int i;

  ValidCards()
  {
   // set up list of known cards. Better system would store in
   // e.g. linked list or file
   knownCards = new Card[8];   // assign memory for 8 valid cards
   // add 6 staff cards
   knownCards[0] = new StaffCard("Fred","Sales","17-11-1999",1);
   knownCards[1] = new StaffCard("Sue","Sales","21-03-2001",2);
   knownCards[2] = new StaffCard("Frank","Research","03-06-2000",3);
   knownCards[3] = new StaffCard("Mary","Testing","29-02-2000",4);
   knownCards[4] = new StaffCard("Bill","Research","05-12-2000",5);
   knownCards[5] = new StaffCard("Jill","Testing","13-01-2000",6);
   // add 2 visitors' cards
   knownCards[6] = new VisitorCard();
   knownCards[7] = new VisitorCard();
  }

  public boolean validCard(int cardNo)
  {
   boolean valid = false;   // initial value
   // search known cards to see if number corresponds
   for (i = 0;i < 8;i++)
   {
    if (knownCards[i].getNum() == cardNo)
    {
     valid = true;       // change to true when one is found
    }
   }
   if (valid)
   {
    System.out.print("Valid card " + cardNo + ". ");
    return true;
   }
   else
   {
    System.out.print("Invalid card " + cardNo + ". ");
    return false;
   }
  }
}
```

Card.java

```java
/* Parent class for cards */

public class Card
{
  int number;  //card number

  public Card(int num)
  {
    number = num;  // constructor copies parameter to number
  }

  int getNum()    // gives card number
  {
    return number;
  }

}
```

StaffCard.java

```java
/* StaffCard inherits the attribute number from Card.  StaffCard contains holder's name
and department and the card's expiry date. */

public class StaffCard extends Card
{
  String name;          // holder's name
  String department;    // holder's department
  String expiryDate;    // card's expiry date

  StaffCard(String belongsTo, String inDept, String expiresOn, int cardNo)
  {
    super(cardNo);        // call parent class constructor to assign card number
    name = belongsTo;     // StaffCard constructor copies parameter to name
    department = inDept;
    expiryDate = expiresOn;
  }
}
```

VisitorCard.java

```
/* VisitorCard inherits from Card */

public class VisitorCard extends Card
{
  String expiryDate;

  VisitorCard()                 // constructor
  {
    super(9);                   //call parent class constructor to set VisitorCard number
    expiryDate = "01-01-2000";  // today's date
  }
}
```

CardReader.java

```
/* Class representing Card reader  */
public class CardReader
{
  private ValidCards okCards;       // list of valid cards
  EntranceBarrier  inBarrier;       // barrier controlled by reader
  public CardReader(CarPark aCarPark, ValidCards centralList) //constructor
  {
    okCards = centralList;          // create association
    inBarrier = new EntranceBarrier(aCarPark);   // create aggregation
  }

  public boolean cardReadOK()     // is card valid?
  {
    int cardNo;               // number of card in machine

    cardNo = Simulator.getCardNo();  // simulate reading

    if (okCards.validCard(cardNo)) // validate card
    {
      inBarrier.raise();
      return true;              // let car in if ok
    }
    else
    {                          // deny entry
      System.out.print("Entry refused, invalid card number ");
      return false;
    }
  }
}
```

Barrier.java

```
/* Class to represent car park barrier
     parent class for entrance and exit barriers */

  public class Barrier

{
  boolean up = false;           // status of
    CarPark ownerCarPark;         // car park to which barrier belongs

    public Barrier(CarPark aCarPark)  // constructor
    {
      ownerCarPark = aCarPark;
    }

    public void raise()           // raise barrier
    {
      up = true;
      System.out.print("Barrier raised ");
    }

    void lower()                  // lower barrier
    {
      up = false;
      System.out.print("Barrier lowered ");
    }
}
```

EntranceBarrier.java

```
  /* Entrance Barrier class which specialises Barrier */

  public  class EntranceBarrier extends Barrier
  {
    public EntranceBarrier(CarPark aCarPark)
    {
      super(aCarPark);  // pass parameter to parent Barrier class
    }

    public void raise() // let a car in
    {
      super.raise();    // use parent's method to raise barrier
      while (ownerCarPark.inSensor.carPresent())
      {
        // do nothing - just wait
      }
```

```
    lower();

  }

  void lower()        // car is now in. 1 space fewer
  {
    super.lower();
    ownerCarPark.decSpaces();
  }
}
```

ExitBarrier.java

```
  /* Class for Exit Barrier */

public class ExitBarrier extends Barrier
  {
    public ExitBarrier(CarPark aCarPark)
    {
      super(aCarPark);
    }

    public void raise()   // let car leave
    {
      super.raise();
      while (ownerCarPark.outSensor.carPresent())
      {
        // do nothing - just wait
      }
      lower();
    }

    void lower()        // car has gone. 1 more space free
    {
      super.lower();
      ownerCarPark.incSpaces();
    }
  }
```

Sensor.java

```
  /* Class to indicate presence of a car at entrance or exit sensor */

  public class Sensor
  {
    public boolean carArriving() // simulated arrival of car
```

```
   {
 return (Simulator.arrivalGenerated());
   }

   public boolean carLeaving()   // simulated departure of car
   {
    return (Simulator.departureGenerated());
   }

   public boolean carPresent()   // simulates sensor detecting car
   {
    System.out.print("Car present.");
    return (Simulator.stillThereGenerated());
   }
  }
```

FullSign.java

```
  /* class for the Full sign */

class FullSign
{
 boolean lightOn;

 FullSign()
 {
  lightOn = false;  // initially
   }

   void switchOn()
   {
    lightOn = true;
   }

   void switchOff()
   {
    lightOn=false;
   }

   void display()
   {
    System.out.print("Full Light is ");
    if (lightOn)
     System.out.println("ON");
    else
     System.out.println("OFF");
   }
  }
```

Simulator.java

```java
/* Class to produce random arrivals, departures and card numbers */

public class Simulator
{

  static int maxCardNo;      // highest card number that could be issued

  public static void setMaxCardNo(int maxNo)
  {
    maxCardNo = maxNo;
  }

  public static boolean arrivalGenerated()
  {
    //This method returns true if an arrival has occurred
    return (Math.random() <= 0.7);    // 0.7 is empirical value
                // to give full range of car park states
  }

  public static boolean departureGenerated()
  {
    //This method returns true if a departure has occurred
    return (Math.random() > 0.7);   // as above
  }

  public static boolean stillThereGenerated()
  {
    //This method returns true if car is still detected by sensor
    return (Math.random() < 0.5);
  }

  public static int getCardNo()
  // generates a card number at random
  {
    return (int)(maxCardNo*Math.random());
  }
}
```

Appendix D: Summary of UML notation

Class

Class Name

Class Name
name : type
opname( )

Example

Car
fuel speed temperature
stop( ) start( ) move forward( ) reverse( )

Object

ObjectName : Class
attribute = aribute value attribute = attribute value attribute = attribute value

Example

Jemima : Car
fuel = 6.4 litres speed = 32 mph temperature = cool

Association

Example

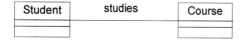

Multiplicities

Examples

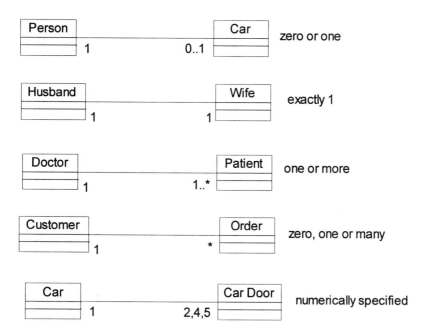

Aggregation

Example

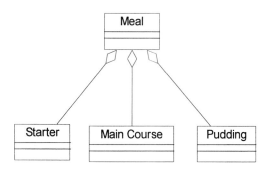

Navigability

Example

Inheritance

Example

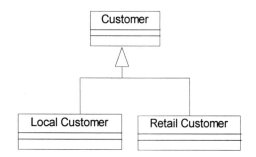

Use case diagram

Example

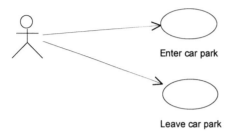

Enter car park

Leave car park

Sequence diagram

Examples

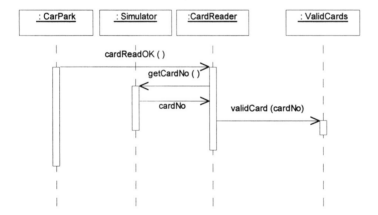

Sequence diagram showing object creation

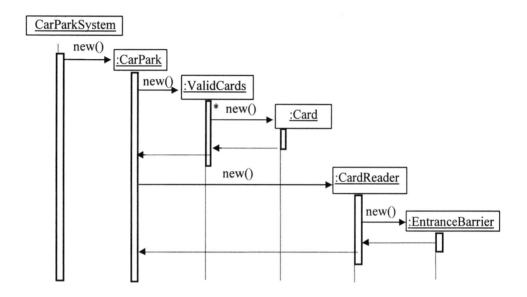

Sequence diagram showing object deletion

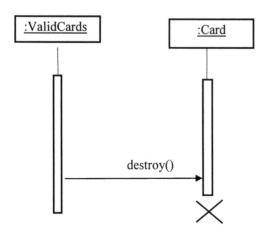

Collaboration diagram

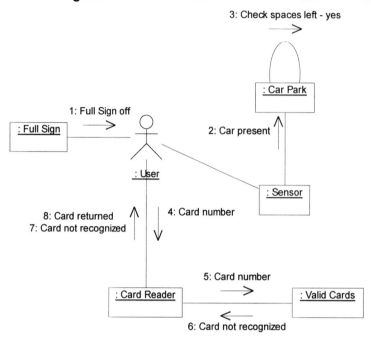

State diagram

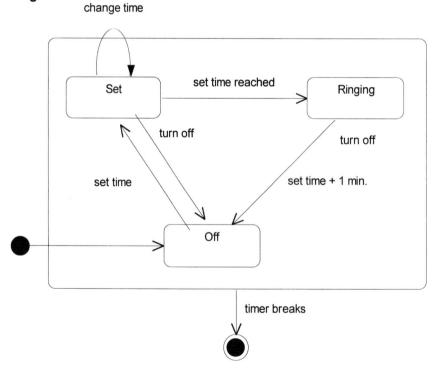

Appendix E: Java code for the family hierarchy example

```java
import java.lang.String;

class Person
{
 String name;

  Person()
  {

  }

  void talk()
  {
    System.out.println("A Person says: I'm not saying anything ");
  }
}

class Baby extends Person

{
 Baby()
  {
  }

  void talk()
  {
    System.out.println("A Baby cries: Wah, Wah ");
  }
}

class Toddler extends Person
{
  String vocabulary;

  Toddler()
  {
   vocabulary = "Mama, NO ";
  }

  void talk()
  {
   System.out.println("A Toddler shouts: " + vocabulary);
  }
}
```

```java
class Teenager extends Person
{
  char gender;

  Teenager(char sex)
  {
   gender=sex;
  }

  void talk()
  {
   if (gender=='M' || gender =='m')
     System.out.println("A male teenager says: Grunt, Grunt ");
   else
     System.out.println("A female teenager says: Where's my mascara? ");
  }
}

class Mother extends Person
{
  Mother()
  {
  }

  void talk()
  {
    System.out.println("A Mother says: Have you tidied your room? ");
  }
}

class Father extends Person
{
  Father()
  {
  }

  void talk()
  {
    System.out.println("A Father says: I'm going to football ");
  }
}

class Grandad extends Person
{
  String currentYear;
  String yearOfBirth;

  Grandad(String thisYear, String birthYear)
  {
   currentYear = thisYear;
```

```
    yearOfBirth = birthYear;
  }

  void talk()
  {
    int age;

    age = new Integer(currentYear).intValue()-
        new Integer(yearOfBirth).intValue();
    System.out.println("A Grandad says: I'm " + age + "years old ");

  }
}

class Granny extends Person
{
  Granny()
  {
  }

  void talk()
  {
    System.out.println("A Granny says: When's the boxing on? ");
  }

}

public class FamilyTalking
{

  public static void main(String[] args)
  {
    Person familyMember[];
    int i;
    familyMember = new Person[8];
    familyMember[0] = new Baby();
    familyMember[1] = new Toddler();
    familyMember[2] = new Teenager('F');
    familyMember[3] = new Teenager('M');
    familyMember[4] = new Mother();
    familyMember[5] = new Father();
    familyMember[6] = new Granny();
    familyMember[7] = new Grandad("99", "01");

    for  (i=0;i<8;i++)
    {
    familyMember[i].talk();
    }
  }
}
```

Answers to selected exercises

Chapter 1

1.1 Discussion on this question should include factors such as the wishes of the client, the preferences of potential users, the amount of money available, the time allowed for development, the nature of the local area. Decisions about the system boundary should consider both the physical area to be covered by the system and the topics to be included, such as maps, transport, local walks and cycle paths, medical centres, shopping and entertainment.

Chapter 2

2.2

a) Class / object

Class: A description of a group of objects with similar properties, common behaviour, common relationships and common semantics, e.g. Politician.

Object: A particular instance of a class which exists in the problem domain, e.g. Tony Blair.

b) Attribute / operation

Attribute: the data items that define a class, e.g. title, author, price for a Book class.

Operation: O-O function or procedure; always defined as part of a class. Operations achieve the class responsibilities, e.g. display title, change price for a Book class.

c) Association / multiplicity

Association: a direct link between classes, e.g. Customer reserves Video.

Multiplicity: indicates the cardinality of the association, e.g. one Customer can reserve up to 5 Videos.

d) Sub-class / super-class

Subclass: in the inheritance relationship the subclass (e.g. Wholesale Order) is the specialization and the super-class (e.g. Order) the more general version of the Class.

e) Message / method

Message: overall system functionality is achieved by objects messaging each other; a message is sent from one object to another requesting that it provide a service, e.g. the message 'set alarm(7.00am)' might be sent to an Alarm Clock object.

Method: is the procedure or function, defined in class, that is executed when a message Is received, e.g. the code for the function set alarm(), which will be defined within the Alarm Clock class.

f) Encapsulation / data hiding

Encapsulation: packaging data and related operations together, e.g. the data 'alarm time' and the operation 'set alarm()'.

Data hiding: data hiding is achieved because the data can only be manipulated by the operations defined to do so, i.e. 'set alarm', 'disable alarm'.

Chapter 3

3.1 What are the main benefits of the system life cycle?

- Provides a framework on which to structure development.
- Can be used to identify milestones, so useful for managers in monitoring and controlling the development process.
- Decomposes the process into a series of stages and identifies inputs andoutputs for each stage; useful for managers when allocating tasks on a largeproject.
- Provides the basis for a common understanding of the development process and supports communication among members of the development team.
- Supports training of staff who are new to system development.
- Encourages clear documentation of the different stages, associated activities, inputs and outputs.

3.2 What do you think are the advantages and disadvantages of developing a system using rapid prototyping?

Advantages.
- Greater client and user involvement generally leads to greater satisfaction with the finished system.
- Prototyping is an excellent way to capture client and user requirements.
- Prototyping is by far the best way of designing and developing the user interface to the system.
- Involvement of clients and users during development means that less training is needed when the system is handed over.

Disadvantages.
- Prototyping demands time and effort on the part of the client and future users of the system. This may cause a problem for the client organization.
- Prototyping can be disruptive for the client's business because of the large amount of involvement required.
- Successful prototyping requires sophisticated support tools and a high-level implementation language. These may not always be available.
- If prototyping is not carried out rigorously, it can result in systems which appear to function correctly and which are attractive, but which are neither robust nor reliable.
- It can sometimes be difficult to know when to stop prototyping, since clients and users may want more and more changes.

3.3 In what ways does the object-oriented approach claim to improve the system development process?

- Provides the basis for a seamless transition from the early stages of development through to implementation.
- Provides fundamental concepts which persist through the system life cycle.
- Provides a common terminology, thus supporting improved communication between members of the development team.
- Promotes traceability from requirements through to code.

- Emphasizes important issues such as maintenance and reuse.
- Supports iteration in the life cycle and is suitable both for traditional development and rapid prototyping.

3.4 Imagine that you are a member of a team developing the following systems:

- a public information system for your local area;
- a system to monitor heart patients in hospital;
- a system to handle orders from a charity's Christmas catalogue;
- a system to control traffic lights at the junction near a village school.

For each case write down as much as you can about the stakeholders, the type of system and the development environment.

A public information system for your local area.
Stakeholders.
- Developers
- Client (presumably local government, or could be a private organization)
- Users (general public, wide range of ages and backgrounds, some will have minimal experience of computer systems)
- People who are going to update the information in the system

Type of system.
- Information system for use by the general public
- Not safety or security critical
- No complex processing or algorithms
- Presentation of information and ease of use are most important issues

Development environment
- Probably a limited budget
- May need to take local politics into account
- Need to think about the type of information in the system and where this information is to be found

A system to monitor heart patients in hospital
Stakeholders
- Medical staff (consultants, doctors, nurses)
- Patients (will not operate the system, but will be very much affected by it)
- Developers
- Hospital technical staff who will run the system on a day-to-day basis

Type of system
- Highly specialized information system
- Safety-critical (failure could be life-threatening)
- Information needs to be well-structured and clearly presented
- May have to interface with other systems in the hospital

Development environment
- Possibly money constraints
- Unlikely that hospital staff will have much time to be involved in development
- May have to be implemented in a particular programming language
- in order to interface with existing hospital systems

A system to handle orders from a charity's Christmas catalogue
Stakeholders
- Charity employees who deal with mail order
- Customers who buy from the catalogue
- People who look at the catalogue out of interest
- Developers

Type of system
- Part mail-order, part marketing
- Not safety-critical
- Not highly security-critical, but must cater for secure payments and credit card transactions
- Hard copy outputs (such as the order form and invoices) must all be clear and easy to deal with
- The system must be easy to operate

Development environment
- Probably limited budget
- Existing manual system will need to be thoroughly investigated
- May be able to use and customize an existing mail-order package

A system to control traffic lights at the junction near a village school
Stakeholders
- People working and living near the junction
- Children attending the village school
- Other road users (pedestrians, cyclists, motorists)
- The local council
- The highways authority
- Developers

Type of system
- Safety-critical
- Processing of data and interface both important

Development environment
- Need to investigate thoroughly how the junction is used at present
- Probably limited budget
- Probably need to be aware of local politics
- Prototyping is feasible, but not at a live junction

Chapter 4

4.1 The following types of information can be found in the interview with Harry and Sue:

- Information that is already structured in lists, forms, company guidelines or policies, e.g. list of staff car numbers.
- Information about company procedures: how certain tasks are carried out at present, e.g. current, minimal, security measures (receptionist at entrance and checks of car park).

- Measurements such as the number of customers or the average size of an order, e.g. ninety-six staff, most of whom use their cars for work.
- Problems that the client has identified in the current system, e.g. anyone can get past the receptionist, and no way of stopping shoppers from using the company car park.
- Initial requirements and wishes for the new system, e.g. better security without antagonizing staff, restrict car park to *Just a Line* staff only.
- Information that is not stated directly, but where there are definite vibes, e.g. difference of opinion over receptionist, who does not appear to be very efficient.

4.2 Other questions that could have been asked during the interview:

- What time do most staff arrive and leave the car park each day?
- Are there any reserved parking spaces, for yourselves or for visitors?
- Apart from lack of space, do you have any other problems as a result of shoppers using the car park, for example, damage to cars?
- Can you give me an idea of the level of security that would be acceptable to your staff?

4.3 Some of the problems with Jane's survey:

- no indication of purpose of questionnaire;
- not clear where to return completed questionnaires;
- not clear how to answer questions;
- questions should be numbered;
- second question ambiguous; what does 'regular' mean?
- fourth question: visitors may see a different person each time;
- should include thanks to people who have filled in the questionnaire.

4.4 Sample criteria for a good requirements modelling technique:

- readily understandable by people who will read the specification;
- precise;
- unambiguous;
- easy to modify;
- facilitates reasoning about the specification.

Chapter 5

5.1
a) Book, Reader, Loan, Reservation
b) Room, Guest, Booking, Payment
c) Customer, Order, Product, Invoice, Payment, Supplier
d) Passenger, Flight, Airport, Airline, Reservation, Payment
e) Doctor, Patient, Appointment, Medical history

5.2
a) name, address, phone number, reader category (adult/child/pensioner)

b) name, employee number, address, phone number, job, salary, tax code

c) surname, forenames, address, date of birth

d) name, address, phone number, member type, registration date, payment method

e) name, address, phone number, date of birth, category (health service/private), dental history

5.3

a) *On the Move* is a small family <u>firm</u> that hires out <u>cars</u>. A car is bought in new or nearly new from a <u>dealer</u> and is given an initial <u>check</u>. It is then available for <u>hire</u>. Between each separate <u>hiring</u>, the car is given a <u>service</u> and a <u>clean</u> for the next <u>customer</u>. When a car reaches a certain <u>mileage</u>, it is sold.

Object	Reason for rejection
firm	too general
dealer	attribute of Car
check	attribute of Car
hiring	duplicate of hire
clean	attribute or operation on Car
mileage	attribute of Car

Objects retained as potential classes:
Car, Hire, Service, Customer.

b) A credit card <u>company</u> with 6.5 million <u>cardholders</u> has arrangements with 500,000 <u>retailers</u> who accept the <u>cards</u>. The retailers include <u>hotels</u>, <u>shops</u>, <u>travel agencies</u>, <u>garages</u> and <u>restaurants</u>. When a cardholder wishes to buy something, he or she presents the card to the retailer. If the <u>sale</u> is for more than £50, the retailer then telephones the credit card company to check that the <u>customer</u> has sufficient <u>credit</u>. If the sale is authorized, the <u>transaction</u> is carried out using a 2-part <u>voucher</u>, which records <u>details</u> of the customer, the retailer and the transaction. Details of the transaction are also included on the monthly <u>statement</u>, which is sent to the cardholder.

Object	Reason for rejection
company	too general
card	same attributes as Cardholder
hotels, shops, travel agencies, garages, restaurants	type of retailer is attribute of Retailer
sale	duplicate of Transaction
£50	value is attribute of Transaction
customer	duplicate of Cardholder
credit	attribute of Cardholder
voucher	means of implementation
details	attribute of Cardholder
statement	derivable from data held in Cardholder, Retailer, and Transaction classes

Objects retained as potential classes:
Cardholder, Retailer, Transaction.

5.4

a)

Employee
name
department
address
date of birth

b)

Credit Card
card number
card type
cardholder name
cardholder address
expiry date

c)

Car
make
model
engine capacity
colour
year of make
registration number

d)

Book
title
author
publisher
year of publication
ISBN

5.5 Sample attributes for some of the classes identified in Exercise 5.1. N.B. If these were part of a class diagram, an association relationship would be used instead of a reference to another class, e.g. reader would not need to appear as an attribute in the Loan class.

a)   Loan:
     book number, reader, date out, date due

b)   Guest:
     name, address, passport number, room number, date of arrival, date of departure,

payment method
c) Product:
name, price, size, colour, supplier, make, quantity in stock
d) Flight:
departure airport, arrival airport, stopover airports, airline, date, time of departure, time of arrival, plane ID, captain
e) Appointment:
patient name, patient address, doctor, date, time, reason

5.6 Sample operations for each of the classes in Exercise 5.4.
a) Loan:
make loan, renew, cancel, change date due
b) Guest:
record new guest, change room, change arrival date, change departure date
c) Product:
record new product, amend quantity in stock, change supplier, change price
d) Flight:
add stopover airport, change date, change time of arrival, change time of departure, change plane ID, change captain, cancel
e) Appointment:
make appointment, change doctor, change date, change time, cancel, confirm

5.7
a)

Father	
Responsibility	Collaborator
satisfy hunger	Mother

Mother	
Responsibility	Collaborator
get tea	Child 1
	Child 2
	Child 3

Child 1	
Responsibility	Collaborator
peel potatoes	

Child 2	
Responsibility	Collaborator
fry sausages	

Child 3	
Responsibility	Collaborator
put kettle on	

b)

Boss	
Responsibility	Collaborator
escape	Mama

Mama	
Responsibility	Collaborator
get funds	Gangster 1
	Gangster 2
	Gangster 3
select team	

Gangster 1	
Respon-sibility	Collab-orator
plan robbery	

Gangster 2	
Respon-sibility	Collab-orator
sort out transport	Accomplice

Gangster 3	
Respon-sibility	Collab-orator
get money to Boss	

Accomplice	
Responsibility	Collaborator
steal car	

5.8

a)

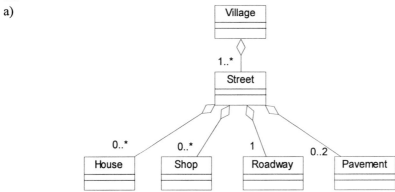

b)

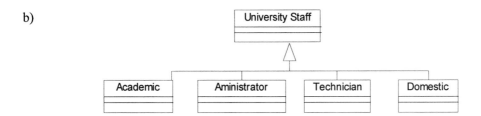

c)

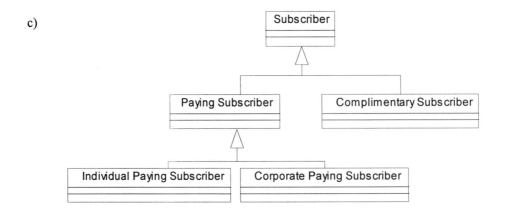

d)

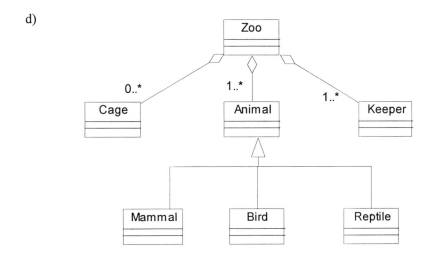

e)

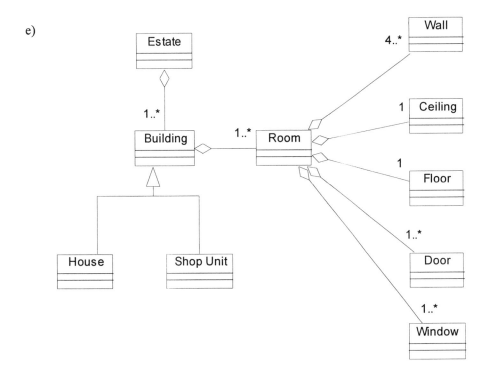

5.9

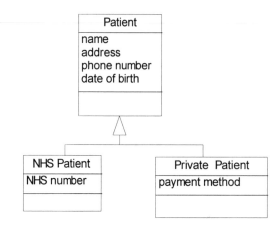

5.10

a) A lecturer teaches at least one course. Each course is taught by one lecturer, and may be studied by zero or more students. A student must study at least one course, and may study several.   A course consists of lectures, possibly tutorials, and at least one assessment. Both coursework and exam are types of assessment.

b) A tennis club owns one or more grounds, which are made up of a clubhouse and 12 courts. A ground can only be owned by one tennis club. The tennis club consists of one or more members, who are either full or social members. Full members are divided into adult and junior members.

c) The set meal in a restaurant consists of one drink and food, which is made up of one starter, one main course and one dessert. The drink may be alcoholic or a soft drink.

5.11

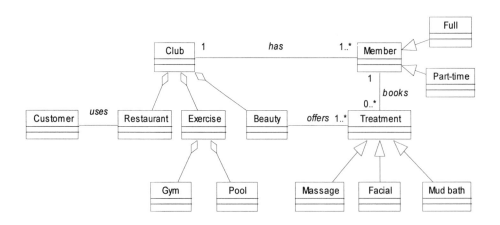

5.12

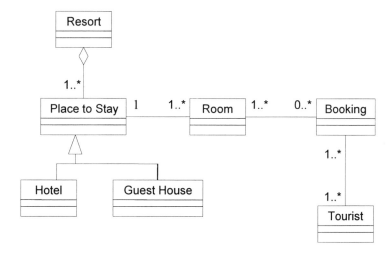

Resort
name
description
beach rating
hours of sunshine
update beach rating
update hours of sunshine

5.13

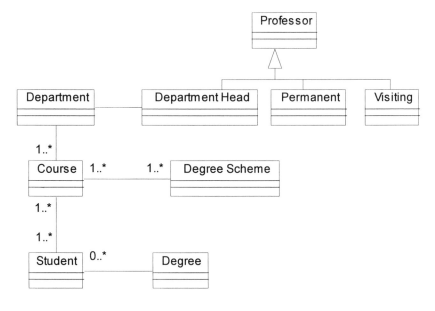

Course
name code topic area lecturer modular value semesters
create course change code add lecturer change lecturer change semester cancel course

Course = name + code + topic area + {lecturer} + modular value + [" A"| " B" | "A&B"]

5.14

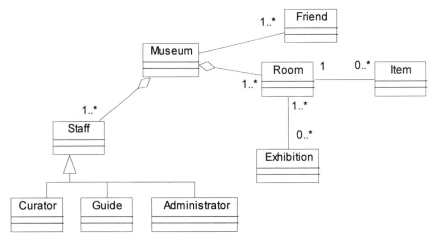

Item
item code name acquisition date source current room exhibition description
change room change exhibition amend description

5.15

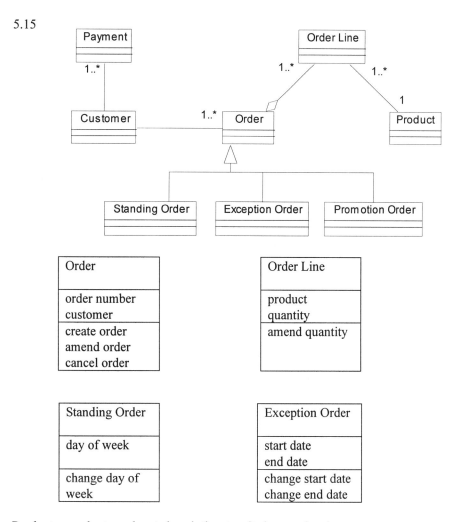

Product = product number + description + unit size + unit price

5.16

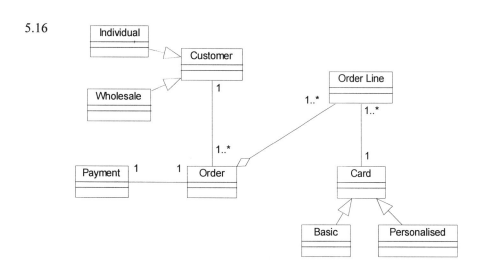

```
┌─────────────────────────────┐
│ Customer                    │
├─────────────────────────────┤
│ name                        │
│ address                     │
│ phone number                │
├─────────────────────────────┤
│ change address              │
│ change phone number         │
└─────────────────────────────┘
```

```
┌───────────────────────┐   ┌───────────────────────────┐
│ Individual            │   │ Wholesale                 │
├───────────────────────┤   ├───────────────────────────┤
│ pre-paid              │   │ delivery address          │
│                       │   │ delivery tel. no.         │
│                       │   │ account number            │
│                       │   │ credit limit              │
├───────────────────────┤   ├───────────────────────────┤
│                       │   │ change credit limit       │
└───────────────────────┘   └───────────────────────────┘
```

5.17   Invoice = order number + customer name + customer address + (delivery address)
        + {order line} + [delivery | P&P] + total cost.

5.18   If Customer lives outside 20 miles radius, then charge P&P
        else (*Customer lives at or within 20 mile radius*)
                if Total Cost of Order < £30, then charge £2.00
                else (*Total Cost of Order =>£30*) no charge.

Chapter 6

6.1
a) A scenario to describe what happens when a card is successfully removed from the list.

    • administrator checks that the number of the card to be removed is in the list
    • administrator deletes the card number
    • administrator informs the Personnel Department that the card is no longer valid

b) A scenario to describe what happens when the card number to be removed is not on the
    list.

    • administrator checks the list, but can't find the number of the card to be removed
    • administrator informs the Personnel Department that the card cannot be removed,
      as its number is not on the list

6.2

a) A simple scenario to describe what happens when someone phones a restaurant to order a large Napolitana pizza to be delivered.

- customer phones restaurant and orders a pizza to be delivered
- waiter asks for the address
- waiter confirms that the address is within the delivery area
- waiter asks if the order is for one of the standard pizzas
- customer asks for a Napolitana
- waiter asks which size the customer wants
- customer states size required
- waiter checks the price of the pizza with the customer
- customer agrees the price
- customer asks how long the delivery will take
- waiter gives the customer an estimated time
- waiter confirms details of the order and the delivery address with the customer

b) A scenario to describe what happens when a requested pizza topping is not available.

- customer phones restaurant and orders a pizza to be delivered
- waiter asks for the address
- waiter confirms that the address is within the delivery area
- waiter asks if the order is for one of the standard pizzas
- customer asks for a pizza with special topping
- waiter says that they do not have any of the topping left
- waiter lists the toppings available and asks if the customer would like one of those
- customer chooses another topping
- waiter asks which size the customer wants
- customer states size required
- waiter checks the price of the pizza with the customer
- customer agrees the price
- customer asks how long the delivery will take
- waiter gives the customer an estimated time
- waiter confirms details of the order and the delivery address with the customer

6.3

a) In the case where a car takes the last space in the car park, the scenario in Section 6.1.3 would have to be amended to show that the Full Sign is switched on once the car has entered the car park.

b)

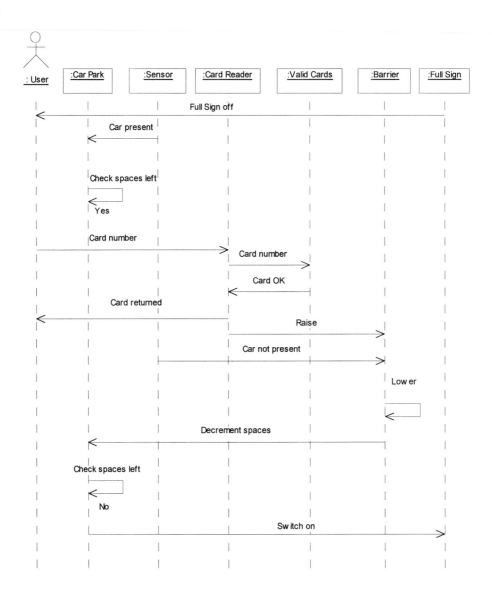

6.4

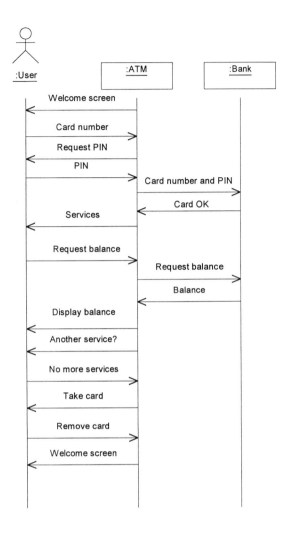

6.5

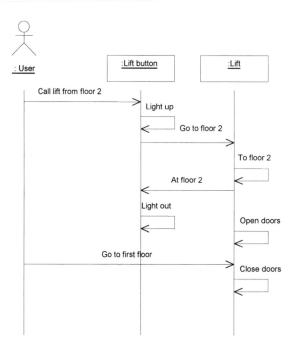

6.6 The user's view of the sequence of events illustrated by the diagram in Exercise 6.6 is as follows:

- the user types in key words relating to the book he or she wants to buy
- a list of book titles appears on the screen
- the user selects a title
- the system displays the availability for the chosen title
- the user places an order for the book
- the system asks for customer details
- the user supplies the customer details
- the system requests credit card details
- the user supplies credit card details
- the system confirms the purchase

6.7
a)
- caller phones Directory Enquiries
- operator asks for the name and location for which the caller wants the phone number
- caller tells the operator the name and location
- operator looks up the number associated with the given name and location
- operator tells the caller the number

b)

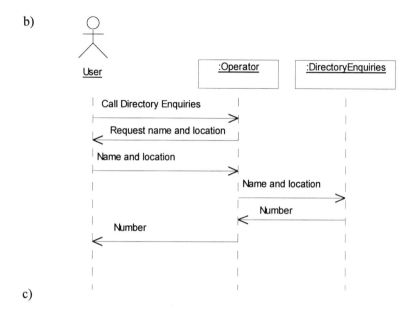

c)

- caller phones Directory Enquiries
- operator asks for the name and location for which the caller wants the phone number
- caller tells the operator the name and location
- operator looks up the given name and location, but can't find the number
- operator asks caller to spell the name
- caller spells name
- operator finds number
- operator tells the caller the number

d)

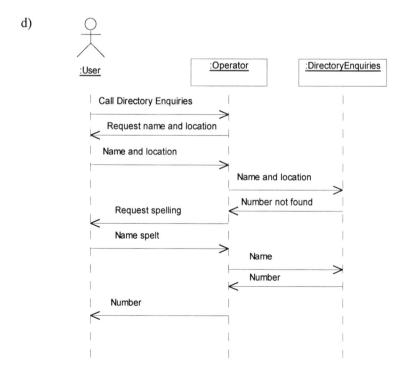

6.8 Simple state diagram for the Full Sign class

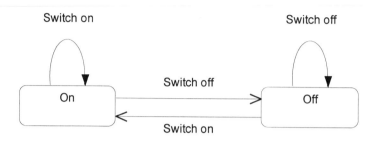

6.9 Modified state diagram for a balloon.

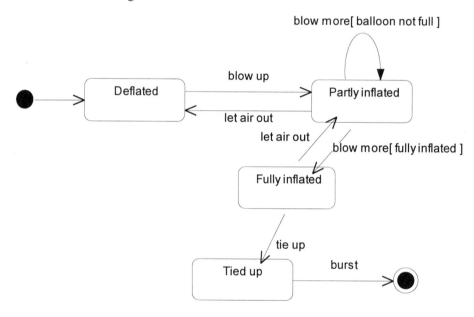

6.10 State diagram for a child's bank account.

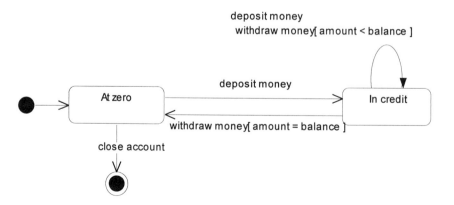

6.11 To start with, the timer is off. It can be set to move it into the Set state, and turned off to move it back to the Off state; in the Set state the time can be changed. Once the timer is set and the set time reached, the alarm rings. The alarm can be turned off, or will stop automatically after one minute. The timer may break at any time.

6.12

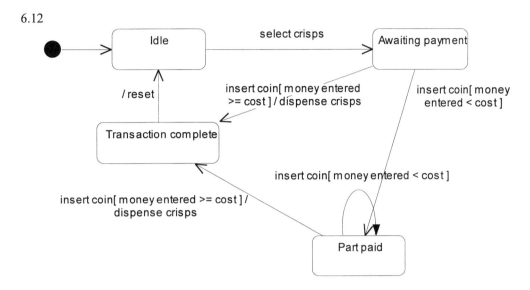

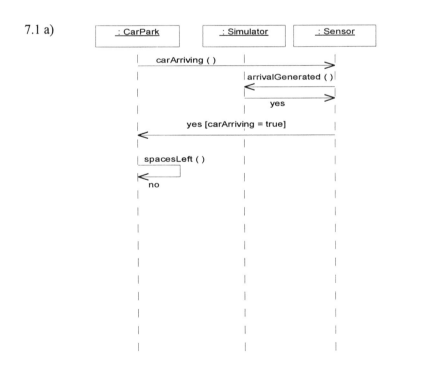

Chapter 7

7.1 a)

7.1(b)

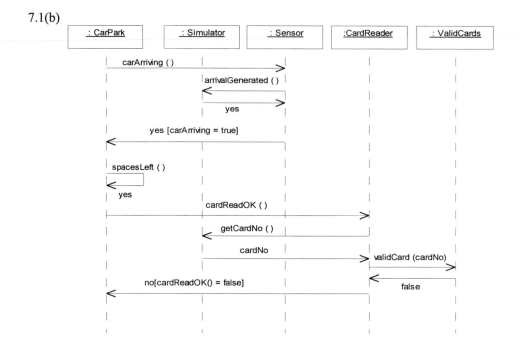

7.2

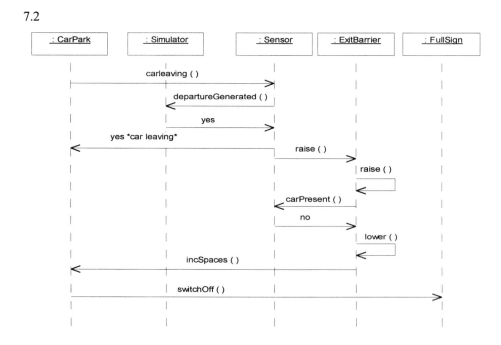

7.3

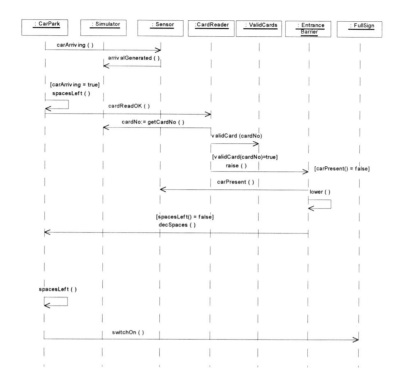

7.4

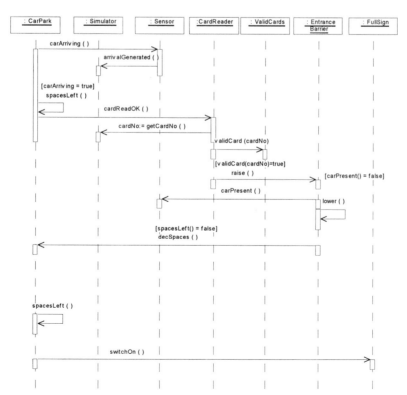

7.5   Collaboration diagram for Figure 7.20.

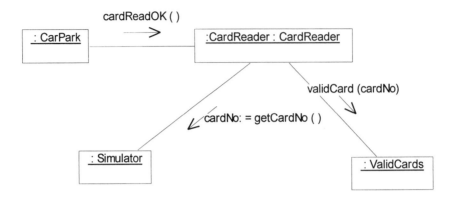

Chapter 8

8.1

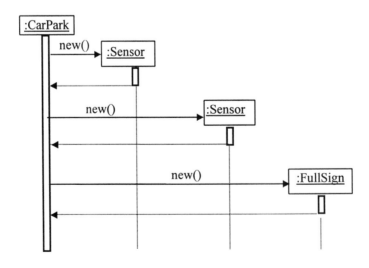

8.3
a)   The carPark attributes are `capacity` and `spaces`.
b)   These attributes are defined in the lines of code:
     private int capacity;   // max number of spaces
     private int spaces;   // actual spaces
c)   These attributes are initialized inside the CarPark class constructor in the lines:
     capacity = inCapacity;   // give value to capacity
     spaces = noSpaces;   // and to spaces
d)   Values for the CarPark attributes are specified, and passed as parameters to the
     CarPark class constructor, within the CarParkSystem class in the line:
     aCarPark = new CarPark(1,1,5,3);
     The first 2 parameters specify the number of exits and the number of entrances; the
     third parameter specifies the value for `capacity`, and the fourth parameter specifies
     the value for `spaces`.

8.4
a)   The CarPark operations are: `decSpaces()`, `incSpaces()` and `spacesLeft()`.
b)   These operations are implemented in the lines:

```
public void decSpaces()
{
   spaces = spaces - 1;
   System.out.print("Spaces left = " + spaces + " ");
}
```

and

```
public void incSpaces()
{
   // add 1 to spaces available
   spaces = spaces + 1;
 System.out.print("Spaces left = " + spaces + " ");
}
```

and

```
public boolean spacesLeft()
{
   // indicates if spaces available
   if (spaces > 0)
   {
      Return true;
   }
   else
   {
      System.out.print("No spaces left");
      return false;
   }
}
```

8.5

a)   In the code fragment:

```
for (i = 0;i<8;i++)
{
   if (knownCards[i].getNum() == cardNo)
   {
      valid = true;
   }
}
```

the operation getNum() is used polymorphically.

b)   The operation getNum() is defined in the Card class.

c)   The operation is applied to objects of the StaffCard (knownCards[0..5]) and the VisitorCard (knownCards[6,7]) classes.

8.6

a)   The class constructors are : Person(), Baby(), Toddler(), Teenager(char sex), Mother(), Father(), Grandad(String this year, String birthYear) and Granny().

b)   The Toddler constructor initializes the attribute vocabulary to "Mama, NO".

c)   The attributes of the Grandad class are currentYear and yearOfBirth. They are initialized by being set to the values of the parameters thisYear and birthYear.

d)   The talk() operation, in line:
     familyMember[i].talk();
     is used polymorphically. It is appled to objects of the classes: Person, Baby, Toddler, Teenager, Mother, Father, Grandad year, and Granny.

Chapter 9

9.1

Employee

EmpNo	Name	Dept
JL209	Chris Doolan	Design
JL437	Sam Parker	Marketing
JL722	Mira Patel	Marketing

9.2

Employee

EmpNo	Name	Dept
JL209	Chris Doolan	Design
JL437	Sam Parker	Marketing
JL722	Mira Patel	Marketing

Room

RoomNo	Floor
A6	1st
A11	1st
C2	4th

EmployeeRoom

EmpNo	RoomNo
JL209	A6
JL209	A11
JL437	C2
JL722	C2

9.3

First option: three separate tables for the one to many association and classes

Employee

EmpNo	Name	Dept
JL209	Chris Doolan	Design
JL437	Sam Parker	Marketing
JL722	Mira Patel	Marketing

Car

RegNo	Make	Model	Colour
R401 CDV	VW	Golf	grey
L43 JKB	Renault	Espace	green
R339 BJS	Peugeot	406	blue
T324 TSS	Ford	Mondeo	red

EmployeeCar

EmpNo	RegNo
JL209	R401 CDV
JL209	L43 JKB
JL437	R339 BJS
JL722	T324 TSS

Second option: implement tables for Employee and Car only, but include foreign key (EmpNo) in the table for the Car class.

Employee

EmpNo	Name	Dept
JL209	Chris Doolan	Design
JL437	Sam Parker	Marketing
JL722	Mira Patel	Marketing

Car

RegNo	Make	Model	Colour	EmpNo
R401 CDV	VW	Golf	grey	JL209
L43 JKB	Renault	Espace	green	JL209
R339 BJS	Peugeot	406	blue	JL437
T324 TSS	Ford	Mondeo	red	JL722

9.4
Implement a single table for the relationship and classes.

Employees

EmpNo	Name	Dept	Salary	Hours/week	Hourly rate
JL209	Chris Doolan	Design	31,000		
JL437	Sam Parker	Marketing	24,000		
JL722	Mira Patel	Marketing		20	15.00

Chapter 10

10.1 Values of i to test that the loop is working under normal conditions are 1 and 10. Abnormal values of i to test that the loop is working are -1, 0,1 to test the lower limit; 10 and 11 to test the upper limit.

10.2 For statement coverage either one of the test cases is sufficient. For branch coverage, both must be used.

10.3

a) For statement coverage either sub-statement 1 or sub-statement 2 must be executed, therefore any one of the test cases may be used, irrespective of whether it evaluates to TRUE or not.

b) For branch coverage both sub-statement 1 and sub-statement 2 must be executed, therefore any test case which evaluates to TRUE may be used (i.e. test case (ii), (iii), or (iv)) and one test case which evaluates to FALSE (test case (i)).

c) Condition testing insists that both parts of the predicate (A OR B) be tested in every possible combination of TRUE and FALSE. All four test cases are required.

10.4 Given the test cases:

i) $(A = 0)$ AND $(B = 1)$
ii) $(A = 0)$ AND $(B = 0)$
iii) $(A = 2)$ AND $(B = 1)$
iv) $(A = 2)$ AND $(B = 0)$.

a) For statement coverage, any one of the four test cases will do.

b) For branch coverage, test case (iv)—which evaluates to TRUE—and any one of the other three will do.

c) Condition coverage requires that all four test cases be used.

Bibliography

This is not a long bibliography; it only mentions a very few of the many books that you can find relating to the subject of object-oriented system development and only a selection of those listed at the ends of chapters. In a bibliography for beginners we felt that it was appropriate to cover only those books which we felt to be accessible and reasonably easy to understand. In particular, we have indicated below books that we feel would be useful in the next stage of learning about object-orientation; these books are marked with an asterisk*.

* Bennett, S., McRobb, S. and Farmer, R. *Object-Oriented Systems Analysis and Design using UML,* London: McGraw-Hill, 1999.
May seem rather large and intimidating for newcomers to the subject, but lots of interesting stuff on O-O and two good case studies.

Booch, G., Rumbaugh, J. and Jacobson, I. *The Unified Modeling Language User Guide,* Reading, Massachusetts: Addison-Wesley, 1999.
Current bible on UML This is a comprehensive and detailed book, though it may be rather daunting for beginners.

Britton, C. and Doake, J. *Software System Development: a gentle introduction*, 2nd edn, London: McGraw-Hill, 1996.
Written for newcomers to the subject of system development. This book contains very little on O-O, but is good for background on the *Just a Line* case study.

Buchanan, W. *Mastering Java,* Basingstoke: Macmillan, 1998.
Lots of examples with the code on the web.

Carter, R., Martin, J., Mayblin, B. and Munday, M. *Systems, Management and Change—A Graphic Guide,* Paul Chapman in association with The Open University, 1988.
Quite an old book, but still an unusual and stimulating introduction to the subject of systems in general , with lots of pictures.

Coleman, D., Arnold, P., Bodoff, S., Dollin, C., Gilchrist, H., Hayes, F. and Jeremaes, P. *Object-Oriented Development: The Fusion Method,* Englewood Cliffs, N.J.: Prentice-Hall, 1994.
Account of a second-generation O-O methodology; may now be superseded by books on UML.

Cook, S. and Daniels, J. *Designing Object Systems. Object-Oriented Modelling with Syntropy,* Hemel Hempstead: Prentice-Hall, 1994.
Another interesting account of how to develop O-O systems, but again, may be superseded by UML.

Davis, A.M. *Software Requirements: Objects, Functions and States,* **Englewood Cliffs, N.J.: Prentice-Hall, 1993.**
This is not a book on the object-oriented approach, but it is a good, standard text for readers who are interested in requirements engineering.

Deitel, H.M. and Deitel, P.J. *C: How to Program,* **London: Prentice Hall International Paperback Editions, 1993.**
This book explains clearly the concepts of structured programming and introduces the reader to C and C++. No prior programming knowledge is assumed. Some topics are covered in depth.

*Fowler, M. with Scott, K. *UML Distilled: Applying the Standard Object Modeling Language,* **Reading, Massachusetts: Addison-Wesley, 1997.**
Great book for this level; very straightforward, sensible and short.

Henderson-Sellers, B. *A Book of Object-Oriented Knowledge,* **2nd edn, Upper Saddle River, N.J.: Prentice-Hall, 1997.**
Clear, well-written introduction to the object-oriented approach.

Jacobson, I., Christerson, M., Jonsson, P. and Overgaard, G. *Object-Oriented Software Engineering: A Use Case Driven Approach,* **Wokingham: Addison-Wesley, 1992.**
The original book on use cases and scenarios.

Kaposi, A. and Myers, M. *Systems Models and Measures,* **Springer Verlag, 1994.**
An interesting and well-written introduction to systems theory for those who prefer a more mathematical approach.

Parsons, D. *Introductory Java,* **London: Letts, 1998.**
A cheap and readable text. Some programming knowledge is assumed. Suitable for a student who is new to the topic of object-oriented programming..

* Quatrani, T. *Visual Modeling with Rational Rose and UML,* **Reading, Massachusetts: Addison-Wesley, 1998.**
A very useful book if you want to get going on the models. Extremely helpful with learning the nuts and bolts of Rational Rose, an object-oriented CASE tool, with clear, step-by-step instructions.

Rumbaugh, J., Blaha, M., Premerlani, W., Eddy, F. and Lorensen, W. *Object-Oriented Modeling and Design,* **Englewood Cliffs, N.J.: Prentice-Hall, 1991.**
A classic; one of the main precursors of UML and still worth reading.

Skidmore, S. *Introducing System Analysis,* **2nd edn, Oxford: NCC Blackwell, 1994.**
A short, easy read, containing good, practical advice on how to elicit and validate requirements.

* **Stevens, P. with Pooley, R.** *Using UML. Software Engineering with Objects and Components,* **Harlow: Addison-Wesley, 1999.**
A good introduction to UML in the context of the software design and development process.

Wirfs-Brock, R., Wilkerson, B. and Wiener, L. *Designing Object-Oriented Software,* **Englewood Cliffs, N.J.: Prentice Hall, 1990.**
Quite an elderly book in computer science terms, but it's still a good read, and the best account of CRC cards.

Glossary

The terminology of object-oriented system development is large and frequently confusing. In books and journal papers you will find the same word used to mean different things and different words used to mean the same thing. This glossary does not attempt to provide definitive meanings for all the terms you need; we simply explain here how we use the various words in this book. Words marked * in the body of a definition have their own definition in the glossary.

Abstract class: a class* that does not have any objects* in the system.

Abstraction: the process of ignoring currently irrelevant details of a problem in order to concentrate on the most important parts.

Acceptance testing: the final testing of the software system in the presence of the client*. The system is then accepted by the client or further alterations are made.

Action: behaviour* that occurs when a transition* takes place.

Actor: a person or organization who interacts with the system in some way. An actor inputs and receives information from the system and is associated with at least one use case* (major functional activity).

Aggregation: the relationship that occurs when one class* is made up of several others, or when one class is made up of many occurrences of another class; sometimes referred to as the 'part-of' or 'consists-of' relationship.

Analysis: one of the stages of the development life cycle*. Analysis involves investigation into and modelling* of both the problem and the developing system.

Architecture: the underlying structure of the system.

Association: a link between two classes* indicating a possible relationship between objects* of the classes.

Attribute: data item defined as part of a class* or object*.

Behaviour: the effects of a system that are visible to an external observer.

Bespoke software: software that is not bought off the shelf, but is designed and developed for a particular client.

Beta testing: testing of a software product by typical users in a working environment before general release.

Boolean: a type that has the values True and False.

Boundary: defines what is to be considered inside the system and therefore under its control. Outside the boundary is the system environment*.

Business application software: software system designed for a specific business area, such as payroll, accounting or stock control.

Cardinality: the cardinality of an association* indicates the number of objects* of each class* that are allowed to participate in the association.

CASE: Computer Aided Software Engineering. The Software tools that automate the system development process.

Child class: a sub-class*, specialization of another class*.

Class: the description or pattern for a group of objects* that have the same attributes*, operations*, relationships and meaning. Template or factory for creating objects.

Class diagram: a diagram showing the classes* in a system* and their relationships to each other. Optionally, attributes* and operations* may be included.

Class library: a collection of fully coded and tested classes* that may be reused in other software applications.

Class-responsibility-collaboration cards: See CRC cards.

Client: the person or organization who requests and pays for the new system. The client will often also be a user* of the system, but this is not always the case.

Client and server: In this context, a client is a class that uses the services of another and a server is a class that provides services to another.

Cohesion: a module is cohesive if it has a clearly defined role, a single, obvious purpose in the application. This makes the module easier for a maintaining programmer to read and understand.

Collaboration: the situation where a class* needs the help of another class to fulfil one of its responsibilities*.

Collaboration diagram: illustrates the behaviour* specified in a scenario*, with the interactions organized around the objects* and the links between them, rather than shown in a time sequence.

Consistency: a specification* is consistent if there are no internal contradictions between different views of the system.

Constructor operation: an operation* that creates a new object* of a class*.

CRC cards: a technique, using small index cards, to identify the responsibilities* of classes* in the system and the classes with which they have to collaborate to fulfil these responsibilities.

Data abstraction: the technique of hiding implementation* details behind a public interface*.

Database: all the data required to support the operations of an organization, collected, organized and maintained centrally in such a way that it can be used by many different programs.

Data decomposition: breaking down a system into smaller parts in terms of its data.

Data dictionary: a modelling technique that uses English and a small set of symbols to define the data in the system.

Decomposition: the process of breaking down a problem into successively smaller parts in order to understand it better.

Deliverable: the output from a stage in the system life cycle*. Deliverables in the early stages of the life cycle are generally in the form of documents and diagrams. In the later stages they include program code and test results.

Design: the stage in object-oriented system development where the architecture of the system is determined: how the system as a whole is to be organized into smaller, more manageable components or subsystems. Whereas analysis* concentrates on understanding the user's* view of the system, system design is driven by implementation* concerns.

Design for reuse: identification of new classes* that can subsequently form part of a class library*.

Design with reuse: identification of existing components in a class library* that can be reused in a new system*.

Documentation: the documentation for the system covers many different aspects. These include instructions for users and operators about the running of the system, information for those concerned with system maintenance*, and documents generated as deliverables* during the system development.

Domain: see problem domain.

Dynamic binding: the binding at run-time of a message* to a particular version of a method*.

Elicitation: see Requirements elicitation.

Encapsulation: packaging data and operations into objects*.

Environment: the system environment refers to anything outside the system that affects it in some way—e.g. people or organizations generating or responding to system data.

Event: an instantaneous occurrence that is of significance to the system. An occurrence that triggers a state transition*.

Feasibility study: part of the traditional system life cycle* which attempts to determine whether there is a practical solution to the problem under consideration.

Feature: a collective term for the attributes* and operations* of a class*.

Fire: when a state transition* occurs, it is said to fire.

Foreign key: if one table* in a database contains an attribute which is the primary key* of another table, this attribute is called a foreign key. A foreign key permits a link between the two tables.

Formal specification languages: languages based on maths or logic that are used in the specification of computer systems.

Functionality: what a system does in terms of the processes that it supports.

Functional decomposition: breaking down a system into smaller parts in terms of its processes.

Functional requirements: describe what the system has to do, what its inputs and outputs are and how these are linked.

Granularity: level of detail.

Guarded transition: a transition* that only fires* when certain conditions are satisfied.

Happy day scenario: a scenario* which records the normal sequence of events in a use case*.

Implementation: the stage of the system development life cycle* where the design is translated into a programming language.

Implementation independent: refers to the design* of a system that is not tied to a particular programming language and can be implemented in a variety of different ways.

Incremental development: an iterative way of developing systems, often using prototyping*, that involves several releases of the system, each one showing an improvement on the one before.

Information hiding: making the internal details of a module inaccessible to other modules.

Inheritance: a relationship between two classes* where one is a refinement of the other; sometimes referred to as the 'is-a' relationship. A mechanism that allows a class to reuse features already defined in another class.

Input: data which is entered into the system by the user.

Instance: an object* that belongs to a particular class*

Instantiation: the creation of a new instance* of a class* (object*).

Interaction: a set of messages* exchanged between objects* for a specific purpose.

Interaction diagram: diagram showing a set of messages* that take place between objects* to accomplish a purpose.

Interface: the system interface is its connection to the outside world. The interface of a module is the information that it presents to its environment*.

ISO/9001: international standard for quality assurance.

Life cycle: a recognizable pattern of steps taken to develop a software system. These generally include the key stages of analysis*, design*, implementation*, testing and maintenance*.

Lifeline: a dotted line connected to an object in a sequence diagram that indicates the existence of the object over a period of time.

Maintenance: the final stage of the system life cycle*, where errors are corrected and minor modifications carried out.

Message: request from one object* to another that it execute one of its methods*.

Methodology / method: recipe for developing a system. The detailed description of the steps and stages in system development, together with a specified list of inputs and outputs for each step.

Method: procedure or function defined as part of a class* or object*; using this term refers to the procedure's implementation.

Modelling: the process of building a representation of all or part of a problem or the system that is designed to solve it.

Modification: changes of any size that are made to the system after it has been accepted and delivered to the client*.

Module: section of a program designed to execute a logically identifiable unit of data and associated operations.

Multimedia: the combination of different forms of media, such as text, graphics, sound, photographs and video, in a computer-based system.

Multiplicity: see cardinality.

Non-functional requirements: the attributes of a system as it performs its job. Non-functional requirements include usability, reliability, security and performance.

Normalization: the process of organizing data into groups in such a way that no redundant data items are stored.

Notation: written language that may include text, symbols and diagrams.

Object: In the early stages of development an object is something that exists independently in the problem domain*. Later on, the term refers to an instance of a class* in the system. At implementation*, an object is a software unit packaging together data and methods* to manipulate that data.

Object-orientation: an approach to developing software systems that is based on data items and the attributes* and operations* that define them.

Operation: procedure or function defined as part of a class or object; using this term refers to the procedure's public interface* with the rest of the software.

Output: information produced by the system for the user.

Override: a feature* in a sub-class* which uses the same name as the feature in the super-class*, but redefines and replaces it.

Parent class: super-class*, generalization of other classes*.

Persistent data: refers to objects* that continue to exist after the program that creates and uses them has stopped executing.

Polymorphism: the ability to hide different implementations* behind a common interface*.

Primary key: attribute* that uniquely identifies a single occurrence of a data item in a relational database table.

Problem domain: the area of knowledge or activity relating to the problem that the system is to solve.

Prototyping / rapid prototyping: an iterative method of developing a system, instead of using traditional structured methods. A working model of the system may be constructed at an early stage in development for the purpose of establishing user requirements* and later discarded. Alternatively, a working model is sometimes used as the basis for design* and implementation* of the final system.

Requirement: a feature* or behaviour* of the system that is desired by one or more stakeholders.

Requirements elicitation: the stage of requirements engineering* which aims to gather as much information as possible about the problem domain*, the clients'* and users'* current difficulties and what they would like the intended system to do for them

Requirements engineering: the process of establishing what is wanted and needed from a software system. Requirements engineering covers the three stages of elicitation*, specification* and validation*.

Requirements specification: the stage of requirements engineering during which the information from the elicitation* process is analysed and recorded using textual and diagrammatic modelling techniques to represent the problem and the proposed solution.

Requirements validation: the stage of requirements engineering which checks that the recorded requirements* correspond to the intentions of the stakeholders* about the system.

Responsibility: an obligation that one class* has to provide a service for another.

Reuse: programming with existing software modules rather than coding them from scratch each time.

Safety-critical system: a system where failure would cause loss of life or severe hardship.

Scenario: a scenario represents one instance of a use case*, describing a particular sequence of events* that may occur in trying to reach the use case goal.

Security-critical system: a system where failure would cause loss of crucial information.

Self-transition: occurs when an object* remains in the same state* in response to an event*.

Sequence diagram: illustrates the behaviour specified in a scenario*, with the interactions shown in a time sequence.

Service: the set of publicly available operations* belonging to a class*.

Simulation: a computer program that models a complex real-world situation.

Software crisis: name given to the situation during the late sixties and early seventies, when software systems were typically late, over-budget, unreliable, difficult to maintain and did not do what was required of them.

Specification: a definition or description of what is wanted and needed from a software system in terms of both functional* and non-functional requirements*. See also requirements specification.

Stakeholder: any person or organization affected by the system, such as users*, clients*, developers, management.

State: represents a period of time during which an object* of a class* satisfies some condition or waits for an event*.

State diagram: diagram illustrating the behaviour* of a single class* in response to events* in the system.

State transition: the response of an object* to an event*; usually involving movement of the object from one state* to another.

Structured English: a sub-set of English that may be used to specify operations*.

Sub-class: a specialized version of another class (the super-class).

Sub-system: a system which is itself part of a larger system.

Super-class: a generalized version of another class (the sub-class).

System: a set of interrelated objects or elements that are viewed as a whole and designed by human beings to achieve a purpose; it has a boundary within which it lies and outside of which is the environment.

Table: repository of data in a relational database*. Tables store data in a row-column format; each column stores a field, or attribute of the data, and each row stores a record, typically the complete set of values for a single data object.

Traceability: the ability to track a requirement* through the development process and identify where it is implemented in the final system code.

Transition: see state transition.

Use case: specifies the functionality that the system will offer from the users' perspective. A use case specifies a set of interactions between a user and the system to achieve a particular goal.

User: any organization or person that uses the system to input or process data, or who receives the results of such processing.

Validation: see Requirements validation.

Index

A

abstract class, 82, 176, 188
abstraction, 21, 66, 69, 113
acceptance testing, 184
Access, 91, 169; Microsoft Access, 5, 6, 168, 170, 171, 178
action: in state diagram, 109
actor, 97-98, 100, 103-105
aggregation, 70, 79-81, 92, 94-95, 114, 128-135, 156, 175; composition, 114; by containment, 114, 132
algorithm, 21-22
alternative solutions, 32, 182
analysis, 4-5, 15, 29, 31- 32, 75, 82, 84, 87, 104, 113, 119, 127-128, 135, 145, 168, 170, 175, 181-182; coverage, 187
ancestor class, 22
application, 8, 10, 13, 33, 37
application domain, 5, 14
architecture: system, 32, 33
argument, 75, 89
assembly language, 13

association, 34, 70, 79-80, 114, 128-135, 152, 156; implementing in database, 172-174
attribute, 15, 17, 21-22, 24, 72, 75-76, 82, 85, 89, 108, 112-114, 120, 143, 145-147, 168, 175-177, 187, 189
automated tool, 29

B

basic functionality, 12, 113
behaviour. See system behaviour
bespoke software, 185
beta testing, 184
black box testing, 183, 191
Booch, 38-39
boot strap, 127
boundary: system, 2-3, 97
brainstorming, 55

C

C++, 13, 34
car park simulation, 119, 132, 143, 151
case study: how to use, 1-2
CASE tool, 37, 120
changeover, 34
child class, 22, 188
choice of methodology,39-41

class,16-25; behaviour,17; 32, 75, 176; child, 22, 188; conditional behaviour, 136; constructor, 131-134, 145-147, 149; decentralized, 112; general, 22; good, 112-113; identify attributes, 73; identify relationships, 79-82; testing, 187, 191
class diagram, 69-82; design stage, 120-127; converting to database tables, 170-176;
class-responsibility-collaboration. See CRC card
client object, 22
client requirements, 28-29, 35, 41, 68, 182
code fragments, 141-158
cohesion: of module, 10-12
collaboration diagram, 103, 106-107
commercial package, 32, 40
COMMON block, 10
computer aided design, 168
computer-based tool, 47

condition: state diagram, 109
conditional behaviour: sequence diagram 135- 136
constructor, 131-134, 145-147, 149, 156
containment: aggregation, 114
co-operative working, 62
CRC card, 70, 75-79, 101, 128
creation: object, 140-141, 146, 148-149, 159
critique: future workshop, 55, 64

D

data abstraction, 20
data dictionary, 74, 82-90; decision construct, 88; level of detail, 87-88; notation, 84-87, 88; repetition construct, 88; sequence construct, 88; value 84
data flow diagram, 9, 37
data hiding, 20-22
data: persistent. See persistent data
data source, 177
data visibility, 10
database, 12, 167-178
database management system, 33
decentralized classes, 112
decomposition, 9-10, 68-69, 148
deliverable, 182

design, 9-10, 15, 19-20, 28-29, 32-34, 72, 104, 148, 151; decision, 105; detailed, 87, 182; for reuse, 34; model, 4-6, 119-120, 128, 131, 135, 145, 168; paradigm, 181, 187; stage, 5-6, 33-34, 84, 88, 119-120, 127, 135, 142, 168, 170, 172, 175, 181-182; view, 120; with reuse, 34
development process, 3-4, 13, 25, 27-35, 69
development stage, 36, 135, 181
distribution of intelligence: class, 112
documentation, 3, 29, 31, 34, 47, 59, 68, 120, 183, 185
documents: describing, 86-87; level of detail, 87-88
driver manager: JDBC, 177
driver program, 183
dynamic model, 32, 75, 128, 135, 148

E

Eiffel, 13
elicitation: requirements, 31, 43, 48-56, 59
encapsulation, 19, 20, 36
end-to-end path: testing, 186

end-user programming languages, 37
entity relationship diagram, 37
environment:system, 2-3, 33, 36, 40, 41
error handling, 184
event:scenario, 103-109

F

fact-finding, 31, 48
Fagan inspections, 59
fantasy: future workshop, 55
feature, 23, 75
foreign key: database, 173-174
form: database, 169
formal methods, 39
formal specification, 56
FORTRAN, 10
fourth generation language, 13
framework, 4, 37, 101
functional decomposition, 8, 9-10, 12, 148
functional design, 10
functional requirement, 47, 101
functional testing, 183
functionality, 2, 10-13, 15, 17-20, 38, 70, 75, 78, 97, 100-101, 105, 112, 119, 148, 184, 191
Fusion, 39, 56
future workshop, 55

G

general class, 22

general knowledge, 72
geographical information system, 168
glass box testing, 183
goal: use case, 97-100
good practice in modelling, 110-114
granularity, 100
graphical user interface (GUI), 12, 14, 33
guard: in state diagram,, 109
GUI. See graphical user interface

H

happy day scenario, 101-103
hard-code, 167
hardware, 3, 28, 32
high level programming language, 13
human-computer interface, 5

I

IEEE, 58
implementation, 13-15, 18, 22, 28, 29, 32-34, 39, 69, 73, 82, 100, 114, 119-120, 140, 143-158, 168, 181; class, 127; class diagram, 143-147; construct, 72; dynamic model, 148-158; environment, 69; database, 168; independent, 32; language, 29, 38, 127; stage, 34; technology, 119
implementation : future workshop, 55
incremental development, 30, 36
index card. See CRC card
Information Engineering, 37
inheritance, 11, 22-23, 29, 34, 36, 70, 79, 81-82, 128, 146, 175-176, 187, 188-191; mechanism, 188; relationship, 23, 128, 146, 175-176
initial class list, 72
initialization, 145, 163
installation: system, 34, 47
instance: class, 16, 133, 145, 173, 188
integration: testing, 183, 184, 187, 191
interaction diagram, 32, 97, 103-107, 120
interface, 5, 11, 14, 33, 40, 41, 57;
interface class, 5; public, 18, 21,22
internal representation: object, 21, 22
internet, 62
interview, 31, 48-53, 59, 63; plan, 49; *Just a Line,* 50-53; summary, 60
irrelevant: objects, 72
IS-A, 23, 188

iteration, 29, 36, 135, in sequence diagrams, 140

J

Jacobson, 26, 38-39, 42
Java, 13, 34, 127, 133, 140, 143-144, 153, 167, 180; linking to database, 177-178
Java Database Connectivity. See JDBC
JDBC, 177, 178
JSD, 37

K

key;primary, 168, 173; foreign, 168,173, 177

L

language: natural, 55, 57, 82, 88; English, 56; formal, 56; programming, 3, 4, 13, 21, 28, 33, 40, 129, 190;
library modules, 11-12
life cycle.   See system life cycle
lifeline: sequence diagram, 104, 122, 139, 140, 149
link: between classes. See relationship
link: to database, 167, 177-178

M

maintenance, 8-11,
22, 28-29, 34-35,
176
many to many
association, 172-
173
Mascot3, 37
message, 14, 18-21,
103, 136, 140, 149-
151
message passing, 15,
19, 143
method: class, 18, 21-
24, 149, 187, 191-
192
method:development.
See methodology
methodology, 4, 27,
31, 36-42, 84;
second generation,
39
Microsoft Access, 5,
168-178
milestone, 27
model, 28-29, 36, 37,
39, 57, 66-69, 82,
110-114, 120, 128-
129, 135, 145, 148;
for communication,
58; to tackle
complexity; 58
working, 28, 57
modelling, 3, 31-32,
37, 66, 68-70, 82,
97, 104, 110, 114,
119; good practice,
110-114
modelling notation, 3,
modelling technique,
5, 13, 38, 48, 58,
68-70, 110
modification, 35, 82
modularity, 8, 10, 20
module, autonomous,
10; cohesive, 10-
12; library, 11-12

monitoring progress,
37, 101
multimedia, 40, 168
multiplicity, 17, 79-
80, 120, 128

N

natural language, 55,
57, 82, 88; English,
56
navigable path, 129
navigability, 129-131
network, 33, 143, 152
non-functional
requirement, 32, 47
normalization, 170
notation, 13, 39, 41,
56, 74, 82, 105,
125, 135, 138, 140,
141; data
dictionary, 84-88;
design model, 120
notational
convention, 120
noun, 70-71

O

object, 2, 4, 11, 14-
15, 17-24, 36, 39,
69-74, 82, 85, 120-
122, 124-126, 131,
133-135, 138, 145,
150; activation,
139-140; client, 18,
22; collaboration
diagram, 106-107;
creation, 140-141,
146, 148-149, 159;
database, 168;
decentralised, 136;
deletion, 140-141;
integration testing,
191-192; internal
representation, 21,
22; lifeline, 104,
122, 139, 140, 149;

sequence diagram,
104; state diagram,
107-109;testing,
187-191; unique
identifier, 113;
object box: sequence
diagram, 121
Object Modelling
Technique. See
OMT
object-orientation, 2,
4, 5, 8, 33, 75, 97,
170; background,
13; concepts, 13-
25; terminology,
14, 36
object-oriented
programming
language, 13, 34,
168, 170
Objectory, 38, 39
OMT, 39
one to many
association, 17,
128, 173-175
operation, 17-18, 23-
25, 75-76, 82, 120,
135, 139, 145, 149;
activation, 139;
describing, 88-90;
overriding, 82,
189; private, 18;
signature, 120,
135; testing, 188-
190
override: operation,
82, 189

P

parent class, 22, 23;
testing, 188
Participatory Design,
55
part-whole
relationship, 114
Pascal, 33

performance behaviour, 184

performance requirements, 47, 182

persistent data, 167-168, 178

physical object, 70, 113

planning, 37, 59

pointer in C++, 131

polymorphism, 23-25, 187, 190

post-implementation testing, 181, 182-184

potential class, 72, 73

pre-implementation testing, 181-182

primary key, 168, 170, 173, 177

priority: of requirement, 57

private operation, 18

problem, 3, 27-28, 35, 37,61, 62, 66, 69; brief, 70-71, 73, 75, 80, 81; description, 47, 75; domain, 2, 14-15, 32, 39, 40, 48, 55, 56, 61, 62, 70, 71, 72, 73, 75, 100, 112, 113, 114, 119, 129, 135

procedural approach, 9, 19

procedural code, 19, 190

programming language, 3, 4, 13, 21, 28, 33, 40, 129, 190; block structured, 10; 88, object-oriented, 13, 34, 168, 170

project management, 41, 79, 100

project manager, 11, 40, 41, 55, 101, 181

prototype, 28-29, 55-56, 61; skeleton, 55

prototyping, 29-30, 41, 55-57, 61; rapid, 28-30, 36, 39

public interface, 14, 18, 21-22

Q

quality assurance, 61, 181

quality control standard, 47

quality of the requirements specification, 57

query: database, 168-169

questionnaire, 53, 54, 59

R

random number generator, 119, 124-125

rapid prototyping, 28-30, 36, 39

Rational Rose, 37

real-time system, 37

receiver. See receiving object

receiving class, 149-150

receiving object, 18, 149-150

regression testing, 184

relational database, 168-169, 175, 177-178

relationship, 17, 22-23, 79-82, 114, 128-135, 146, 152,

188; in database, 175, interpretation, 135

release testing, 184

repetition; in data dictionary, 87, 88; in sequence diagrams, 140

requirements, 43-62; capture, 15, 25,29; client, 28-29, 35, 41, 68, 182; elicitation, 31, 48-56, 68, 100, 103, 191; engineer, 43-46, 47, 48, 50, 61, 66, 68, engineering, 31, 43-62, 66, 82, 97, 120; difficulties, 61-62 functional, 47, 101; non-functional, 32, 47; reliability, 47; sources, 56; specification, 48, 56-58, 61, 62, 66, 69; validation, 48, 58-61, 66

responsibility: class, 19-20, 75-79, 129, 146. See CRC card

Responsibility-Driven Design, 38, 39

returns: sequence diagram, 136-139

reuse, 11-12, 20, 33, 34-35, 78, 82

role, 72

round-trip gestalt design, 38

Rumbaugh, 39

S

safety-critical: system, 40-41, 56

scenario, 55, 97-99, 100-107, 112; advantages, 100-101; event, 105-109; happy day, 101-103 *Just a Line*, 101-107
scheduling, 37
seamless process, 29
seamless transition, 36, 168
security-critical: system, 40-41, 56
selection: data dictionary, 85-86
self-transition: state diagram, 109
sender, 18; class, 149-150
sequence diagram, 103-106, 107, 110, 112, 121, 128, 130, 135, 141, 148-151, conditional behaviour: 135-136 direction of navigation, 129; iteration, 140
server, 18, 76, 183
service, 18, 76, 130
Simula, 13
simulation, 124-127, 144, 149
simulator class, 124-126
Smalltalk, 13
software crisis, 8, 25
software library, 12, 21
software reuse. See reuse
software testing. See testing
specialization, 22-23, 81, 189
specialized class, 22-24, 188, 190

specification. See requirements specification
spreadsheets, 12, 20
SSADM, 37
stakeholder, 40, 46, 61
start state: state diagram, 108-109
state, 107, 108-109, 110, 187, 191
state diagram, 107-110; action 109; condition, 108-109; start state, 108-109; stop state, 108-109; transition, 109
stop state:state diagram, 108-109, 118
storage tests, 184
storyboard, 100
structured approach, 8, 10, 12, 41
structured English, 88
structured meeting, 55
structured methods, 8, 25
stubs, 183
sub-class, 22, 82, 175, 176
sub-path: testing, 186
sub-system, 9, 184, 191
super-class, 22, 82, 175-177, 179
superstate: state diagram, 109
survey, 54
Syntropy, 39, 42, 56
system, 2-3; architecture, 32, 33; behaviour, 97-114; boundary, 2-3, 6, 97; development, 3-4; environment, 2, 3,

33, 36, 40, 41, 42; large and complex, 12-13; life cycle, 27, 28, 29, 31, 34, 35, 36, 41, 42; requirement, 28, 55, 57, 62; testing, 181, 183, 184, 187

T

table: database, 168
terminology, 14, 36
test coverage, 11
test harness, 183
test plan, 34
testing, 11, 34, 62, 101, 181-192; acceptance, 184; activities, 181, 184; beta, 184; black box, 183, 191; branch coverage, 186, 187; code, 182; condition coverage, 186, 187; end-to-end path, 186; functional, 183; glass box, 183; integration, 181, 183, 184, 187, 191; O-O, 187-191; path coverage criteria, 185, 192; pre-implementation, 181; post-implementation, 182; regression, 184, release, 184; stages, 181; storage, 184; sub-path, 186, system, 184; unit, 183-185, 187; team, 181, 182, 184, 185; white box, 183

tool, 13; automated, 29; computer-based, 47
top-down functional decomposition, 9, 148
traceability, 36
transition: state diagram, 109

U

UML, 5, 15, 38-39, 41, 114
Unified Modelling Language. See UML
unique identifier: object, 113
unit testing, 183-185, 187
usability, 47
use case, 38, 79, 97-103, 107, 148, 191; advantages, 100-101; goal, 97-100; *Just a Line*, 101-103
user interface, 15, 29, 32-33, 57, 69
user-friendly, 33, 68, 105, 169

V

validation, 181-182; requirements, 31, 43, 48, 58-61, 66
verification, 181-182
verb phrase, 75
video conferencing, 62
visibility of data, 8, 10
Visual Basic, 33, 37

W

walkthrough, 181
web site, 6, 178
white box testing, 183
Whitehead, 13
working model, 28, 57
workshop, 55
World Wide Web, 56

X

Xerox Palo Alto Research Center, 13

Y

Yourdon, 37